Stretching the School Dollar

*How Schools and Districts Can Save Money
While Serving Students Best*

Frederick M. Hess and Eric Osberg
Editors

HARVARD EDUCATION PRESS
CAMBRIDGE, MASSACHUSETTS

Library of Congress Control Number 2010931317
Paperback ISBN 978-1-934742-64-8
Library Edition ISBN 978-1-934742-65-5

Published by Harvard Education Press,
an imprint of the Harvard Education Publishing Group

Harvard Education Press
8 Story Street
Cambridge, MA 02138

Cover Design: Perry Lubin
The typefaces used in this book are Minion and Helvetica Neue.

The Educational Innovations Series

The *Educational Innovations* series explores a wide range of current school reform efforts. Individual volumes examine entrepreneurial efforts and unorthodox approaches, highlighting reforms that have met with success and strategies that have attracted widespread attention. The series aims to disrupt the status quo and inject new ideas into contemporary education debates.

Series edited by Frederick M. Hess

Other books in this series:
Bringing School Reform to Scale
by Heather Zavadsky

What Next?
Edited by Mary Cullinane and Frederick M. Hess

Between Public and Private
Edited by Katrina E. Bulkley, Jeffrey R. Henig, and Henry M. Levin

Contents

Acknowledgments   vii

Introduction   1
Frederick M. Hess

1   A Warning for All Who Would Listen—America's Public
    Schools Face a Forthcoming Fiscal Tsunami   19
    James W. Guthrie and Arthur Peng

2   What's Happening in the States   45
    June Kronholz

3   Now Is a Great Time to Consider the Per-Unit Cost
    of Everything in Education   71
    Marguerite Roza

4   Managing for Results in America's Great City Schools   97
    Michael Casserly

5   The Efficient Use of Teachers   125
    Steven F. Wilson

6   More Productive Schools Through Online Learning   155
    John E. Chubb

7 Large-Scale Cost Cutting and Reorganizing   179
   Jill Corcoran, Reginald Gilyard, Lane McBride, and Jamal Powell

8 Investing in Improvement—Strategy and Resource
   Allocation in Public School Districts   209
   Stacey Childress

9 First-Person Tale of Cost-Cutting Success   235
   Nathan Levenson

10 Overcoming the Political Barriers to Change   263
   Martin R. West

11 Conclusion   289
   Eric Osberg

Notes   303
About the Editors   321
About the Contributors   323
Index   331

Acknowledgments

THIS PROJECT HAD ITS genesis in early 2009, when the drumbeat of negative economic news and collapsing state and local budgets made it clear that school finances could be in for a rough period. As districts sought to adjust budgets and the nation debated the Obama administration's $787 billion stimulus plan, we argued that the silver lining of these tempestuous clouds was the opportunity for states and districts to tackle inefficiency and impose spending discipline. When reporters would ask us to provide examples of how this might work, we consistently found ourselves pointing to public, nonprofit, and for-profit enterprises from *outside* of K–12 schooling, simply because efforts to aggressively wield the budgetary axe are neither celebrated nor much documented in K–12. In fact, we found ourselves debating representatives from the professional associations who argued that there was no fat to trim in K–12 spending and that suggesting we could smartly trim education budgets amounted to a hostile attack on schooling. From those experiences, it became clear to us that there was a crying need for a book that would celebrate (and not bemoan) budget-cutting, provide strategies and approaches for identifying waste, offer concrete examples of where it had been done, and talk seriously about the political and practical challenges.

As the tumultuous economy continued to languish through 2009, the need for a book of this kind became increasingly clear. When we look forward, to a landscape in which the wreckage of the real estate bubble has not yet fully played out, where the aid from the massive 2009 federal stimulus bill is tapering off, to states and districts struggling for years to come with projections of tight budgets and underfunded pensions, it strikes us that the analyses and guidance provided by the contributors to this volume could not be more timely.

We are deeply appreciative to those who aided in the crafting of this volume. In particular, we thank the authors, both for their conference drafts presented at the January 2010 conference and for the final chapters that appear here. We also thank the discussants who participated in that conference and gave invaluable feedback on those early papers. That stellar list of public officials, leaders, and scholars includes: Lily Eskelsen, vice president of the National Education Association; William R. Hite Jr., superintendent of Prince George's County Public Schools; Kartik Jayaram, a partner at McKinsey and Company, Inc.; Dwight Jones, commissioner of education for Colorado Department of Education; Michele McLaughlin, vice president of federal and state policy for Teach for America; Michael Podgursky, professor of economics at University of Missouri, Columbia; Michael R. Sandler, chairman and CEO of the Education Industry Group; and José M. Torres, superintendent of School District U-46 in Illinois.

We're also indebted to our terrific staff at the American Enterprise Institute and the Thomas B. Fordham Institute for their dedicated labors in compiling and editing this volume and for making the January 2010 conference a success. Our special thanks go to Jenna Schuette for her tireless efforts in overseeing the project, as well as particular gratitude to Jack Byer, Amy Fagan, Marisa Goldstein, Claire Moore, Janie Scull, and Juliet Squire for their critical support.

We sincerely appreciate the support of the Searle Freedom Trust, which helped make this volume possible, as did the support of the Fordham Institute's sister organization, the Thomas B. Fordham Foundation. We are also grateful to Fordham and to the American Enterprise Institute and especially their presidents, Chester E. Finn Jr. and Arthur Brooks, for their unflinching support of this research. Finally, we would like to express gratitude to our publisher Doug Clayton and production manager Marcy Barnes for the outstanding work that they did at Harvard Education Press in translating the manuscript into this finished product.

Introduction

Frederick M. Hess

THE HEADLINES TELL THE TALE. In newspapers like the *New York Times,* the *Washington Post,* the *San Francisco Chronicle,* and the *Las Vegas Sun,* the drumbeat has been incessant. "State government revenues fall 16 percent." "Budget gap endangers valued school programs." "School budget cuts threaten gains." "Public schools getting snared by recession." "School budget cuts 'going to be ugly." "Hard times hitting districts and schools." "District schools lay off teachers." "Education, state workers hit in bare-bones budget." Projections make clear that the situation may very well get worse before it gets better.

Looking to the 2010–2011 school year, a national survey of superintendents conducted in spring 2010 found that most see no sign of daylight ahead. Nearly half of superintendents are planning to cut health-care benefits in the next year, up from barely one in ten who did so in 2009–2010. One in five is contemplating trimming pension contributions, one in three is contemplating furloughs, and 90 percent are planning for personnel cutbacks.[1] And the situation will likely continue to worsen in 2011 and beyond, as the impact of declining property values, massive fiscal shortfalls, and underfunded pension and healthcare systems continue to play out.

The challenge is clear. What to do about it isn't so clear. And, in a nation where educational outlays have risen consistently for decades, hard-pressed state and district leaders find disconcertingly little guidance when they seek to lead. So this is a book about what can be done. More than that, this is a book which argues that this bleak landscape may actually be rich with opportunity. In the memorable phrase of President Obama's chief of staff, Rahm Emanuel, "Never let a serious crisis go to waste." And the current fiscal straits offer a chance for savvy state and district leaders to launch a much-needed overhaul of school systems by wringing out inefficiencies, infusing them with a new sense of operational acuity, and rethinking outdated practices and routines.

In a sector buffeted by shrinking revenues, state budget shortfalls, and the first sustained cutbacks in memory, interesting educators in how they might stretch a buck is not a hard task. At the same time, some of the analyses in this book also involve asking policy makers and educators to rethink some basic assumptions about how schooling is organized and delivered. For instance, in this volume various authors make the case for revisiting our attachment to reducing class size and advocate for much more expansive use of virtual schooling—a kind of rethinking that can be a much more uncomfortable challenge.

When I teach aspiring district leaders or talk to state and district leaders, one of the things that has struck me in the past year or two is the degree to which concerns about budgeting have become much more pressing. It was only a few years ago, in the heart of the No Child Left Behind era, that such concerns seemed to be regarded as almost tangential next to questions of student achievement. Now the relative standing of cost-effective management seems to have bounced back. This is, on the whole, a good thing. School improvement strategies pursued with insufficient attention to cost-effectiveness or sustainability are no more than a recipe for disappointment.

Grappling with a severe recession and an unprecedented downturn in school spending, educators and policy makers across the land are asking how schools can squeeze budgets and, perhaps, use this as an opportunity to boost efficiency and promote reform. Newspapers are filled with stories about schools and districts responding to budget challenges by turning up thermostats, canceling sports and arts programs, adding new fees for parents, limiting bus routes, and delaying the purchase of new texts. And a sizable portion of the $100 billion in federal "stimulus" that Congress provided in 2009 was dedicated to limiting teacher lay-offs.

The problem with these strategies is threefold. One, they're mostly stop-gaps. Two, they don't hold any promise of promoting improved teaching and learning. And three, some of them—like the use of stimulus funds to preserve teaching jobs—just serve to aggravate the challenges ahead.

The pressure to reduce costs without sacrificing student achievement will only intensify as declining real estate values depress local and state revenues, as the growing welfare state saps federal budgets, and as an aging and retiring teaching force creates greater pension obligations for states and districts. Indeed, the Nelson Rockefeller Institute reported in late 2009 that states would be looking at budget shortfalls exceeding 6 percent into 2013 and beyond.[2] And that calculation preceded the dramatic health-care reform act of 2010, with its new demands on state Medicaid systems. The reality is that state and district budgets are likely to be under significant pressure at least through the middle of this coming decade. And, absent sensible reform, perhaps even longer.

Even the most admired and efficient public and private organizations can almost inevitably benefit from a hard scrubbing and scouring after a long run of prosperous years. When times are good, there's a natural tendency for hard decisions to get pushed off, for programs and personnel to accumulate, and for management to accept a certain degree of inefficiency in order to maintain a tranquil and collegial workplace. That's why we saw even profit-able, successful private firms like Cisco, IBM, and Microsoft quickly respond to the economic downturn in 2008 by cutting thousands of positions. Microsoft CEO Steven Ballmer said of the cuts in January 2009, "We will emerge an even stronger industry leader than we are today."[3] As Jonathan Chadwick, Cisco Systems corporate controller said in February 2009 of the cuts, "We think of this as Portfolio Management 101."[4] Indeed, within weeks of letting thousands go, Microsoft turned around and made a slew of new hires. The firm used the urgency and cover provided by the economic turbulence to facilitate a number of personnel moves and strategic decisions that would have been painful to do in smoother seas. That's not the way educational leaders have traditionally approached these issues, but we think they can and should. And this is a book intended to help them do so.

THE CONTEXT OF EDUCATIONAL COST CUTTING

There are many in the world of K–12 schooling who recoil at the notion of slicing education spending. After all, parent groups, teachers' unions, and policy makers have made the crusade to boost school spending a crusade and even a moral litmus test. Parents, teachers' unions, and policy makers deem it wrong-headed. This book is not for them. This is a book for those seeking to do the best they can with the resources they have. At the same time, squeezing out operational efficiencies is an obviously smart and useful thing to do even in boom times. Indeed, as the chapters that follow suggest, one persistent problem for schools is that they have too rarely obtained the full benefit of each dollar spent.

I'm always perplexed by the notion that there's something unsavory about trying to boost educational productivity and wring out inefficient spending. After all, these are tax dollars collected for the purpose of funding our children's education. Taxpayers want their dollars to be spent carefully, and all of us want a given amount of educational outlays to provide the best possible schooling. Given those simple truths, attention to maximizing productivity and minimizing inefficiency should have broad and obvious appeal (not least from the perspective of educators, because taxpayers and voters confident that dollars are being well-spent are going to be more supportive of requests for additional funds).

All of this is somewhat academic, because the reality is that districts have come to the end of a historic streak of steadily increasing revenues and have been trimming budgets for two years now. In 2008–2009 more than 40 percent of superintendents reported altering thermostats; more than 15 percent eliminated field trips, deferred textbook purchases, and reduced custodial services; and more than 10 percent increased class size or cut bus transportation. In 2009–2010 more than 40 percent raised class sizes or laid off personnel, and more than 30 percent deferred textbook purchases or eliminated or delayed instructional initiatives.[5] These figures show two things. One, like it or not, districts are having to make tough choices. And, two, the difficulty and significance of those choices is becoming progressively more significant.

For long decades, as Jim Guthrie points out in chapter one, districts have been growing staff and spending at a pace that outstrips student enrollment (or achievement gains). The piper was going to come calling eventually. That's especially true in a nation with a steadily aging population, where the percentage of Americans over age sixty-five is going to nearly double between 2000 and 2050 and where growing outlays for health care are going to increasingly compete with state funding for K–12 and higher education. On top of all of this, states and localities are struggling with massive pension and health-care obligations for public employees, including teachers; the need to fund existing commitments is going to eat into operational expenditures. Given this landscape, including both current challenges and those looming on the horizon, it is a propitious time for educational leaders to get serious about getting their houses in order.

Cost-cutting may be a necessity in this era of constrained resources, but it can also be much more than that. Erasing inefficient spending is a critical step in freeing up the resources to drive reform and fuel school improvement, and the process of wringing out waste can leave schools and systems better prepared to succeed at the core work of teaching and learning. Every dollar spent on unnecessary staff or maintenance is a dollar that comes at the expense of teaching and learning. Equally important, however, is that lean organizations send a signal that efficacy is valued and make clear that they're addressing lethargic human resource systems, unreliable procurement operations, or haphazard data systems that can otherwise be a distraction or a hindrance for educators and school leaders—burdens and barriers that can otherwise hamper educators.

Unfortunately, the precedents for significant belt-tightening, restructuring, and reorganizing within education are pretty sparse in K–12 schooling. While states and districts have wrestled with these challenges, their efforts have not been documented or studied. Similarly, little has been done to help explain how educators might import sensible practices from other sectors.

The result is that when it does come time to trim, districts often make cuts that are more harmful than helpful. Perhaps not surprisingly, given that they are public entities managed by public officials, they tend to opt for popular measures even when those may not be the most productive. They fire promising young teachers in favor of less effective and more expensive veterans. Or they gut music instruction rather than close down underenrolled schools. To be sure, districts' hands are often tied by collective bargaining agreements, state and federal laws, and the size of their operations. But even within those constraints, there is opportunity for bolder and savvier responses.

Thus, we believe that the time is right for an analysis and book aimed at education leaders, policy makers, and the wider public, one that explains how schools could save money while enhancing achievement, provides evidence that such changes are actually possible, and urges leaders to alter the policies and practices that too often inhibit such reform today. Can we cut budgets and improve education at the same time? We believe we can, and this project will show how.

Today there is surprisingly little research or writing that demonstrates, in specific and compelling ways, the savings and efficiencies that could be possible in K–12 education. We propose to develop such a resource, a single volume that shows education leaders and policy makers exactly what is possible—not by applying loose analogies from other sectors but via specific analysis, detailed examples, and thoughtful studies of how school systems currently work, what could be done differently, and what savings these changes would yield. In short, we aim to publish a "how to" guide for both school system leaders and policy makers as they navigate these new fiscal times. In so doing, we aim also to arm them with greater confidence that such moves can successfully be made—and should be.

TWO WAYS TO THINK ABOUT COST-CUTTING

This volume will encompass two schools of thought when it comes to saving pennies. One consists of relatively straightforward efforts to improve the operational efficiency of today's schools and districts. Authors Michael Casserly and Marguerite Roza will discuss how districts might use buses more efficiently or construct class schedules in more cost-effective ways.

The second school, addressed in chapters by authors John Chubb and Steven Wilson, includes efforts to more radically rethink today's schools and systems in order to take advantage of new technologies and use talent more cost-effectively. Which avenues hold the most promise for a given district are a product of local conditions and local needs; we think all of these approaches have a place in the toolbox of reform-minded district leaders.

In popular discussions, these strategies are often characterized as opposites. Those skeptical of virtual schooling or computer-assisted instruction frequently label efforts to use these measures as cost-cutting tools as an attack on teachers or schools. Meanwhile, moves to boost cost-effectiveness in facilities maintenance or procurement are regarded as desirable and relatively nonthreatening. We are suggesting that these strategies are actually points along a continuum, one ranging from more to less ambitious efforts to rationalize spending. The desirability of any particular tack depends on local need, opportunities, and politics.

The leaders of any organization, public or private, would typically rather sidestep thorny problems than confront them. In good times, budgets expand, payrolls grow, new people come on board, and managers delay difficult decisions. Tough times come to serve as a healthful, if bitter, tonic, forcing leaders to identify priorities and giving them political cover to trim the fat.

What's unique about public education is that, unlike their private-sector counterparts, few school districts ever face this day of reckoning. Superintendents squawk when they are told to hold spending growth to "just" 1 or 2 percent the next year.

Per-pupil spending today is roughly double (in inflation-adjusted terms) what it was in 1983, when the United States was declared "a nation at risk." That huge increase in public outlays has funded all manners of questionable practices, including ever-shrinking class sizes (popular with parents and teachers but mostly unrelated to student achievement), an ever-growing number of teachers and other school employees, a uniform salary schedule that treats incompetents and all-stars identically, an unsustainable pension-and-benefits system, and a tenure system that protects instructional dysfunction. In other words, taxpayers have spent decades funding an enormous, inefficient jobs program.

Indeed, in many ways, today's schools illustrate the perils of uninterrupted job creation. Thanks to teacher ranks having grown twice as fast as student enrollment over the past five decades, we today employ 3.3 million teachers. The resulting press of numbers has made it difficult to be as selective or as purposive about training as we might like. It has also meant that dollars for teacher salaries go toward attracting more bodies rather than boosting compensation.

The contributors tend to share the presumption that K–12 schooling has long stood to benefit from a good belt-tightening. Tough budgets compel and enable administrators to rethink staffing, take a hard look at class sizes, trim ineffective personnel, shrink payrolls, consolidate tiny school districts, replace some workers with technology, weigh cost-effective alternatives to popular practices, reexamine statutes governing pensions and tenure, and demand concessions from the myriad education unions.

Because public schools are publicly funded and publicly governed, addressing inefficiencies and identifying savings is inevitably an issue of political will, incentives, and overcoming cultural and political barriers. This volume is less focused on grand political debates, however, than on illuminating some problematic practices and promising responses in order to encourage concrete strategies and help muster the political will to adopt them. Ultimately, however, this volume will not offer a magical remedy for deep-seated political and cultural challenges; rather, our hope is that it can promote practical problem-solving by exposing challenges and surfacing solutions.

A NECESSARY CONDITION

Cutting expenditures or squeezing out budgetary fat is not the same as improving schools. However, tightening up a school system, sloughing off unnecessary facilities or personnel, and focusing resources where they are needed most can help create the conditions for sustained, disciplined improvement.

In early 2010, Kansas City superintendent John Covington, who had months earlier inherited a district plagued by a $50 million budget shortfall, half-filled schools, and lousy performance, opted not to keep on muddling through as so many of his predecessors had done. Instead, Covington and the school board agreed to shut down almost half the district's sixty-one schools, sell the district's downtown central office, eliminate 700 of its 3,000 positions, and require teachers at six low-performing schools to reapply for their jobs.

All this was made necessary because the district had lost 75 percent of its students in the past four decades, with enrollment shrinking from 75,000 to 17,500. After long years of superintendents who were happy to preside over steady decline and keep open half-empty buildings, Covington opted for a different course. The move freed up crucial dollars and eliminated distractions, while enabling the district to shutter troubled schools and to focus on teaching, learning, and school improvement. This kind of aggressive response to "business" challenges can help set up leaders for instructional success.

While most districts are not Kansas City, Covington's plight isn't as unique as one might imagine. Districts across the land are gearing up to face the dreaded funding "cliff," a situation aggravated by the end of federal stimulus aid. States are looking at tens of billions in budget shortfalls for fiscal year 2011. And the accelerating downturn in commercial real estate and the soft housing market mean that districts will likely be looking at tight budgets into 2014 and beyond.

Thus far districts have dealt with collapsing revenues and the possibility of a new fiscal reality mostly by postponing building maintenance, adjusting thermostats, and cutting bus routes. Now, more are starting to ham-handedly increase class sizes, reduce the use of instructional materials, and do away with electives. While I'm all in favor of strategically increasing class size (for particular students, grades, and subjects), those cuts will only take districts so far. And the last thing superintendents need is encouragement from would-be allies to just demand more money and dismiss calls to run a tighter ship.

It's time for more district leaders to consider taking a page from Covington's book by addressing structural shortfalls and scrutinizing the cost-effectiveness of programs and staff. This requires a different mindset than traditional "more, better" education leadership, which has historically promoted improvement by layering new dollars atop existing spending. Covington may well be seen as the avatar of an era in which leaders increasingly fuel improvement by stripping and recycling excess and inefficiency from lethargic systems.

A MODEL IN NEED OF RETHINKING

Serious cost-cutting, as in Kansas City, is going to involve tough choices and creative thinking. Trimming raises from 4 percent to 2 percent will certainly save dollars, but it also amounts to "a little bit less of the same." Given that few educators or reformers are currently happy with the status quo, the same thing, but a little less of it, hardly holds out much promise. Needed is an array of much more aggressive and far-ranging efforts to rethink how we staff schools, pay educators, and organize the core work of teaching. In some cases, this will necessarily mean rethinking the teacher's job description, the number of students in a classroom, how technology is used, and how teachers are paid. In this volume, the chapters by Steven Wilson and John Chubb are particularly focused on these kinds of strategies.

By far, the biggest expenditure in K–12 schooling is people. Salaries and benefits account for roughly 80–85 percent of all district spending, and the majority of that is for classroom teachers. This means that any discussion of how to shore up the financial position of school systems inevitably comes back to questions of staffing.

To improve schooling, the United States has adopted the peculiar policy of hiring more teachers and asking them each to do the same job in roughly the same way. This dilutes the talent pool while spreading training and salaries across more bodies. Chester Finn Jr., president of the Thomas B. Fordham Institute, has wryly observed that the United States has opted to "invest in many more teachers rather than abler ones . . . No wonder teaching salaries have barely kept pace with inflation, despite escalating education budgets."[6] Since the early 1970s, growth in the teaching force has outstripped growth in student enrollment by 50 percent. In this decade, the ranks of teachers grew at nearly twice the rate of student enrollment. If policy makers had maintained the same overall teacher-to-student ratio since the 1970s, we would need one million fewer teachers, training could be focused on a smaller and more able population, and average teacher pay would be close to $75,000 per year.

Today's teaching profession is the product of a mid-twentieth-century labor model that relied on a captive pool of female workers, assumed educators were largely interchangeable, and counted on male principals and superintendents to micromanage a female teaching workforce. Preparation programs were geared to train generalists who operated with little recourse to data or technology. Teaching has clung to these industrial rhythms, while professional norms and the larger labor market have changed. By the 1970s, however, schools could no longer depend on an influx of talented young women, as those who once would have entered teaching began to take jobs in engineering and law. The likelihood that a new teacher was a woman who ranked in the top 10 percent of her high school cohort fell by 50 percent between 1964 and 2000. Meanwhile, policy makers and educators were slow to tap new pools of talent; it was not until the late 1980s that they started tinkering with alternative licensure and midcareer recruitment. Even then, they did little to reconfigure professional development, compensation, or career opportunities accordingly.

Even "cutting-edge" proposals typically do not challenge established routines but instead focus on filling that 200,000-a-year quota with talented twenty-two-year-olds who want to teach into the 2040s. Perhaps the most widely discussed critique of teacher preparation of the past decade, the hotly debated 2006 study by the National Center for Policy Analysis, *Educating School Teachers*, simply presumed that teacher recruitment ought to be geared toward new college graduates who would complete beefed-up versions of familiar training programs before being cleared to enter the same old jobs. Absent was any reconsideration of who should be teaching or any inclination to question the design of the enterprise.

There may be smarter, better ways to approach the challenge at hand: expand the hiring pool beyond recent college graduates, staff schools in ways that squeeze more value out of talented teachers, and use technology to make it easier for teachers to be highly effective. A twenty-first-century human capital strategy for education should step back from the status quo and revisit existing assumptions.

A DEARTH OF GUIDANCE

Even as we ask district and school leaders to do more with less, we see a research landscape that offers remarkably little analysis or guidance on how they should proceed. Perhaps it's because education spending has historically risen year after year. Perhaps it's because educators and reformers prefer to focus on boosting achievement rather than cost-effectiveness. Perhaps it's because the data systems to track and monitor cost-effectiveness have not traditionally been available. Perhaps it's a question of educational culture. Yet, for whatever reason, researchers and analysts who have rafts of suggestions to proffer when districts are seeking to spend money on professional development or new school models have little or nothing to say when districts are seeking advice on how to cut.

While the subject of educational spending is hardly a new one, most previous efforts to address school spending have focused on exploring its relationship to academic outcomes rather than the question of how and where school systems might find savings. For instance, previous volumes, such as W. Norton Grubb's 2009 *The Money Myth: School Resources, Outcomes, and Equity* and Gary Burtless's 1996 book *Does Money Matter? The Effect of School Resources on Student Achievement and Adult Success*, examine the relationship between school funding and academic achievement. This is a vital question, but one profoundly different from figuring out how districts might cut spending in smart ways. Other notable books, such as Helen Ladd's 2007 volume *Handbook of Research in Education Finance and Policy* and James Guthrie's 2006 *Modern Education Finance and Policy*, provide useful summaries of the state of education finance—but, again, are not intended to help districts find cost savings or manage in lean times.[7]

In fact, a search of major academic databases for titles in the past decade that coupled either "school" or "education" with the phrases "cost-effective," "cost-efficient," "strategic budgeting," "cutting costs," "reducing costs," "cost savings," or "cost-benefit analysis" revealed no articles directly relevant to the focus of this volume. In all, that search yielded about one hundred results, almost all of which addressed issues such as distance learning, vocational education, and technical education in developing nations. The most directly relevant article in evidence was the 2005 "Higher Education Strategies for Reducing Cost and Increasing Quality in Higher Education," which, needless to say, did not focus on K–12 schooling.

Perhaps the existing work most similar to this current effort was Allan Odden and Carolyn Busch's 1998 *Financing Schools for High Performance: Strategies for Improving the Use of Educational Resources*, a volume penned over a decade ago and in a very different era of school reform.[8] This volume that you hold in your hands inevitably touches on many popular debates in contemporary school reform, including merit pay, accountability, school governance, and turnaround strategies. Rather than provide one more set of thoughts on these broad strategies for school improvement, however, the contributors to this volume provide guidance and concrete suggestions to help policy makers, district leaders, and reformers decide how to free up the dollars they need to fuel reform.

THE BOOK FROM HERE

In chapter one, James Guthrie, of the George W. Bush Institute, and Arthur Peng, of Vanderbilt University, sketch the history of school spending in America, showing its consistent growth over time. Guthrie and Peng explain that the primary causes have been the steady growth of the teacher workforce, the federal dictum of "supplement, not supplant," the skyrocketing costs of special education, and a broad disinterest in labor-saving devices or practices.

In chapter two, former *Wall Street Journal* reporter June Kronholz takes a look at how an array of schools and districts are trying to shave costs and get creative about budgeting. Her account flags a number of district strategies, ranging from more to less ambitious, and offers the chance to see how some cash-strapped districts are wrestling with the challenge.

In chapter three, Marguerite Roza, an expert on district budgets at the Center on Reinventing Public Education at the University of Washington, explains how districts can analyze their data in new ways in order to shine a light on cost-effectiveness of programs and offerings. Without even realizing they are doing it, districts and schools concentrate resources on certain programs and classes at the expense of core priorities like math and English. Roza points out how the arbitrary nature of these spending decisions highlights tremendous opportunities for savings and efficiencies in how dollars and staff are allocated.

Michael Casserly, executive director of the Council of Great City Schools (CGCS), has been working with urban school systems for nearly two decades. For most of that time, the primary push has been for those districts to dramatically boost levels of student achievement and attainment. In the past few years, of course, the new imperative has been to do that in increasingly cost-conscious ways. In chapter four, Casserly discusses the ongoing efforts by CGCS to compile performance data from its sixty-six member districts across more than one hundred indicators, in such areas as transportation, building maintenance, food service, financial management, and information technology. Casserly explains how these data can help flag districts that are faring especially well or especially poorly when it comes to operational efficiency and offers districts a benchmark for identifying vast potential savings in those areas where they are underperforming.

Teachers are by far the largest cost for schools. In chapter five, Steven Wilson, the founder and president of the Ascend Learning charter school management organization, explores how teachers could be utilized more strategically and cost-effectively. Taking one district as a case in point, Wilson makes the case that sensible rethinking could shave district costs by perhaps 15 percent while putting the district in a stronger position to support high-quality teaching and learning.

In addition to making better use of their teachers, schools could make profoundly better use of technology. In chapter six, John Chubb, former chief development officer and senior executive vice president at Edison-Learning, explains how schools can deploy new distance learning and virtual technologies to save money and improve learning.

Several members of the Boston Consulting Group's education practice share in chapter seven the kinds of analysis and insight that are usually revealed only on a proprietary basis to paying clients. Examining strategies that several states and large school systems have employed to yield dramatic cost savings and sharp increases in operational efficiency, they paint a cheery picture of what is possible with strong leadership.

In chapter eight, Stacey Childress, formerly a senior lecturer in management at the Harvard Business School and a cofounder of the Public Education Leadership Project at Harvard University, and now deputy director of innovation for the Bill & Melinda Gates Foundation, explores how three districts have worked to improve productivity and efficiencies at the district level. Using the cases of Montgomery County, Maryland, New York City, and San Francisco, Childress examines how districts can strategically align spending decisions to advance their priorities and to promote more efficient, effective operations.

All of these strategies have the potential to be enormously useful, but they all also require that state and district leaders negotiate political and organizational challenges. Historically, reform has been pursued in large part by "buying off" threatened constituencies with new resources. In today's fiscal environment that course is less available. In chapter nine, former Arlington, Massachusetts, superintendent Nathan Levenson, who came to the job with extensive consulting and private-sector management experience, shares some of the lessons he learned trying to bring hard-nosed business analyses to public schooling. He explains why importing cost-benefit analysis to public schooling can be made more difficult by statutes, policies, and contracts. While Levenson found savings in a number of budget areas, including special education (he lowered costs while increasing higher student achievement), administration (he reduced the number of administrators and added teacher leaders), and ineffective programs in the areas of reading, remediation and alternative education), he was caught off-guard by cultural resistance to seemingly innocuous management strategies. This is a chapter that offers a look at the thorny, practical challenges of controlling district costs.

In chapter ten, Harvard University Graduate School of Education professor Martin West picks up where Levenson leaves off and explores the kinds of political and structural barriers that can make it difficult for districts to tackle their costs. West notes that there are many reasons why the reforms described in the chapters above have not taken hold in most districts, including the pressure to forge consensus, state mandates and rules on spending and staffing, the inertia inherent in large bureaucracies, and the preferences of teacher unions and parents. After exploring the nature of these factors, West offers some suggestions as to how leaders can start to surmount them.

Finally, in the concluding chapter eleven, my coeditor Eric Osberg, vice president and treasurer of the Thomas B. Fordham Institute, pulls together some of the contributors' key insights and recommendations. He surveys some of the varied strategies for stretching school budgets, from those that simply fine-tune the familiar schoolhouse to those that use the fiscal crunch as an opportunity to envision a fundamentally more cost-effective approach to schooling.

The current budget crunch, and the bleak financial situation of schooling, has led some to bewail the cruel fates and hold out hope that new dollars will materialize. That course seems both misguided and ultimately irresponsible.

Fortunately, that reaction seems to be confined mostly to the ideologues and professional Washington money-seeking associations. Most educational leaders, board members, and policy makers seem to have a far more practical response. They want to know how they can stretch a buck. They want to know where they might look for savings, how other districts have tackled these challenges, and what tactics they might try. This book is intended for them, and for all those who believe that responsible stewardship is a matter of doing the best we can with the dollars available.

1

A Warning for All Who Would Listen—America's Public Schools Face a Forthcoming Fiscal Tsunami

James W. Guthrie and Arthur Peng

A HUNDRED-YEAR ERA of perpetual per-pupil fiscal growth will soon slow or stop. The causes of this situation are far more fundamental than the current recession. Schools should start buckling their seat belts now.

Even when controlled for inflation, school spending has been increasing substantially for a century. Political and fiscal pressures, however, will soon coincide to reverse this trend, and issues of productivity and performance will become paramount.

Historically, public schools' per-pupil real-dollar revenues have increased almost every year. Moreover, these added dollars have kept coming even when the economy, as measured by Gross Domestic Product (GDP), took downward turns. The number of school employees relative to the number of students has followed a similar trajectory for the past five decades. Only during the Great Depression and in the World War II years were there significant slowdowns in per-pupil spending and in added personnel, and these periods of slow growth lasted only a short time.

Teacher salaries, while not benefitting proportionately from historic per-pupil revenue gains, increased more than 42 percent in constant dollars over the last half-century. Moreover, educators' working conditions, heath benefits, and retirement arrangements have become ever more commodious. Education's stable fiscal condition has stood in contrast to the volatility in virtually every other economic sector.

A unique set of constitutional, structural, financial, and political arrangements has, up to now, ensured that school systems and professional educators are buffered from revenue losses when the economy declines. Other sets of state rules surrounding local school district budgeting procedures contribute to the exact opposite impression, making it appear to the public that schools are in a perpetual financial crisis.

Such was the past. The future appears quite different; the nation's long-standing positive funding trend appears about to slow and possibly reverse itself.

The Obama administration's stimulus injection of unprecedented billions in additional federal funding likely ensures that education's comfortably cushioned resource condition will continue during the current economic downturn. However, this stimulus injection may have dramatically added to the federal function in education. Unlike ever before in history, the federal government now appears to be the fiscal flywheel protecting the nation's schools during economic downturns. This change has occurred with hardly any national debate.

Ironically, however, the role of the federal government as a major funding partner may portend the end of automatic spending increases for schools. As school funding becomes more centralized, both at the state and federal level, it is forced to compete more intensely with other public sector services and is positioned against a far less favorable political backdrop. Whereas local school districts are often free to shift future salary increases, pension liabilities, and retiree health-care costs onto state authorities, the greater the federal and state funding roles, the larger these previously extraneous conditions become as funding obstacles.

Such fiscal dynamics, coupled with the long-standing static nature of student achievement, do not bode well for future school revenues. A new era of fiscal stringency is emerging, and it may come quickly.

A COMFORTING GLANCE BACK THROUGH EDUCATION'S FISCAL HISTORY

For the past hundred years, excepting brief periods during the Great Depression and World War II, America's public schools invariably have had more money and fewer pupils per employee in year two than in year one (after controlling for inflation).

Episodically, school districts do become insolvent. And on occasion states do have to step in and take over a district. California experienced a string of such costly and highly visible insolvencies in the last decade of the twentieth century and in the first decade of the twenty-first century. The state had to elbow locally elected school boards aside and install all-powerful administrative overseers in large districts such as Oakland and Richmond. In the Midwest, Detroit is the poster child for a similar situation. However, school district insolvencies are rare and most often are due to unusual individual instances of administrative or school board mismanagement and malfeasance rather than diminished revenues and systematic budget cuts.

The larger picture is far different, however. As seen nationally in Figure 1.1 and by classification of school district (rural, suburban and urban) in Figure 1.2, America's public schools districts have long been on an upward per-pupil revenue trajectory. Moreover, with the exception of the enrollment decline and recessionary period of the late 1970s and early 1980s, teacher salaries also continually increased over time, though they have flattened out since 1985.

And, as displayed in Figures 1.3, 1.4, and 1.5, the number of employees, teachers, administrators, and other education employees has also continually increased for the last four decades, with the exception of the early 1980s enrollment decline and recessionary period.

FIGURE 1.1

Historic per-pupil expenditure

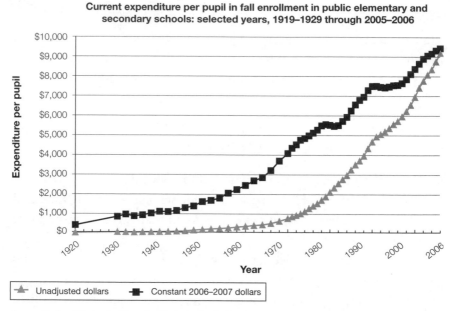

Current expenditure per pupil in fall enrollment in public elementary and secondary schools: selected years, 1919–1929 through 2005–2006

Legend: Unadjusted dollars — Constant 2006–2007 dollars

Source: National Center for Education Statistics, *2008 Digest of Education Statistics*.

FIGURE 1.2

Historic per-pupil spending by school district type

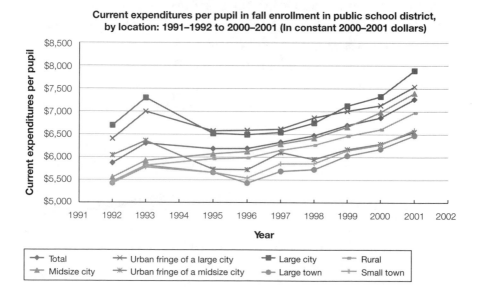

Current expenditures per pupil in fall enrollment in public school district, by location: 1991–1992 to 2000–2001 (In constant 2000–2001 dollars)

Legend: Total — Midsize city — Urban fringe of a large city — Urban fringe of a midsize city — Large city — Large town — Rural — Small town

Source: National Center for Education Statistics, *2004 The Condition of Education*.

FIGURE 1.3
Historic numbers of school teachers in elementary and secondary schools

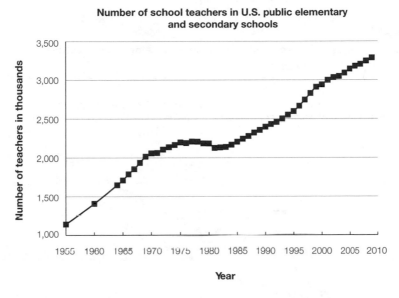

Number of school teachers in U.S. public elementary and secondary schools

Source: National Center for Education Statistics, *2008 Digest of Education Statistics.*

FIGURE 1.4
Historic change in pupil-teacher ratios

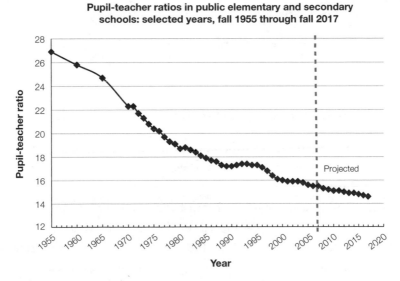

Pupil-teacher ratios in public elementary and secondary schools: selected years, fall 1955 through fall 2017

Source: National Center for Education Statistics, *2008 Digest of Education Statistics.*

FIGURE 1.5

Displays number of elementary and secondary employees relative to growth in GDP over time

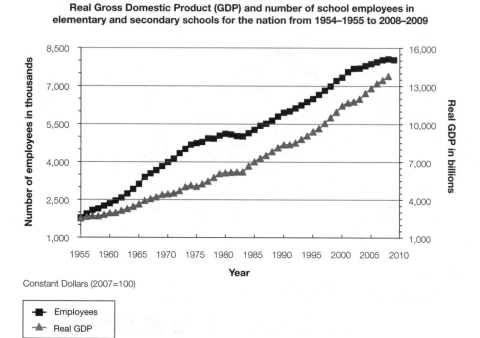

Real Gross Domestic Product (GDP) and number of school employees in elementary and secondary schools for the nation from 1954–1955 to 2008–2009

Constant Dollars (2007=100)

Source: GDP data retrieved from National Economic Accounts, Bureau of Economic Analysis, April 9, 2009; school employment data extracted on December 8, 2009 from Bureau of Labor Statistics.

WHY AND HOW IS EDUCATION SO PRIVILEGED?

Public schools have done well when the economy is in a growth mode and, particularly when compared to other sectors, are remarkably insulated from downturns.

Figure 1.6 shows a seventy-five-year historic pattern for per-pupil revenue change (percent year-over-year growth or decline) relative to the GDP (in constant dollars) change. Since 1929 there have been only two times when per-pupil spending declined, once during the Great Depression and once

FIGURE 1.6

Gross domestic product and mean national per-pupil expenditure change compared

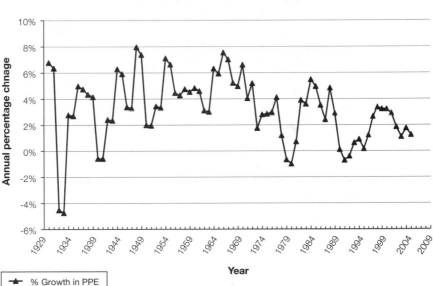

Annual percentage growth in per pupil expenditures (PPE)
in constant 2006–2007 dollars: 1928–1929 through 2006–2007

Source: GDP data retrieved from National Economic Accounts, Bureau of Economic Analysis, April 9, 2009; *U.S. Business Cycle Expansions and Contractions,* National Bureau of Economic Research. Retrieved on November 9, 2009; National Center for Education Statistics, *2008 Digest of Education Statistics.*

during World War II. Conversely, there have been eleven periods during which the GDP declined but mean total real per-pupil revenues increased.

Figure 1.7 displays historic (1972–2008) employment information in nine selected sectors other than education: construction, finance, government, information, manufacturing, professional and business services, retail trade, transportation, and warehousing.

Here one can see that employment levels are linked to economic conditions and, except for government (which includes educators), that the historic employment trend in other sectors is a modest upward line. Contrast

FIGURE 1.7

Number of employees in eight selected sectors

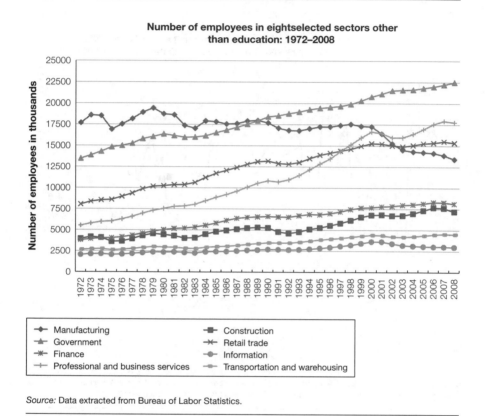

Source: Data extracted from Bureau of Labor Statistics.

this picture with the perpetually steeper slopes in previously cited figures 1.3 and 1.5 regarding education employment.

Figure 1.8 displays almost four decades of defense appropriations relative to the real GDP. Here one can see that from 1990 until September 11, 2001, Pentagon appropriations occupied a falling share of the real GDP and, despite recovering since the inception of the War on Terror, have not begun to reclaim their historic share.

Historically, an interlocking and reciprocally reinforcing set of conditions has protected education from the direct effects of macroeconomic ups and

FIGURE 1.8

Real GDP and national defense expenditures

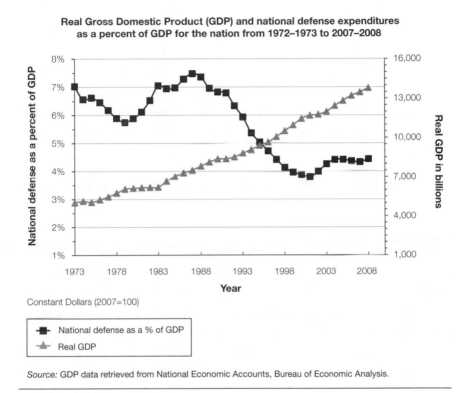

Real Gross Domestic Product (GDP) and national defense expenditures
as a percent of GDP for the nation from 1972–1973 to 2007–2008

Constant Dollars (2007=100)

- ■ National defense as a % of GDP
- ▲ Real GDP

Source: GDP data retrieved from National Economic Accounts, Bureau of Economic Analysis.

downs. These conditions include education's privileged legal status within most state constitutions; schooling's almost unique decentralized operation and diffuse revenue generation structure; local political dynamics and institutions that generally foster a favorable fiscal environment for public schools; a multitiered responsibility for funding schools with complicated intergovernmental funding incentives; and reliance on inelastic tax sources—property—at the local level. Almost no other economic endeavor enjoys such a spectrum of insulating conditions. However, as described in the second part of this paper, many of these conditions appear to be eroding and will likely be less able to buffer public school revenues in the future.

Constitutional Privilege

The U.S. Constitution is silent regarding education and schooling. This omission, taken in tandem with Tenth Amendment prescriptions reserving unspecified powers to states, the people, and state-level constitutional provisions, renders education principally a state function.[1] Moreover, state constitutions actively assume responsibility for provision of schooling. State constitutional provisions are generally of three kinds. They assign the legislature a responsibility for provision of an education system that is "thorough and efficient" or "general and uniform" or a product of the legislature's "paramount duty."

The precise language of the state constitution is not as important as is the explicit specification or acceptance of the state's responsibility for providing education. Criminal justice, transportation, welfare, public health, higher education, recreation, and even public safety are not privileged to the same degree as education. A state can decide to create or abolish numerous activities—for example, prisons, highways, parks, welfare payments, or colleges—but it cannot decide to abandon its K–12 education system. Indeed, sometimes a state, almost regardless of the economy, is hamstrung when it comes to school spending. Several states have constitutional provisions that prevent less being spent on education in any one year than in a prior year. In addition to constitutional and statutory protections for state education systems, courts have frequently made clear that education comes first when it comes to appropriating funds.[2]

Decentralized Operation

No modern nation has an education system that is more decentralized or multitiered than the United States'. The consequence is that, most often, U.S. school systems are buffered structurally and politically against resource competition more than any other state or local government service.

The United States has relied on fifty distinct state education systems conceived in the colonial period and evolving well into the twenty-first century. These state systems, in turn, delegate selected dimensions of operational authority to more than 13,000 local school districts. Eighty percent of these local districts have property taxing authority. Those that do not have such taxing power rely on county or municipal governments to generate their required local revenue share.

Local school districts are overseen by boards of education. Eighty percent are comprised of elected members; the other 20% rely on appointees. The remaining are appointed by mayors, city councils, or other elected authorities (such as the Court of Common Pleas in Philadelphia). However, regardless of membership selection procedures, these boards place education in a privileged government position. Most publicly provided services must depend on more general governments for revenue and are subject to the resultant and more intense intersegmental competition for resources that such arrangements imply.

Political Protection

Political transaction costs privilege parents and public school system employees over citizens, particularly citizens who do not have children enrolled in public school. School policy and operational matters can be complicated. It takes a great deal of personal time to become informed regarding details of issues such as racial desegregation, charter schools, curriculum content, testing, graduation standards, geographic placement of a new school, and the configuration of attendance boundaries. These are illustrative of issues with which local school boards routinely deal with and that directly affect parents and educators more than they do other citizens.

Hence, school district politics, including those surrounding funding issues and taxation, tend to be dominated by self-interested coalitions of parents and school district employees. For these constituents, the costs of becoming informed and active in school district decision making are low relative to the benefits to be gained. Hence, it is this employee-parent coalition that tends to dominate local school district school board elections and ballot measures regarding school funding. Their self-interest and favorable predisposition provides schools with added political protection against budget cuts when the overall economy turns down.

Opponents of added school spending or higher taxes for schools can be mobilized and, on occasion, dominate an election. This was dramatized in the 1978 enactment of California's famous tax limitation provision, Proposition 13.[3] Usually, however, incremental costs of proposed school budgets involve only a fractional addition to local property tax rates. Property owners may find themselves projected to pay but a hundred or so additional dollars in the forthcoming year. Hence, most taxpayers, who are not immediate benefactors of schooling or school employment, are unwilling to assume the high transaction costs involved in actively opposing added or sustained school spending at such a low level.

High transaction costs partially explain general citizen apathy toward school spending. There are several more active political elements, however, that favor school funding. Educator employees, those with the most direct interests in sustaining or elevating school spending, are frequently well organized politically. Employee groups can offer sympathetic candidates more electoral campaign resources than most any other school-related constituency. Union members are themselves probably the voters most predisposed to turn out at an election and vote. These dynamics provide schools and school spending with local-level advocates that are long lasting, politically sophisticated, and well-resourced for electoral campaign purposes.

There is an additional political dynamic contributing to the preservation of local school funding levels. A frequent metric, however misguided, for measuring school quality is the amount of operating money a district annually spends per pupil. Many posh suburbs actively compete on this dimension, proudly proclaiming their per-pupil spending status ranking relative to competitor districts. Citizens, parents, and others who have purchased homes in such districts perceive the sustained high value of their property linked to high per-pupil spending levels and accordingly acquiesce to advocate implorations for more money.

Finally, in most states education employee unions have the right to bargain with school boards and to embed collectively derived agreements regarding salaries and working conditions into legally enforceable multiyear contracts.

These extended-year contracts, often bridging or outlasting economic recessions, act as an inertial flywheel to smooth revenue reduction threats.

Multiple Revenue Sources

The distribution of revenue-raising responsibility over three levels of government—federal, state, and local—contributes to education revenue stability. Schools are highly resource dependent, but they are not dependent on a single source. Figure 1.9 demonstrates the three-tier longitudinal mix of government-contributed education revenues from 1920 to 2006.

There are three trends of note in this figure. First, the initial pattern is of dominant local school district support, with states and the federal government as only minor partners. By convention, local district and municipal

FIGURE 1.9

Percentage distribution of revenues

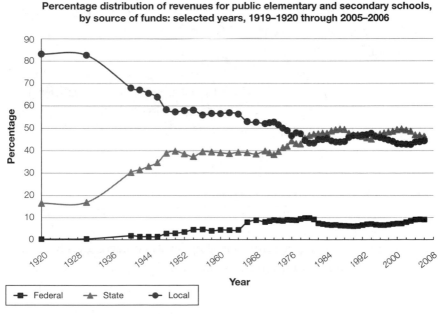

Percentage distribution of revenues for public elementary and secondary schools, by source of funds: selected years, 1919–1920 through 2005–2006

Source: National Center for Education Statistics, *2008 Digest of Education Statistics.*

revenue support have been generated through property taxation. Historically, this arrangement has assisted in insulating schools from economic
ups and downs. Property taxes are relatively inelastic when the economy
swings up. It takes assessors two to three years to capture escalating property values and, thus, to give school districts the full measure of benefit
from economic growth and housing inflation. However, this same inelas-
ticity protects schools during economic downturns when property owners
continue to pay taxes, even if their income is reduced and when assessors
do not reduce property values in a timely manner.

The second trend began in the post–World War II era with state funding
supplanting and matching, or slightly exceeding, local district revenues. This
pattern appears to have resulted, at least partly, from the "equal protection"
legal litigation movement launched in the 1970s in which state courts em-
phasized that once-rampant intrastate spending inequalities were the states'
responsibility to rectify. Remedies to this problem could have taken various
paths that would have left local funding as the principal revenue source for
schools. However, state legislatures chose another course of action, providing funding centrally from state coffers and reducing the relative contributions of local school districts.

This is a double-edged sword. State revenues, generally from sales and
income taxes, can dampen interdistrict per-pupil wealth inequalities. But,
at the same time, state revenues are also more closely linked to economic
fluctuation and more volatile than property tax receipts. Also, added state
funding places education in a more competitive resource arena. Local
school boards concern themselves, and focus their taxing authority, only
on education issues, while state legislatures, even acknowledging education's privileged constitutional position, have to consider a far wider range
of services in deciding who gets what.

The third trend of note pertains to the federal contribution. Even prior
to ratification of the U.S. Constitution, Congress contributed to education policy. This began with the 1780s Land Survey Ordinances specifying
resources in newly opening territories for the support of local schools and
continued with the enactment of vocational education programs, the pas-

sage of so-called "impact aid" to compensate local school districts for lost revenue and enrollment consequences stemming from federal land ownership and program activity, and the 1958 National Defense Education Act (NDEA) response to the surprise Soviet Union launching of Sputnik, the world's first orbiting satellite.

In 1965 the federal government launched its most significant education endeavor when the Johnson administration initiated the Elementary and Secondary Education Act (ESEA). Appropriations from this legislation pumped federal spending all the way to the then-unheard level of 8 percent of total school revenues. The currently controversial No Child Left Behind Act (NCLB) is a 2001 addendum to ESEA. While this statute did not dramatically increase federal funding for education (at least as a percent of total local, state, and federal revenue), it ushered in a completely new era of accountability in education and attendant educator and educator-sympathizer resistance.

Regardless of ESEA and NCBL's long-standing and escalating influence, the federal contribution has seldom been of much revenue consequence. Prior to 2009, the highest historic federal contribution rate to public school spending was 10 percent. The Obama administration's economic stimulus plan ($44 billion for states and schools under the American Recovery and Reinvestment Act [ARRA] of 2009) dramatically altered this trajectory and contributed to a more evenly balanced revenue portfolio for schools. Now the federal government is less and less a junior partner and more and more an equal partner in the tripartite American method of funding schools

Indeed, the 2009 ARRA stimulus package may signal an entirely new source of fiscal stability for America's schools. If the economy turns down, the federal government may be the major fiscal safety net for schools.

WHY THE EVER-PRESENT SENSE OF FISCAL DOOM FOR SCHOOLS?

If school revenues do indeed enjoy such remarkable financial stability, why is there a perception of fiscal calamity? There are two related answers to this question: media dynamics and protectionist personnel provisions.

School district budget cycles are imperfectly synchronized with legislative appropriations processes. While the fiscal year for state and local governments routinely begins on July 1, it is increasingly rare that legislative bodies enact spending bills much in advance of this date. Yet school districts are legally obligated to have balanced budgets. They cannot balance anticipated expenditures through deficit financing. As local school boards begin their winter and spring budget planning, in the face of what they and their administrative officers perceive as state and federal fiscal uncertainty, they publicly discuss, as state sunshine statutes mandate, their contingencies for budget cutting.

In that 80 percent of school district budgets are absorbed in personnel costs, when pressed fiscally local school boards give consideration to personnel cutbacks and salary freezes. State statutes and collectively bargained employee contracts make it necessary to inform school employees, usually in April or May, if there are to be layoffs. School districts sensing financial vulnerability and needing to comply with personnel notification deadlines issue layoff notices and hold mandatory public hearings, even if the probability of actual layoffs is slim. Such negative publicity triggers a media frenzy, alarms employee and parent advocates, and exacerbates a prevailing public perception that, yet again, schools are headed for fiscally stringent times.

Though the reality of resource reductions is remote, it is a rare reporter— or teacher who receives a layoff notice (however unlikely to be acted on), or parent who was expecting to have that teacher for her third grader in the fall—who sees the matter in historic perspective or with objectivity.

A DISCONCERTING LOOK INTO THE FUTURE

Education's short-run fiscal prospect is likely quite different from the long-run outlook. The short run, through 2011, will probably not be terribly different from that which school districts are now experiencing. If anything, money matters may improve somewhat as state and local government fiscal conditions improve.

However, the longer term, beginning in or near 2012, may be character-ized by vastly different and more perilous conditions. This fiscal reversal will have little to do with the outcome of the presidential election in November 2012. Indeed, the structural conditions described here will likely have a nega-tive impact on school revenues regardless of electoral outcomes.

Public frustration with four decades of stagnant school achievement, the apparent unproductive increasing labor intensity, the slow pace of infusing instructional technology into classrooms, the overall decline in education productivity, frightening financial liabilities associated with current and future retiree pensions and health-care obligations, added political compe-tition from other publicly funded services, increasing centralization of rev-enue generation, the diminishing number of households with school-age children, and overarching pressures of soaring national debt all warn of a downwardly spiraling funding dynamic that may be more powerful than any partisan electoral forces. Future presidents, governors, mayors, school board members, and superintendents will likely face a perfect storm of fis-cal obligations, revenue restrictions, and resource competition not seen for a hundred years.

In the years 2009–2011, these revenue stabilizing factors likely will protect schools and per-pupil revenues. This prediction is based largely on the un-precedented congressionally authorized ARRA stimulus recovery package for education. The dramatic escalation of the federal government's revenue con-tribution, close to 15 percent of education's national spending total, almost ensures that, when finally compiled, 2008–2009 per-pupil national mean revenues will not have declined (and if they did it will not be by much).

We do not dispute the reality of the current recession. State and local tax receipts, heavily dependent on consumption and income, were down 4.6 percent for 2009 from the previous year. Retail sales are down. Hous-ing foreclosures and personal bankruptcies continue to climb. Purchasing managers anticipate continued cutbacks in orders placed. Consumer con-fidence is still close to a three-decade low.

More positively, aside from President Obama's efforts to jawbone the economy upward, the federal government's monetary and fiscal recovery plans have been enacted into policy with remarkable speed. Congressional willingness to subsidize the economy has never been higher, and the international community has coordinated and elevated stimulus spending as never before. In mid-2009, the U.S., European, and Asian stock markets seem to have bottomed out and turned upward. Durable goods inventories are becoming slender. Job loss rates, while continuing, are slowing. And nationwide unemployment has stabilized near 10 percent with no indication of coming close to catastrophic Great Depression rates.

Balancing these factors leads to the projections in Figure 1.10a and Figure 1.10b, which provide bounded estimates of near-future national total

FIGURE 1.10a

Current expenditures per pupil

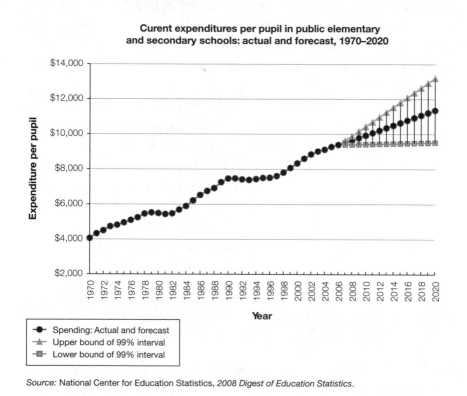

Curent expenditures per pupil in public elementary
and secondary schools: actual and forecast, 1970–2020

Source: National Center for Education Statistics, *2008 Digest of Education Statistics.*

FIGURE 1.10b

Current expenditures in public elementary

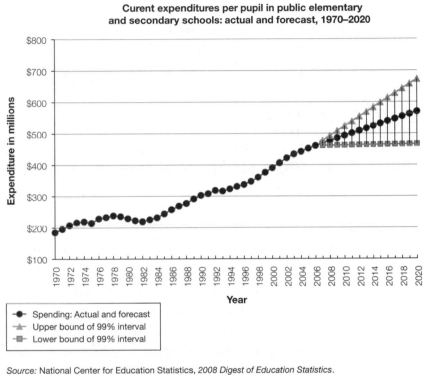

Curent expenditures per pupil in public elementary
and secondary schools: actual and forecast, 1970–2020

Spending: Actual and forecast
Upper bound of 99% interval
Lower bound of 99% interval

Source: National Center for Education Statistics, *2008 Digest of Education Statistics*.

operating revenues by per pupil and in the aggregate. The major assumption here is that the federal government K–12 contribution will be close to $90 billion. The $37 billion in the stimulus package intended to replace reduced state and local education revenue will be sustained at least another fiscal year and continue to cushion what would otherwise likely have been the first per-pupil spending reduction in sixty years.

The probability that the recession will end quickly and result in a dramatic upward increase in the GDP and school spending seems remote. The lower bound of the projection, sustained school spending, seems the likely outcome.

EDUCATION'S LONGER-RUN FISCAL FUTURE IS FAR LESS OPTIMISTIC

Like a tsunami amassing momentum far out at sea but not yet visible from land, a set of ominous economic conditions has been building that portends a far less fortunate fiscal future for America's public schools. Early effects of the tsunami are already starting to be felt, even if the full tidal impact has yet to surge.

Early Warnings

Even as mean national per-pupil revenues continued to trend upward, in the 1990s public education ceased to capture its historic share of the fiscal dividend resulting from GDP growth.

Figure 1.11 displays a sixty-year (1947–2007) perspective of national mean per-pupil expenditures as a percentage of the GDP. (In that mean per-pupil spending is a small dollar figure relative to the huge number for the GDP; the quotient is a very small percentage. Thus, it is the trend line that matters, not the actual percentage). Evident here is that up to the 1980s, education spending was capturing an ever-larger per-pupil share of GDP growth. In the 1980s this trend reached a plateau, and in the 1990s it actually reversed with inflation-adjusted national mean per-pupil spending occupying a smaller and smaller percentage of the GDP.

Public Intolerance Regarding Stagnant Student Achievement

While the reduction in the GDP share may be an early warning sign, more ominous signals are coming from other sources. The United States expects much of its schools. Preparation for career, college, and citizenship; racial and gender equity lessons; leisure, aesthetic, and environmental appreciation and awareness; expectations of scientific sophistication; instruction on personal health, hygiene, safe driving,sex, reproductive, alcohol, drug, and social mobility issues are all part of the booming, buzzing, and sometimes antithetical public discourse that results in assigning purposes to the nation's schools. America's solution to a public policy issue is to add a course

FIGURE 1.11

Real GDP and current expenditures per pupil

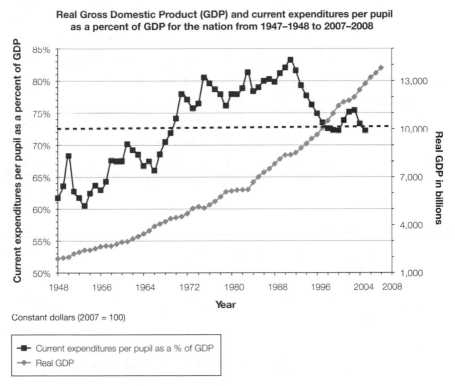

Real Gross Domestic Product (GDP) and current expenditures per pupil as a percent of GDP for the nation from 1947–1948 to 2007–2008

Constant dollars (2007 = 100)

- ■- Current expenditures per pupil as a % of GDP
- ◆- Real GDP

Source: GDP data retrieved from National Economic Accounts, Bureau of Economic Analysis; National Center for Education Statistics, *2008 Digest of Education Statistics*.

to the public school curriculum. The consequent spectrum of purposes impedes easy appraisal of the system's outcomes.

However, regardless of the range and complexity of purposes, there are two fundamental areas in which schools must maximize performance in order to make progress toward the hierarchy of other desired education outcomes. These fundamental activities are children learning to read and perform mathematics and students staying in school. When viewed longitudinally, America's schools have not done well on either of these.

As shown in figure 1.12, despite sustained upward revenue growth, National Assessment of Educational Progress (NAEP) reading scores have been flat for four decades. And graduation rates, as recently calculated by Nobel Laureate economist James Heckman, display the same regrettable pattern (see figure 1.13). For a half-century nearly a third of the nation's high school students have failed to graduate. Many of these subsequently obtain high school equivalent training, such as the GED, but schools themselves have somehow failed each year in retaining more than a million adolescents.

What explains this stagnant condition? The reasons are varied and complicated and cannot be treated adequately here. Suffice it to proclaim that the inability of the public education system to elevate student achievement will assuredly trigger increasing political pressures for reforms.

FIGURE 1.12
Trends in average reading scale scores

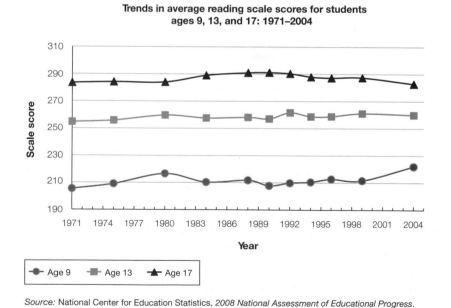

Source: National Center for Education Statistics, *2008 National Assessment of Educational Progress.*

FIGURE 1.13

Heckman calculated high school graduation rates

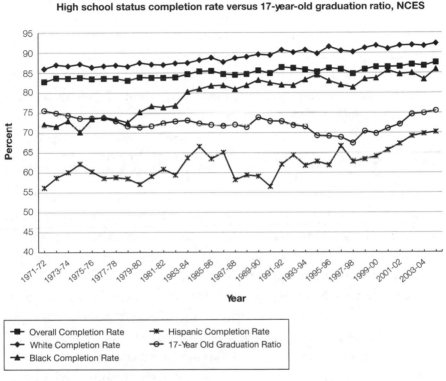

High school status completion rate versus 17-year-old graduation ratio, NCES

Legend:
- Overall Completion Rate
- White Completion Rate
- Black Completion Rate
- Hispanic Completion Rate
- 17-Year Old Graduation Ratio

Source: Laird et al., June 2007; National Center for Education Statistics, *2004 Digest of Education Statistics*.

Matters Are Changing

There are reasons to be guardedly optimistic that public schools are adapting to the new global reality and grappling with the new achievement challenge. Increasing numbers of states are independently adjusting upward their learning objectives and achievement goals. There is an expansion and political acceptance of charter schools. Approximately 20 percent of the nation's classroom teachers are now paid by performance measurement means, in addition to or in place of the conventional single salary schedule.

And technology appears to be creeping into the interstices and margins of schooling through means such as distance learning and private-sector-marketed new curricula.

The question is whether or not these or a combination of these changes will be adopted with sufficient speed and intensity to preserve the resource privilege that public education has long held.

This stagnant achievement has occurred despite the investment of billions of dollars for added education personnel. Figure 1.5 compares education personnel growth to enrollment trends. There is nothing new here, but it is apparent that increases in educator employment outstrip growth in numbers of enrolled students. At some point decision makers have to question whether or not this strategy should be sustained.

Other economic sectors have had great success and gained significant productivity by substituting capital for labor. Communication, agriculture, finance, and manufacturing have all become much less labor intensive and much more dependent on technology to provide services. To date, education has been remarkably impervious to such changes.

Public-sector employees generally, and education employees in particular, are typically provided with generous fringe benefits, namely retirement plans and health care. Health care is expensive for those who are currently employed. It is also expensive for those who have retired. Pensions in education are said to be heavily back-loaded; that is, they do not provide much benefit for those who have been employed for a short time. However, for those teachers and administrators willing to be patient and remain for a long time in a school system or state pension plan, the benefits are generous when compared to private-sector employees in comparable positions.

The problem is that school districts and states have not been setting aside sufficient funding to cover fully these employee and retiree pension and health obligations. And now there is a big bill coming due. Robert Novy-Marx and Joshua Rauh estimate unfunded pension systems liability to be approximately $3 trillion, possibly as high as $5 trillion.[4] Clark estimates unfunded teacher retiree health costs liability to be in the range of

$0.5 to $1 trillion. All other public employee retiree health cost liabilities are probably the same amount or higher.[5]

Resource Competition

Paying interest on and striving to reduce the $13 trillion national debt; ensuring that Social Security is fiscally stable; funding the health-care needs of an aging and unhealthy population; addressing the nation's deteriorating physical transportation and waste infrastructure; converting the economy to an ecologically sound basis; buoying banks and other fragile financial institutions; bailing out fundamental industries such as automobile manufacturing; and sustaining the War on Terror are increasingly intense competitors for public dollars. What the total bill is for the foregoing list is difficult to say. However, it is not difficult to see that the aggregate consequence of the foregoing assuredly will have a diminishing effect on allocations to operations such as the support of schools.

For much of the twentieth century, education had a protected revenue base.[6] Most school dollars were generated from local property taxes, which are resilient in times of economic duress. However, as plaintiffs have successfully pursued equalization suits, a larger and larger share of school spending has shifted to state sources. States depend on income and sales taxes, revenue sources much more tightly linked to economic ups and downs. As education shifts from local to state and federal funding, it forfeits its privileged revenue base, finds itself in competition with added sectors for scarce resources, and is more vulnerable to the vagaries of the larger economy.

There is an additional demographic threat to public schools' politically protected resource privilege. Many of the contemporary resource resiliency arrangements were politically promulgated in the 1960s and 1970s at the height of the post–World War II baby boom. In 1963, 57 percent of the nation's households had children under age 18 at home, marking the high point in the nation's history. By 2008 this figure had fallen to 46 percent and was still dropping. Moreover, the number of children at home had itself dwindled to an average of 1.8 per female. Finally, only 36 percent of households had enrolled or were intending to enroll their children in public schools.

The political base for public education is shrinking. The competition for resources from other sectors—for example, the aging baby boomers—will assuredly imperil schools' historic resource privilege.

CONCLUSION

Public schools have enjoyed a century-long period of relative full funding. Year-over-year per-pupil spending, even when controlled for inflation, has climbed even higher, as have teacher salaries and benefits and the total number of school employees. But an emerging coincidence of unfavorable fiscal and political conditions suggests that this era of plenty is about to end and a new era of intense public policy concern for education efficiency and productivity is about to begin. This new era of necessity must cope with personnel costs. Savings assuredly can be gained from greater scale economies and greater resource efficiency. However, regardless of progress in these areas, it is eventually augmenting labor with capital that will have to provide the "penny saved" solution.

2

What's Happening in the States

June Kronholz

FIRST, SCHOOL THERMOSTATS WERE lowered a couple of degrees. A secretarial spot was left vacant. Maybe a junior varsity sport was dropped or the library budget was trimmed. That was the easy stuff.

As the nation's recession has worsened and state tax revenues have withered, school districts almost everywhere have had to look for deeper, wider, more painful cuts to budgets that most of them already felt were stretched too thin. In its December 2009 Fiscal Survey of States, the National Governors Association reported that twenty-nine states cut K–12 spending as a way to close budget shortfalls in the fiscal year that ended in September 2009 and that thirty planned K–12 cuts in the year ending in September 2010. In Polk County, Florida, that translated into a 5.36 percent hit to the school system's 2009–2010 budget. In Clark County, Nevada, it meant a 6 percent cut, even though three thousand more children enrolled in the schools that year than had the year before.

Superintendents are predicting worse to come. Federal stimulus dollars prevented thousands of teacher layoffs for two years, but by the 2011 school year, "We are definitely at the budget cliff,"[1] said David Peterson, chief business officer of the Scottsdale, Arizona, Unified School District.

There is a certainty, too, among many superintendents that they are running out of often-used options such as tapping reserve funds, trimming supply budgets, and foregoing academic conferences. When the New York State Council of School Superintendents polled its members about their 2010–2011 budget plans, "they all said they'd done the easy stuff," said the council's deputy director, Robert N. Lowry Jr. By the 2010–2011 school year, "we will have run out of the easier options," added Don Phillips, superintendent of Poway, California, United School District, which already has gone from two assistant principals to one in all its elementary schools, cut its custodial staff, and set up a bridal-type registry where donors can help fill the district's supply cabinet.

In researching this essay, I interviewed superintendents and chief financial officers in dozens of school districts around the country—big and small districts, urban and suburban. States particularly hard hit by the recession—Arizona, California, Florida, and the industrial Midwest—face massive budget shortfalls, and, not surprisingly, their superintendents reported making the most drastic cuts. In farming and mining states and in those states where real estate prices have held steady—Texas, the Dakotas, Nebraska, and Missouri, among others—federal stimulus dollars have lessened most of the pain.

Some of the cost-cutting strategies those districts reported using go to the heart of school-improvement efforts and may end up undercutting student and teacher performance in the long run. Colorado Springs District No. 11 cut $1 million from a bonus plan that rewarded schools for improved student achievement. The Paradise Valley, Arizona, Unified Public School District has just one half-time reading specialist for each of its elementary schools, each of which typically enrolls nine hundred students.

Other strategies are stopgap and cannot be sustained for very long. In Fairfax County, Virginia, teachers agreed to forego raises and cost-of-living adjustments rather than face layoffs and larger class sizes. Almost no one plans to buy textbooks any time soon. "We don't have any books that say, 'Some day a man will land on the moon.' I don't know what they say about Pluto," said Poway's Don Phillips. Still, some strategies adopted by superintendents and CFOs take a longer view that may benefit their districts for years to come. Scottsdale has invited private investors to install solar-power installations on the roofs of its schools. Jefferson County, Colorado, schools have begun training teachers how to handle larger classes.

The biggest challenge for school districts is that the overwhelming majority of their costs are in personnel salaries and benefits—and that most personnel are teachers, whose benefits are often protected by union contracts, state legislation, or both. Nationwide, personnel costs typically account for at least three-quarters of school district operating budgets, and even more in some Sun Belt states and inner-city districts. In Scottsdale, salaries and benefits account for 90 percent of spending, with another 6 percent going to utilities. "I have 4 percent for everything else," said Chief Business Officer David Peterson.

That gives school districts three options for closing their budget gaps:

Trim personnel: That is easier said than done, of course. State mandates, laws, and constitutional amendments have cut class sizes in many states by increasing the number of teachers. But "if you can't do something to reduce the number of teaching positions, you can't do something to reduce costs," said Michael Griffith, a policy analyst at the Education Commission of the States. Tracie Rainey of the Colorado State Finance Project added, "You either pay teachers less or you pay less teachers."

Trim everything else: Even 10–25 percent of a multimillion dollar budget amounts to real money. So districts are joining purchasing co-ops, doing more online professional development, beginning more intensive use of buses, and adopting smarter energy management (solar power isn't limited to the Sun Belt states; Milwaukee is trying it).

Find new sources of revenue: With sales, property, and income tax revenues lagging, school districts are looking at other ways to raise money. Sometimes that means just new and different taxes. But some districts have set up foundations to raise money, have imposed new fees, or have turned to modest entrepreneurial enterprises.

There's no silver bullet when it comes to trimming budgets—it is a long, tough slog with savings often measured in the tens of thousands of dollars rather than the millions. Arlington County, Virginia, for example, a district facing a 2009–2010 budget gap that it estimated would be between $12 million and $16.5 million, opted against providing new uniforms for its maintenance staff at a savings of $20,000.

The bright side of the budget crisis, said Scottsdale's David Peterson, is that "it is making us look at how we operate" and, in that way, may be positioning the most cost-conscious districts for the new realities of public education. Declining enrollment in most big cities and even in high-growth states like Colorado has left districts with unsustainable overhead but with little political will to close schools. Traditional schools are in stiff competition with charter schools for students and state-paid per-pupil allocations. Years of tough negotiations with unions have saddled districts with potentially crippling retirement and medical obligations. For example, for every dollar Milwaukee pays in salaries, it pays another sixty-three cents in benefits, about twice the cost of benefits in most public-sector jobs. Among part-time kitchen workers, benefits tack on eighty-one cents for every dollar in salary.

Perhaps most inauspiciously, taxpayers almost everywhere are letting governments know that they are not willing to shoulder higher public spending. According to the Pew Center on the States, education accounts for 29 percent of state spending in New York, 30 percent in Florida and Pennsylvania, and 45.5 percent in Michigan. "We can't afford to keep doing education as we've always done it," said Jeff Weiler, CFO of the Clark County School District. "There won't be a huge infusion of money even when the recession ends. We'll be lucky to get back to where we were."

TEACHER-LED SCHOOLS, TEAM CLEANING, CLASS SIZE, AND MORE

Until someone figures out how to automate the classroom—and the bus route, the cafeteria, and the coaching staff—a school district's biggest costs will be in personnel. Districts typically spend from 75 percent to 80 percent of their budgets on salaries and benefits, according to the Education Commission of the States; and 65 percent of total education spending goes to teachers, it adds.[2]

Union contracts often give districts little flexibility to trim workforces or salaries, though, and state legislatures can frequently add to the problem by approving benefits increases that they pass along to the districts to pay. "The biggest savings are the ones that are the least accessible—salaries and benefits," said James Langlois, superintendent of the Putnam/Northern Westchester, New York, Board of Cooperative Educational Services. "Everything else is picking around the edges."

That has been tempered a bit by the budget crisis facing most states. The Poway United School District, like many others in California, negotiated a 2.7 percent salary rollback with its teachers to prevent any layoffs. Non-unionized Fairfax County, Virginia, negotiated an agreement with its school employees' association that requires teachers to forego $72 million in step increases and cost-of-living adjustments in the 2009–2010 school year.

Paradise Valley Unified School District, which includes parts of Phoenix and Scottsdale, Arizona, negotiated salary cuts that will depend on the size of the decline in its state funding. The worst-case scenario would mean a 6.2 percent salary cut, but that could likely be reduced to "the high 4's" if sales tax revenues pick up, said Tom Elliott, the district's assistant superintendent for business services. Salary cuts or freezes are not a long-range strategy, though, and that has superintendents and CFOs looking for other, more sustainable ways to trim their personnel costs.

One of the biggest recurring savings that districts can realize comes from closing underused schools. With America deep in another baby boom, it seems hard to imagine underused schools. But even in fast-growing Colorado, 108 of the state's 178 school districts have declining enrollment, according to the Colorado State Finance Project. Upstate New York districts are losing enrollment at the rate of 1 percent a year. Meanwhile, inner-city districts are seeing steep declines as students move to the suburbs and, increasingly, to charters. Washington, DC, where more than one in three public school students attend a charter, closed twenty-three district schools in 2008.

The Colorado School Finance Project, a nonprofit that has been studying such issues as funding adequacy in Colorado for more than a decade, estimated that Colorado districts can save from $300,000 to $400,000 a year by closing an elementary school with fewer than 300 students, and $400,000 to $600,000 by closing a middle school. The Pittsburgh school district realized $14 million a year in savings by closing twenty-two of its eighty-six schools in 2006. Colorado Springs District No. 11 anticipated savings of $4 million a year from closing nine schools in a community whose enrollment had fallen by 12 percent, to 28,000, in twelve years.

A big share of those savings is in maintenance and building costs, but there are also significant savings in personnel. Lynn Bragga, director of budget and financial reporting for the Richmond, Virginia, public schools, estimated that the district will cut sixty-two full-time-equivalent jobs in 2010 when it closes a middle school whose enrollment had declined to 300—or about five students for every adult job.

A school's staff doesn't necessarily decline with its enrollment—you still need a third-grade teacher even if there are only ten third graders. As enrollment declines, the number of students per teacher does too, leading to huge staff inefficiencies. In districts that use site-based budgeting—where schools are given a salary allowance based on their enrollment—that also can lead to a hollowing-out of the program. A school paying that third-grade teacher with ten students and a fourth-grade teacher with just as few might have to forego a music teacher or a math specialist.

Richmond's Lynn Bragga said that is pretty much what happened in the middle school slated for closure. It had already lost its guidance counselors, much of its clerical staff, and its assistant principal, and—surprise!—was in the seventh year of failing to meet No Child Left Behind progress goals.

It is painful to close a school, of course, but budget woes can give administrators the political cover and community support to "right size" their infrastructure. Milwaukee calculated four years ago that excess capacity was costing it $26.5 million a year. The district estimated it would need five years to shed that capacity and began by closing nineteen schools, although it re-opened two as specialized high schools. So far, those closings have shed only enough excess capacity to save $6.5 million a year. With one year to go on the right-sizing plan, "we have a considerable amount more to close," said the district's CFO, Michelle Nate.

Increasing class sizes may be even more unpopular than closing schools, but it can create even bigger savings. Kristen Michael, director of budget services for Fairfax County, Virginia, Public Schools, said the district saved $9 million in both 2008–2009 and 2009–2010 by increasing its general education class size by half a student. Countywide, that increased elementary school classes to an average 21.2 students and middle school school classes to 24.1 students. Of the $150 million in cuts the district planned to make in 2009–2010, about $20 million of it will come from staff reductions.

Long Beach, California, is restrained by state mandate from increasing class sizes beyond twenty students in kindergarten through grade three, so it negotiated a contract with its teachers union that allows classes of up to thirty-five in grades four and five and thirty-one in grades six through twelve. Elsewhere, though, districts are bypassing class size requirements that have boosted their personnel costs. Poway Unified, in San Diego County, opted to ignore the state mandate and increase classes to twenty-three students, with the option of raising them further to twenty-five. Poway will pay $3.1 million in class size fines in 2009–2010—that is, California will withhold a percentage of its per-pupil funds for each child in each class that is larger than twenty. But that still is cheaper than the $3.7 million Poway says it would cost to hire enough the teachers to meet the state 20:1 mandate. Moreover, the fines stop accumulating after twenty-five children per class; there is no further penalty on the twenty-sixth child. "We could go to thirty [without adding to the penalties], and we may get there" in 2010–2011, said Poway superintendent Don Phillips.

Florida is granting waivers to a state mandate that eventually would have reduced classes to eighteen students in elementary school, twenty-two in middle school, and twenty-five in high school. That plan was originally to be phased in, starting with the lowest grades and working up by grade level, but after meeting early targets, "we won't go to the next level," because of the cost, said Polk County Public Schools finance officer Audra Curts-Whann.

Superintendents are looking beyond increasing class size in an effort to cut their personnel, of course. The most endangered job in education may be the assistant principal, as districts opt to cut jobs in the office rather than the classroom. Long Beach, California, will have fifty-six vice principals in 2010, down from seventy-one in 2009, while Richmond, Virginia, has eliminated the second assistant principal in all of its elementaries.

School librarians are also vulnerable, with many being cut back from full-time to part-time employment. Poway is offering just two languages instead of four in its high schools—Spanish in each, plus Mandarin in its newest high school and German in two others where the program was particularly strong. And Blind Brook-Rye Union Free School District in New York dropped French altogether. The Littleton, Colorado, schools are trying to share a chemistry teacher with a nearby district, according to the Colorado School Finance Project. In tiny Woodlinn, Colorado, has hired a part-time superintendent. Among other things, his reduced salary offsets the perception in a poor community that school leaders are too highly paid. And in Milwaukee, where schools have wide latitude over their hiring, a few schools are sharing a principal and a few others are teacher led. In those schools, a teacher-leader does the administrative work and a neighboring principal does the evaluations. The arrangement saves a salary, which the school can use for other purposes.

Clark County, Nevada, meanwhile, has eliminated block scheduling, which district CFO Jeff Weiler said cost $500,000 per school in extra staffing costs, or about $11 million for the district. Block scheduling created additional time for students to take noncore classes like music; on nonblock days they could squeeze in two classes in a two-period block. Now the district is offering core classes, for a fee, on Saturdays so that students can stay in their weekday enrichment courses. Taking another tack, Hillsborough County, Florida, estimated it would save $38 million a year by having high school teachers teach six periods a day, up from five.

James Langlois of Putnam/Northern Westchester Board of Cooperative Educational Services in New York said he is advising member schools of his co-op about other ways to reduce personnel. His suggestions include hiring technicians to run science labs, freeing higher-paid teachers to teach another period each; paying department chairs a stipend instead of giving them the typical two periods of release time; scheduling larger physical education, art, and music classes; reconsidering or rescheduling teachers' before- and afterschool activities, which require extra pay; and rethinking the one-on-one aids that have become increasingly common in special education. According to Langlois, the reason most special education children have aids is to help them become more independent, "but the opposite is happening. The child becomes dependent on the aid" to help him or her control behavior or complete work. He instead proposes an annual review of each child to determine if he or she still needs an aid.

Many urban districts still have paper-based systems to keep track of purchases, work orders, and the like because they have found it politically difficult to eliminate white-collar jobs in high-unemployment inner cities. Those systems are ripe for automation. Pittsburgh has turned its old triplicate forms—which were filled in by anyone seeking a repayment, an advance, or a leave, among other things—into interactive computer PDF files. Its work-order system, also now paper based, will go online in 2009–2010.

Similarly, Milwaukee saved seven jobs by putting its purchasing system online. Under the old purchasing system, schools called in their orders to a central office staffer who filled in a purchase-order form. Seattle Public Schools CFO Donald Kennedy said he is doing an analysis of the district's business office with the aim of automating more of its functions and, as a result, has already eliminated twenty-nine jobs.

Automation is also likely to eliminate some waste. Richmond's Lynn Bragga said the district spends $52 million a year for supplies but has no central database to track its purchases. Moreover, half of those purchases are documented only by paper receipts. An audit found some schools paying one dollar for a box of paper clips that could have been purchased for less than thirty cents under a centralized contract.

Under pressure from taxpayers and tech-savvy parents, suburban districts have already automated many clerical jobs, but apparently there's still room for more. School co-ops in St. Louis and New York operate online placement services where teachers can post resumes and schools can post job openings, saving districts advertising dollars, paperwork, and time.

Some jobs cannot be automated, of course, so districts are finding ways to redefine them. Colorado Springs District No. 11 reduced the number of workers who manage the heating, air conditioning, and ventilation systems at each of its buildings from two to one but set up a team of "floaters" who can respond to emergencies around the district. Long Beach Unified eliminated thirty-five custodial jobs and saved $1.6 million by switching to "team cleaning." Instead of assigning a custodian to each school, Long Beach assembled cleaning teams that each tackle four schools a night.

Districts are also looking at their use of substitute teachers. In Scottsdale, Arizona, all administrators and curriculum writers are now obliged to substitute teach five days a year. That will save only $100,000 out of the district's $1.4 million substitute budget, but "it helps" and is "good for everyone to see what it's like in a classroom," said David Peterson, the chief business officer who also substitute teaches math, chemistry, and physics.

Grand Rapids, Michigan, Public Schools has contracted with a private company for substitutes. The arrangement saves the district human resources chores like payroll processing, said Superintendent Bernard Taylor Jr. And most schools are rethinking the practice of hiring substitutes so full-time teachers can attend meetings, crunch test-scores, or design professional development presentations. New hand-held computers can do the number crunching and keep teachers in their classrooms—*if* districts can afford the technology, of course. As for relief time, "We won't have the money for that," said Poway's Don Phillips.

The need to cut staff—as well as fuel and equipment costs—is forcing schools to take a good look at their bus schedules as well. Fairfax County Public Schools will save $4.7 million in 2009–2010 by having each bus and driver complete three runs in the morning and evening instead of two.

Seattle expects $2.2 million in savings by centralizing school start times so it can use its buses more efficiently and plans to eliminate forty-nine buses in 2009–2010.

It is possible that no city has a more complicated busing system than Milwaukee, which has long allowed youngsters to attend the schools of their choice, with the city providing transport. That has resulted in buses criss-crossing the city and a $27 million general education bus budget. At the suggestion of parents, teachers, and other community members, Milwaukee has begun limiting how far it will bus students and has started to offer door-to-door van service to students who return to neighborhood schools in high-crime areas, forsaking schools in safer but more distant neighborhoods.

Cutting transport is not painless, though. Centralizing bell schedules takes away some of the autonomy that districts allow their schools, for one thing. Clark County's magnet and "empowerment" schools formerly kept to a different schedule than the rest of the district, with longer hours on some days and bus service to accommodate their needs. Now the county has adopted a uniform bell schedule aimed at cutting bus runs and transport costs.

Other districts are debating widening the busing radius—typically ending bus service to anyone who lives within a three-mile radius of school rather than a two-mile radius—or eliminating busing altogether, where state law allows. But that creates safety issues in neighborhoods without sidewalks and could raise dropout rates among youngsters who already may have little motivation to go to school. Moreover, general education busing helps underwrite special education busing, which districts are required to provide under federal disabilities law. Poway Unified saved $1 million in 2008–2009 by cutting underused bus routes and reducing ridership from 6,000 to 4,000 students, each of whom pays a transport fee. But those fees help pay for the mechanics, schedulers, and others who maintain Poway's special education transport system, which is free. "If we went to no [general ed] ridership, that would increase our [special ed] costs," said Don Phillips.

HEALTH FAIRS, EARLY RETIREMENT, AND WORKMEN'S COMP

Benefits add a third or more to most compensation packages and require the same degree of creativity to trim. For example, union contracts in Milwaukee are so sacrosanct that the district is required to deliver or mail paper paychecks to four thousand employees who refuse direct deposit and online notification. Postage for those workers costs the district $80,000 a year, said CFO Michelle Nate—not a lot in the scheme of things, "but a teacher costs $90,000." Still, districts have begun nibbling around the edges of worker benefits, sometimes achieving substantial savings.

Retirees' benefits seem the most vulnerable in this economic climate. The Palo Alto Unified School District, among many others, pays medical benefits for retirees for five years or until they reach age sixty-five—a benefit that currently costs the district $500,000 a year, said Superintendent Kevin Skelly. In 2008–2009 Palo Alto renegotiated its union contract to drop that benefit. The district's 1,100 current workers are still eligible for the benefit, which means it will run for another two decades or so, but new hires are excluded. One upside of the recession, Skelly added, is that fewer workers are taking early retirement, and the district is paying medical benefits for a smaller number of retirees for fewer years.

Pittsburgh had a similar arrangement that required retirees to pay 5 percent of health insurance premium costs and 20 percent of any year-to-year premium increase. Workers could retire at age fifty-five, which means the district was committed to paying the bulk of their medical insurance premiums until they reached Medicare eligibility. The district now has increased retirees' share to 50 percent of any premium increases. One early result of the change is that the cut in potential benefits "scared" a lot of workers into early retirement before any further cuts are made, enabling the district to shed a substantial number of jobs, said CFO Christopher Berdnik.

Milwaukee has had less success negotiating a change in retiree benefits, however, which suggests the peril at hand. The district pays full health-care benefits and 100 percent of the premium cost for all of its employees, including part-timers, who can retire as early as age fifty-five. The district currently faces a $2.2 billion liability for retiree health-care benefits, and because the district failed to win any relief in arbitration, that liability will grow to $4.9 billion in 2013. It's "going to eat us alive," said CFO Michelle Nate.

A few years ago retirement incentive plans seemed a good way to shed high-salary veteran teachers. But in the light of budget gaps, that now seems an expensive benefit that districts are trying to eliminate. Richmond, Virginia, for example, had an incentive plan that paid teachers 35 percent of their salaries for five years or 25 percent for seven years if they would retire early. But the benefit cost the district about $4 million a year and did not attract the teachers that the district most wanted to shed. Even after the district shut down the program, employees who had taken the option retained their payouts, eventually costing the district $28 million. Similarly, Clark County, Nevada, dropped an early retirement program that had been in place since the 1980s and expects salary savings of $2.5 million a year from the move, said CFO Jeff Weiler.

Arizona, which has experienced huge growth and a shortage of public-sector workers until just recently, has long allowed retired teachers and other state employee to return to work and collect both a salary and their full retirement benefits. That benefit is changing in the new economic environment, though. In Paradise Valley three hundred of those retirees were the first teachers let go as the district struggled to close its budget gap.

Districts are taking back or reducing benefits for current employees as well. Palo Alto had long allowed its administrative staff to accrue unused vacation days and take a cash payout at retirement. That created a liability of $450,000 in unused vacation days—"not a huge amount" in a $150 million budget, but eliminating it also solved a bookkeeping nightmare. "I didn't know how that time built up," Superintendent Kevin Skelly said.

Almost everywhere districts are asking employees to shoulder a bigger share of medical premiums or pension contributions, although many increases are fairly marginal because of union contracts. The Education Commission of the States estimates that health-care costs are rising by 7–10 percent a year for teachers, even while education spending is flat or in decline. In Polk County, Florida, the union contract still requires the district to pay 100 percent of health-care premiums.But other districts are increasing co-pays or deductibles. Jefferson County Public Schools in Golden, Colorado, allocates each employee $515 a month to purchase benefits. It formerly paid out the balance to anyone who didn't spend the full $515, but it now has withdrawn that perk. Ann Arbor, Michigan, Public Schools announced plans to pay up to 5 percent of health-care premium increases but no more.

Districts are seeking to rein in benefits in other ways. Arlington, Virginia, Public Schools will cut its pension contribution from 2.3 percent of an employee's salary in 2008–2009 to 0.2 percent in 2009–2010, saving an anticipated $3.7 million. Nevada raised retirement contributions—they are now equal to 21.5 percent of salary, up from 20 percent—but employees will have to pay 0.5 percent of the 1.5 percent increase.

Arlington, Virginia, also has begun hiring teachers on so-called "terminating contracts" that typically expire at the end of the year and save the district from becoming overstaffed. Richmond ended a tuition-reimbursement plan that offered teachers up to $1,000 a year in education benefits and nonteachers up to $500. There will be some education vouchers available this year, but they will be on a first-come-first-served basis and redeemable only for courses needed for teacher certification. Pittsburgh has added an additional step in its pay schedule: There's now a step 10A and a step 10B, so that teachers will need an additional six months to reach the highest step and pay level—a six-month savings in salary for the district.

Pittsburgh's CFO, Christopher Berdnik, has developed two other programs that promise far-reaching savings. In 2008 the district began to self-insure its own catastrophic-illness medical plan and, at year's end, found itself with a surplus in the fund. The district's Health Care Cost Containment Committee—a joint effort of the teachers union local and management—recommended putting $200,000 of the surplus into a health fair that offered cholesterol tests, bone-density screening, blood tests for prostate cancer and diabetes, and other tests that could point out potential health problems. Some 70 percent of the district's teachers participated.

"We're planting seeds that will pay rich fruit" both in employee wellness and reduced health-care costs, Berdnik said.

Similarly, Berdnik stepped up efforts to reduce the district's workmen's compensation claims, which were approaching $20 million. The district more thoroughly investigated injury claims and aggressively litigated some of them. And it moved the processing of claims from the personnel office to the finance office, which took a closer look at costs. The value of outstanding workmen's comp claims dropped by half. At the same time, the district became more aggressive on safety. The local electricians' union sponsored a week-long course on worker safety—including such topics as first aid and scaffolding training—that at least one representative from each school attended. The district also solicited a donation of defibrillators—one for each building—and trained two thousand employees in their use. (A defibrillator saved one life in 2008-2009.) "We won this fight by winning a thousand skirmishes. That's how you gnaw away at a structural gap," Berdnik said.

THERE GOES THE PLANETARIUM

After paying their personnel bills, superintendents and CFOs typically have only 10–25 percent left in their budgets to pay for fuel, buses, computers, books, utilities, professional development, office equipment, supplies, cafeteria operations, transport for the band to Friday night's big game, and everything else that goes into running a school district.With teacher salaries and benefits often untouchable, most districts have turned first to this "everything else" category when they've gone looking for budget cuts. Around the country, bus and computer purchases have been shelved. Thermostats have been turned up in summer or down in winter, and even off. Glenn Gustafson, CFO of Colorado Springs District No. 11, predicts his 28,000-student district will save $250,000 in 2009–2010 by dialing down the heat to 66 degrees (from 68) in the winter and raising the air conditioning temperature from 72 to 74 degrees in the summer. And Scottsdale Unified, like many districts, cut back to a Monday-through-Thursday work week for central office staff in the summer and saved $500,000 on utilities, said David Peterson, the district's chief business officer. Peterson was catching up on work one Friday in August 2009 when he reported that the temperature in his office was "in the high 90s. Most people don't come in," which seemed hardly surprising.

Almost everywhere, textbook purchases have been put on hold. California is allowing its districts to shift money from their state-funded textbook budgets into their general operating funds and to stretch out their textbook adoptions, which currently are every seven years in math and reading. That will save Poway Unified $1.8 million in 2009–2010 on new science texts for its 33,000 students, who now are not likely to get new science books for another three years, said Superintendent Don Phillips. Some reading texts in Long Beach will be twelve years old by the time the district buys new ones in 2013, said Superintendent Chris Steinhauser, who calls the state-mandated adoption cycle "one of the biggest areas of waste" and maintains that the district will save "at least" $5 million by stretching out the cycle by a few years.

Summer school, Saturday academies, afterschool programs, and test-prep courses all are vulnerable, although districts have looked for ways to lessen the effects those cutbacks could have on student achievement. Long Beach Unified eliminated remedial summer school for elementary students but will require that those children attend afterschool tutoring. Poway kept its remedial summer school programs for high schoolers who need credits to graduate or to meet state college entrance requirements. But it eliminated summer classes for students who simply want to accelerate their learning schedule; the district gave them the names of local adult education and community college programs instead. Richmond cut its summer school budget by 25 percent by consolidating classes at fourteen schools rather than running them at twenty-eight schools, as it has done in the past. The move raised transport costs but saved on building costs and personnel.

Most districts also have taken a closer look at their sports and activities budgets. They are playing teams closer to home to save on transport, dropping a junior varsity or junior high sport or two, combining boys' and girls' track, and sending the marching band to fewer away games and the orchestra to fewer festivals. Clark County, Nevada, will cut its sports and activities budget by 15 percent, or $1.7 million, in 2009–2010.

Districts everywhere are dropping little luxuries. Fairfax County, Virginia, Public Schools has cut the planetariums at nine high schools at a savings of $350,000. It will use online resources instead, said Kristen Michael, the director of budget services. Paradise Valley, Arizona, will consolidate evening programs and meetings at a few schools rather than keep the air conditioning churning in every building to accommodate parent and community groups. That and other energy economies are expected to save $1.5 million a year.

But along with cutting their budgets, many districts are looking at new— and potentially cheaper, faster, smarter—ways of doing things. Colorado Springs District No. 11 used $6 million of a $150 million bond issue passed by voters in 2006 to build a fiber-optic "ring" around the district. The new fiber-optic system replaces Internet lines that the district formerly leased from a commercial provider for $550,000 a year.

In 2009–2010 Scottsdale was scheduled to launch a solar power system to power its buildings. The school district does not have the capital to build the solar system, but CFO David Peterson saw a boon for investors who can realize generous tax credits from investments in alternative power. Under Peterson's plan, which is seen in Arizona as a template for other school districts in the state, investors would build solar power collectors on school roofs and covered parking lots. The systems would heat, cool, and light the schools during the day and potentially feed power into the electricity grid on weekends and during the summer. The benefit to investors is tax credits of up to 50 percent in the first year of their investment, Peterson calculated; that includes federal alternative energy tax credits and rapid depreciation. The benefit to the district is a steady energy price. Peterson said he has locked in a rate with the investors of 11 cents per kilowatt hour for the next twenty years, compared to 12 cents the district is currently paying the local utility in peak hours. But there is another bonus: Peterson plans to charge students and staff up to $400 a year to park in the new covered lots, up from the $100 they pay now for an uncovered parking spot.

Alternative energy doesn't have to be limited to Sun Belt states. In Milwaukee one elementary school is already running on solar power, and a high school will begin solar generation in 2009–2010. The district's CFO, Michelle Nate, said the high school power system is being funded with federal stimulus money and will be used by the school as part of a "green" curriculum. State regulators shot down another school's proposal to build a wind power system, but the district is using wind turbines to partially power the milking machines at its experimental farm.

Careful monitoring of energy—"green" or conventional—can also produce huge savings. Clark County, Nevada, launched an energy-use incentive program that saved $9 million in energy costs in 2008–2009. Of that, the district returned $500,000 in bonuses to schools that cut their energy use. The $9 million "is money we don't have to spend on electricity or gas, so we're spending it on teachers," said CFO Jeff Weiler.

Other districts are rethinking how they deliver services. Pittsburgh recentralized its printing operations in 2004, outfitting a new print shop with copiers that were more expensive than individual schools could afford but more efficient. Now teachers email their printing jobs to the shop, which sends back the finished copies on the district's food service trucks. The district saves in printing costs and manpower: The print shop can produce color images for about 10 cents a page, compared to about 25 cents if the same page were produced at the school or by a commercial printer, said CFO Christopher Berdnik. Moreover, low-skill workers do the job instead of higher-paid teachers, who otherwise might have to give up planning time to stand in front of a copier. The bigger bonus, though, is what it means for the classroom. "We're rewriting a lot of the curriculum, so we had to replicate and distribute it," said Berdnik. The district's print shop "allows us to do real-time curriculums and lesson plans."

Milwaukee, meanwhile, is rethinking books. In 2007 the district began a pilot project to give $400 laptops to its sixth graders. The district is paying for the computers with $24 million that class-action plaintiffs in the federal antitrust case against Microsoft failed to claim and that Microsoft offered the district in the form of vouchers. The computers would allow teachers to use so-called "open source" books instead of texts—that is, books and other online material that is free to the public to download or otherwise use. There are plenty of problems with open-source books, which many legislators and others see as a low-cost alternative to publishers' textbooks. If open-source books or chapters are merely downloaded and printed out for everyone in class, printing can soon exceed the cost of a text that is re-used for years. The other option—providing a computer or text reader to everyone—is even more expensive and would require technicians to support it. But in districts like Milwaukee, where the technology already exists and where the annual textbook budget is $7–8 million, "we could save some significant money," said CFO Michelle Nate.

Milwaukee and other districts also are rethinking their food service. In 2009 McKinsey & Company, a management consultant, produced a massive study of Milwaukee's nonacademic operations and identified $103 million in potential savings. Among them, McKinsey proposed the district switch to bagged lunches, which can be assembled at a central kitchen instead of prepared onsite. "Kids love them," said Nate, and the centralized system helps with portion control. But the real savings is in labor costs: Kitchen workers, although they are part time, receive full-time benefits. But Milwaukee did reject another McKinsey recommendation—that it use cheaper food. Nate said the district will continue to provide fresh fruit rather than fruit cups.

Seattle is also centralizing its kitchens, moving all of its elementary kitchens to a site in the central office complex. The secondary school kitchens are next. The district's food service still isn't self-supporting, but the new arrangement is saving $600,000 a year so far, said CFO Don Kennedy.

In an entrepreneurial move, Fairfax County, Virginia, services its school vending machines instead of contracting with a supplier and splits the profits between its cafeteria operations and the schools. The county also hires the district's food service to provide snacks for county-funded senior citizen and afterschool programs. With the added revenue, the district's food service is self-supporting. Richmond, whose food service was $1 million in the hole in 2007, hired a new manager who started a profitable catering service for in-house meetings and other gatherings. With that and other changes, Richmond's food service now is also self-supporting.

Technology offers some cost-control promise, although so far not nearly as much as state legislators and community activists seem to think. Virginia, South Carolina, and Texas, among others, are moving their standardized tests online, which saves printing and delivery costs, and should speed up grading and the analysis of results. Grand Rapids, Michigan, Public Schools began in 2009–2010 piloting an online curriculum for students in its alternative education center. In a summer school trial, the program saved on staff. Classes were as large as forty students, and hourly paid tutors provided additional help. Next, said Superintendent Bernard Taylor Jr., "we want to see if there's applicability to general ed."

Clark County, Nevada, is looking at a similar program for students needing to repeat classes to graduate. According to CFO Jeff Weiler, the courses are cheaper than conventional classes and popular with students, who can choose to take them at night or on weekends. In northeastern Colorado some districts have joined an instructional television collaborative that broadcasts lessons to small or rural schools that can't afford, say, a physics teacher. But the project is hard to replicate in other low-population parts of the state, where valleys and mountains make broadcast reception poor, said Tracie Rainey at the Colorado School Finance Project.

Indeed, technology seems more likely to add to or improve education rather than make it less expensive. It can provide virtual science labs and offer long-distance AP courses that a school otherwise might not be able to afford. But it also requires schools to buy licenses and make updates and hire techies and systems managers. "I see progress; I don't see savings," said Polk County, Florida, finance officer Audra Curts-Whann. Her district uses a computerized program for credit recovery, but licensing and other fees make the course no cheaper than one that uses a teacher and textbooks, she said.

Cooperative ventures among school districts, or between school districts and other government departments, also offer some promise of cost savings—but, again, with limits. Boards of cooperative educational services or BOCES have flourished in many states for decades, providing member districts with everything from technology training and accounting services to access to purchasing, medical insurance, and investment consortia. The Cooperating School Districts, a nonprofit consortium in the St. Louis area, also lobbies the state legislature on behalf of its sixty-five members, guides districts through federal stimulus fund red tape, offers public relations advice to districts asking taxpayers to pass bond issues, and manages a natural gas purchasing consortium.

Among other things, co-ops give districts access to higher-level professionals than they could afford alone—a CFO instead of a bookkeeper, for example. The Putnam/Northern Westchester BOCE runs an investment pool wherein districts can park their reserves; with assets of $1 billion, the pool gets a better interest rate than districts could expect individually, said its superintendent, James Langlois. And districts get better rates on their medical insurance policies because of the purchasing power of the consortium.

Larger districts, meanwhile, are working cooperatively with city governments to leverage better prices for their purchases. Pittsburgh's schools bid jointly with the city and county for natural gas, office supplies, and even rock salt for the roads. A committee of the three jurisdictions meets monthly to coordinate contracts. The Fairfax schools and county do joint fuel purchases, and the county maintains its own buses and those of the district as well.

But there are limits to the cooperation. Few neighboring districts can agree on a common textbook, which reduces their ability to negotiate discount prices. Richmond's school district has asked for bids on a plan to combine its finance department with the city's, but the two have different computer systems, and there is also "bad blood" between employees of the two jurisdictions, who fear layoffs, said the district's Lynn Bragga. Moreover, small districts fear that cooperation, if it appears too successful, would encourage state legislatures to demand more district consolidation as a cost-saving measure. "We've been through that," said Michael Griffith of the Education Commission of the States. Small-town residents worry that losing a district will mean losing a school and, ultimately, the slow withering of their community.

A BRIDAL REGISTRY AND RECOVERING TAX LIENS

Cutting money for schools is tough enough, but raising it is even tougher. Still, some superintendents and CFOs are finding ways to increase their revenues to fill in budget gaps.

The most direct, of course, is to ask voters for more money. Dozens of California schools are doing that by asking voters to pass parcel taxes, which are levies on individual parcels of real estate first proposed in the 1980s after California voters passed Proposition 13, which severely limited the ability of local jurisdictions to raise property taxes. Parcel taxes, which require approval by a two-thirds majority of voters to pass, typically must be renewed every three to eight years and levy from $50 to $200 on each parcel in the jurisdiction, regardless of the property's value. The ballot measures have a fairly successful record: 17 of 21 parcel taxes that were up for a vote in California in November 2008 passed, as did 11 of the 17 on California ballots between March and June 2009, according to ballotpedia.org, which tracks election results. The measure put on the June 2008 ballot by the Los Gatos, California, Unified School District, for example, promised it would "support high academic achievement for local students by retaining quality teachers, keeping small class sizes, and maintaining science, literacy, art, music and other programs." It passed for the fifth time since 1990.

Colorado districts, similarly constrained from raising taxes by a Taxpayer Bill of Rights (TABOR), have gone to voters for tax overrides. Those overrides allow districts to raise taxes temporarily, typically for four or five years, to generate a predetermined sum of money. Denver voters agreed to an override to pay for the district's performance-based compensation plan for teachers, and Jefferson County passed a $35 million override that, among other things, is protecting the district's innovation budget. But voters in the Douglas County, Colorado, School District voted down an override that would have funded a performance-based pay system, and some Arizona districts reported a similar lack of success at the polls.

In Missouri, the Cooperating School Districts is taking a different tack. The group compiled a report in 2009 on the effect that tax abatements and "holidays," such as those given to big housing developments, were having on school revenues. The consortium is using the report to lobby legislators to rethink Missouri's tax structure, said John Urkevich, the group's executive director.

But taxes aren't the only way to raise revenues. In the mid-1990s Pittsburgh's city government, school district, and water authority packaged their outstanding tax liens and sold them to a debt collector. The three jurisdictions got cash for the liens "but nothing happened to the properties," said schools CFO Christopher Berdnik. So in 2006 Pittsburgh Public Schools bought back its tax liens for $2 million, or what Berdnik called "pennies on the dollar." The district began its own tax collection and in two years recouped its $2 million. Using the city's enforcement powers, the district got some property owners to pay up and forced others into treasurer's sales, with any proceeds going to satisfy the tax liens. Those properties bought by new owners are now back on the tax rolls. "It's like the gift that keeps giving," said Berdnik.

Monitoring school attendance can raise money too. In California, districts receive state funding based on how many days each student actually attended school the previous year, rather than on how many were merely enrolled. That comes to $40 a day when a student attends and nothing when he does not. In 2009–2010 Long Beach Unified will shift ten of its social workers and counselors into a new truancy strike force that will identify and work with frequent truants. A 2 percent increase in attendance in 2009–2010 would translate into an additional $3 million in state support in 2010–2011, said Superintendent Chris Steinhauser.

Similarly, Jefferson County, Colorado, is funding a dropout prevention program that protects the district's per-pupil state allocation, even while it's helping more students graduate. Many districts are also becoming aggressive about protecting their enrollment from an assault by charter schools and about attracting students back. Ann Arbor Public Schools said in a budget presentation to the community that it planned to increase enrollment by two hundred students in 2009–2010, which would increase revenues by $1.9 million.

Grand Rapids Public Schools, among other districts, is rethinking special education. It is providing tutoring and counseling when problems first appear so that students with only a reading difficulty or a behavior problem are not channeled into expensive special education classes and services. "Special ed is such a regulations-driven endeavor that the only opportunity to save money is dependent on how many students are identified as being in need," said Superintendent Bernard Taylor Jr.

Schools are looking everywhere for new fee income. Fairfax County Public Schools is raising student parking fees to $200 a year from $150, a move that will bring in an additional $250,000. Paradise Valley, Arizona, Unified is offering to sell advertising on its buses: $7,200 a year for one side of a bus, with a 30 percent discount for seventy-five buses or more. Clark County, Nevada, is piloting similar ads on its food service trucks. "We're not ready to do it on buses, but that's not off the table," said CFO Jeff Weiler, who projected potential revenue of "several" million dollars a year.

Many districts are levying—or at least considering—sports fees. Those are controversial because of their potential to exclude low-income youth from participating. And while many districts offer scholarships, they worry that students who need them will not apply. The fees may run afoul of state laws guaranteeing free public education, but "no one tests them in court because they're afraid the school would cut the activity instead," said Dan Raisch, coordinator of the Department of Educational Leadership at the University of Dayton. Arizona schools have found perhaps the surest way around those concerns. The state legislature gives families a tax credit to pay for extracurricular activities. When Paradise Valley raised its fee to $200 per sport from $180, the move "went off without a blink," said Tom Elliott, assistant superintendent for budget services.

Districts also have begun to rely on community-funded foundations to help them fill budget gaps. Poway, California, Unified and its teachers' federation set up a bridal-type registry with local stores after the district cut its supply budget by 30 percent in 2008–2009. Parents and other community members can go online to order goods from a wish list compiled by each teacher. The teacher gets the name of the donor so she can send thanks; the donor gets a receipt for her tax records.

In Long Beach, a sprawling district with ninety-one buildings, foundations at the elementary schools raise "easily $1.5 million" each a year, while a separate districtwide foundation raises another $1 million a year, said Superintendent Chris Steinhauser. Together,they pay for extra science, computer, and language teachers and enable the district to reduce class sizes in grades four and five. Meanwhile, the business community donates money to hire tutors for Algebra I and II students.

YES TO LIBRARIES, NO TO EDUCATIONAL TV

It is not easy cutting school funding, which is why districts increasingly are enlisting parents, taxpayers, unions, teachers, school staffers, and anyone one else who is interested to help. Superintendents claim that those additional voices can come up with money-saving ideas and give the school district some sense of a community's priorities. Just as importantly, they can give a school district political cover when it has to make unpalatable choices.

Clark County, Nevada, compiled a six-page list of potential cuts that it presented to the community in a series of meetings and surveys as it was preparing its 2009–2010 budget. "There wasn't much consensus," except that the central office should take the brunt of the cuts, said CFO Jeff Weiler. But the process "allowed people to own the problem and understand it."

Long Beach Unified conducted an online survey in three languages, including Cambodian, asking community members to rank what was most-to-least important to them in the elementary, middle, and high schools. The survey generated 7,000 online responses and another 2,500 were mailed in. Among the findings, counseling and sports were the highest priorities in high school, and assistant principals were among the lowest. Libraries were the highest priority in elementaries, and instructional television was the lowest.

Similarly, Colorado Springs asked a budget committee that included parents and community members for help in identifying $4 million in cuts from a three-page list of possibilities compiled by the CFO. The group rejected such ideas as eliminating a school directory that cost $7,000 to print and reducing the cleaning budget by $225,000 (the district made both cuts anyway). But they gave the administration support for other unpopular cuts, including eliminating $1 million in bonuses to schools based on student achievement, attendance, and graduation rates.

Jefferson County, Colorado, increased its technology purchases in 2009–2010 while cutting teaching jobs—a "controversial" move, said Superintendent Cindy Stevenson. "What protected us," she added, was that a "budget working group" of community members endorsed the idea before sending it to her own budget committee for review.

Paradise Valley Unified established a committee with representatives of the parents' council, the teachers union, classified employees, and the administrators' association. The committee helped compile a "huge list" of budget recommendations and acted as "another filter to run our decision-making process through," said Tom Elliott, the assistant superintendent. Elliott said his budget writers also "met with everyone a lot more" than usual as the budget process developed. "We want to be sure everyone knows what's going on. We don't want anyone to say, 'We didn't know what's happening,'" he added.

Fairfax County held twenty "community dialogue meetings" where attendees were asked to break into small groups and discuss what the district shouldn't cut, what it could cut, and what services it should eliminate. Community members proposed cutting back bus service, raising student parking fees, charging for sports, and shifting the charge for AP and IB tests to families. The school board accepted the first two and rejected the next two.

Indeed, the recession is making taxpayers acutely interested in their schools, which may be one of the few bright spots in a grim economic situation. James Langlois of the Putnam/Northern Westchester, New York, Board of Cooperative Educational Services predicted that that new interest may cause parents and community members to push for such innovations as student achievement benchmarking and differentiated pay that the teachers' unions now resist. "The goal shouldn't be just to cut dollars; it should be to use them more wisely," he said.

Who could argue with that?

3

Now Is a Great Time to Consider the Per-Unit Cost of Everything in Education

Marguerite Roza

THERE IS NOTHING quite like a serious fiscal crisis to inspire a sober assessment of an organization's finances. So it is with the current recession and our nation's schools. Whether policy makers are staring at the exponents on projected budget gaps or scrutinizing budgets to find what to cut or even sizing up the stimulus package, they are dealing with dollar signs like never before. Yet, in the frenzy of renewed interest in finances, many education officials miss the one step that can often provide the best insight into the implications of all those dollar signs: convert the money into *per-unit* terms.

In education, putting money in per-unit terms often means "per student," particularly when examining those funds used more directly to serve students. For instance, an oft-cited statistic is that the United States spends, on average, around $10,000 per pupil per year on K–12 education. But for many education leaders that is where much of the per-pupil analysis ends. Rather, education finance documents summarize finances across categories, reporting instead the millions spent on teacher salaries, benefits, or debt service or on broad categories like "instruction" and "instructional support." And then there are the reams of accounting and compliance data reported to states and federal agencies to ensure that funds are not misused in some way. What is not clear from all this fiscal documentation, however, are the per-unit costs of what it is that schools or districts deliver. For instance, what does the district spend per pupil for math, science, or physical education? What is the per-student price tag on different sports offerings or on counseling or drama productions? And how does spending on a range of efforts intended to improve teaching compare on a per-teacher basis?

The practice of breaking down budgets to find the cost of what is provided is an important lens on an organization's expenditures, particularly in a time of constrained revenues. Not only can spending be broken down as a way to optimize it on routine business and operational services (as is described elsewhere in this volume), but the same can be done for spending on those services more central to the organization's purpose of serving students (for example, delivering courses). Consider the following six applications of converting dollars into per-pupil, per-teacher, or other per-unit terms:

1. Convert big numbers to per-unit costs to better convey relative magnitude.
2. Compute per-unit costs of various services to enable districts and schools to look for out-of-whack spending.
3. Use per-unit costs as a way to consider trade-offs.
4. Examine per-student costs across schools as the basis of school budgets.
5. Put spending in per-unit costs in order to better communicate with the public.
6. Budget in per-unit terms to stabilize the budgeting process.

For each of these applications, this chapter describes the relevance to district leaders and policy makers dealing with education budgets. Where relevant, basic instructions and examples are provided that draw on over a decade's worth of fiscal analysis on school and district spending at the University of Washington's Center on Reinventing Public Education.

CONVERT BIG NUMBERS TO PER-UNIT COSTS TO BETTER CONVEY RELATIVE MAGNITUDE

Recent headlines tell of proposals like a $698 million cut to New York's schools, an $800 million cut from Alabama's state budget, and a $40 million cut in the Sarasota County district in Florida.[1] Surely these are large numbers, but, intuitively, it is difficult to understand or compare the relative importance of figures like these in part because the federal government, states, and districts operate at such large and different scales. But by converting the millions or billions to their per-pupil terms, we find that the above figures would amount to cuts of $256 per student in New York, $1,082 in Alabama, and $966 in Sarasota. By putting the figures into the same terms (per student) that most of us use to run our own households, we can better understand and compare how significant or potentially disruptive cuts of this scale might be.

The same can be done with the funding provided by the American Recovery and Reinvestment Act (ARRA). Much has been made of the opportunity provided to use the one-time funds to spur innovation, reinvention, or other major overhauls of schooling. And while the funds will serve different purposes in different states, understanding the magnitude of all the zeroes in the $100 billion ARRA figure is difficult even for a numbers junkie like myself.[2] But when we divide this twelve-figure number among the nearly fifty million public education students in the United States, the education stimulus funds translate to about $2,032 per student.[3] If the funds are distributed over a two-year period, they are closer to $1,000 per pupil per year, or roughly 10 percent of what our country spends on education. Those who hope that schools will be overhauled ought to be looking for innovations that can be achieved within this scale. Here again, putting the funds in per-pupil terms allows for better intuitive understanding of the relative magnitude of funding and the potential for its use.

Districts, too, can convert their bigger numbers into per-pupil terms to better understand their relevance. School construction and other capital projects, for instance, often come with price tags in the millions. With simple division, districts can break these figures down in terms of the yearly cost per student over the life of the investment in order to put the cost in context. In one northwestern district, for example, a planned investment in a new track was scrapped after the per-unit costs were made clear. The district had drafted a plan to remodel a stadium to improve the track, making it suitable to host state competitions. The project boasted an impressive lifespan of fifty years and came with a $4.3 million price tag to be paid by local levies. The school board had decided to move ahead with the project until an analyst calculated the per-unit costs.[4] Even over fifty years, in present-day dollars, with a projected track team of forty students per year, the cost per runner per year of the course still exceeded $2,000. For a district spending only $9,000 per student, the project suddenly seemed extravagant and was scrapped. Instead, students continued to practice and compete on their existing course detached from the stadium.

Conversely, investments in information systems at first may seem shockingly expensive when confronting the total price tag. New York City's Achievement and Reporting Information System (ARIS), which tracks and analyzes student and school performance, cost an unimaginable $81 million, prompting concerns about the amount of funds that "could be going directly to the classroom."[5] Broken down in per-pupil terms, however, the investment is just $81.17 per student. And if ARIS stays running for just ten years, that initial investment becomes just $8.11 per pupil per year. Compare that to the nearly $15,000 per pupil spent by the district each year, and ARIS doesn't appear quite so expensive. For those claims that funds spent on ARIS might have been diverted back to the classroom, the question becomes: what else could have been purchased per classroom at a similar expense of less than $200 per classroom per year? For those who had visions that the funds spent on ARIS could have gone toward smaller classes, more teaching assistants, or other similar investments in staffing, the reality is that at $8 per pupil, the average classroom would not have seen much of any increased staffing.

COMPUTE PER-UNIT COSTS OF VARIOUS SERVICES TO ENABLE DISTRICTS TO LOOK FOR OUT-OF-WHACK SPENDING

Some of the most pertinent per-unit figures are those that are computed per student on the different operations of the system. Here again, while budgets can detail spending by department (e.g., curriculum or food services), budgets typically miss any financial analysis that follows the money to each school building or classroom to price out the services actually delivered to students. And yet per-student spending can be computed for the various services students receive, such as for the different courses taken in high schools, for tutoring, or even for various athletic offerings. By partitioning the primary cost drivers (usually salaries) and dividing them among their courses and students (units), the resulting analysis has surfaced some unexpected per-unit costs in some schools and classrooms.

Take, for example, one district studied by the Center on Reinventing Public Education, where our researchers computed the cost per pupil for every course offered in the district's high schools and then looked for patterns. We found that the per-pupil staffing costs for electives averaged $512 per course, whereas math classes came in at $328 per pupil. In another district, one in a higher-spending eastern city, we found that Advanced Placement (AP) courses came at a cost of $1,660 per pupil versus $739 per pupil for regular core courses.

While these are interesting patterns in the context of school district priorities, what may be most relevant in the face of budget gaps is the use of these spending data as a way to surface practical cost-saving measures. And, in fact, in a few of the districts mentioned here, the costs did prompt investigation on how to deliver the service at a lower cost. It was in the process of identifying the per-pupil cost of different services that district leaders were able to recognize the potential savings and then act on them.

Recently, the Council of Great City Schools launched its effort to collect and share data to enable districts to manage for efficiency (see chapter 4 by

Michael Casserly). While the analysis differs in that it focuses more directly on operational services, such as transportation, and thus the units are less often students, many of the same principles are applied.

The process of computing per-unit costs of services, deemed "service costing" or "spending-on-services," however, is not new in education, although historically it was applied more as a research technique than as a management tool.[6] In 1996, researcher David Monk and his associates determined per-pupil expenditures for various courses in six high schools in four New York districts. They calculated per-course spending using actual teacher and aide salaries, course schedules, and course enrollments.

In 1999, Jay Chambers of the American Institutes for Research merged unique state-level databases containing information on teacher salaries, teacher course assignments, and course enrollment data to calculate per-pupil expenditures by course for students in Ohio. The results indicated wide variations in spending by course, with some elective courses—including Latin, AP Spanish, and drafting—costing twice as much on a per-pupil basis as algebra, literature, and composition.

These research teams relied on the same basic approach applied here toward cost cutting. In cost cutting, districts provided information on teacher salaries and stipends, teacher assignments and teaching loads, course offerings and schedules, teachers' aide salaries and placements, and student participation in various courses. Each teacher's actual salary (including stipends, where relevant) was then divided proportionately among the courses taught and the number of participating students. The approach yields a per-pupil expenditure based on the proportionate teacher and aide compensation. Clearly, this per-pupil figure does not fully recognize all inherent expenditures (for instance, the costs of school leadership, school facilities, and district-provided shared services). It does, however, provide a means of making comparisons in spending across courses, as the excluded costs do not vary within schools.

In these districts, the results were combed for oddities, those courses where costs seemed unexpectedly high. Similarly the expenditure data were aggregated across subjects and teachers, again looking for places where the costs called attention to potential problems in how a set of courses was organized, staffed, or otherwise delivered.

Next, the key cost drivers for each course or set of courses were broken out in order to identify what was driving the high price tags. Figure 3.1 illustrates how key cost drivers were compared across the core and AP courses in our eastern district. As is clear, the much higher costs for the AP courses stem from both smaller class sizes and higher teacher salaries.

It came as no surprise that salaries were higher for AP teachers, many of whom had been teaching longer and had worked their way up in the system and into the AP courses. (In many districts, more senior teachers have preference in selecting their courses and, not surprisingly, choose honors and AP classes.) The differences in class size, however, were less expected. The district's research director looked into the issue and found that the smaller AP class sizes had been prompted by a state policy that tied funding to smaller classes for AP. The district had in turn capped these classes. What the research director realized, however, was that the district did not need to cap AP class size in order to get the state reimbursement and thus had the

FIGURE 3.1

Smaller classes and higher salaries drive up AP course costs

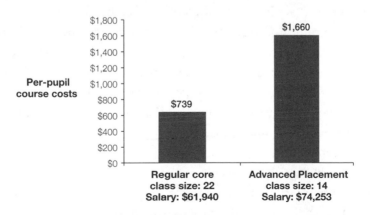

Note: Sources for figures and tables in this chapter, if required, are in endnote citations.

option of removing the cap on AP classes as a way to save funds. Districts may want to regularly check their assumptions about state requirements around caps and class sizes in order to better inform their own policies.

The same kind of process played out in a western district, where higher per-pupil spending on music courses uncovered much smaller classes for these electives. In this case, district leaders acted on the data by combining some music course sections and thereby freeing up funds that were then applied elsewhere. In the same district, analysis of per-pupil staffing costs for athletics suggested particularly high spending on certain sports. Cheerleading, on one end of the cost spectrum, cost $1,348 per cheerleader, whereas golf, on the other end, cost $217 per golfer. The wide disparity prompted a discussion of how this activity was structured. Indeed, the high relative cost was tied to the manner in which the course was offered (as a class and also with a stipend). Intuitively, district officials recognized that there are no fundamental reasons cheerleading should cost so much. Faced with this analysis, the superintendent moved immediately to restructure the way cheerleading was offered, shifting it to an afterschool sport subsidized only by the stipend, not a teacher's salary. In the end, the effect was to lower the per-pupil cost of offering cheerleading and thereby free up funds. Notice that the services were not eliminated, as we often hear is the only option.

In another western district, district leaders explored reducing high spending on electives by having students take some of those classes at the adjacent community center, which offered pottery, guitar, and other electives at a much lower price point than it was costing the district to provide these options. Unfortunately, since the district had passed a levy to pay for these electives, the district had no choice but to continue in-house delivery. The idea, however, may have some potential for districts exploring how to reduce costs without eliminating course options for students.

Certainly it might be argued that making changes to current service delivery models will degrade the quality of the service. The community center's pottery program may indeed be inferior to the school's offering. Similarly, perhaps cheerleading is a better program when offered during class hours than when shifted to a less expensive afterschool arrangement. The clear question for policy makers and school leaders is one of trade-offs: What are the available funds? What else could the district be doing with those funds to improve outcomes for students?

By converting spending into this more standard metric, districts can benchmark service costs against the costs for districts or from other providers. School districts can investigate per-pupil costs of services like tutoring and then compare their spending to the rates offered by Sylvan Learning, for example. Custodial, security, food services, or maintenance costs can be compared to those of numerous other vendors. Our analysis of these four services revealed one district with substantially higher rates than its neighbors in the same urban region. For instance, where custodial services cost $431 per pupil in one large district, the average for their neighbors was $342 per pupil. Clearly, benchmarking alone will not save districts money. However, understanding which other districts are providing similar services at reduced cost, and how they do so, can be the first step in deciding whether custodial or other services might be restructured or redesigned to save money.

Districts might begin to think more about per-unit costs of key services as more viable alternatives emerge. For instance, as online courses advance to the point where they can replace selected course offerings, district leaders may increasingly consider the per-student costs of traditional versus online options. Similarly, there are some cities where students have access to high-quality offerings outside of schools for sports, electives, higher-level college coursework, and other options. Comparing per-pupil costs of alternative offerings for students may increasingly be the first step in gauging the fiscal viability of pursuing the new alternatives.

Making the Calculations Toward Identifying Savings

An important note to district leaders embarking on this kind of cost analysis is that much of the fiscal manipulation must be done on data not readily available in standard finance documents. While the data are not difficult to access, and the metrics rely only on simple math, these kinds of cost manipulations are not typical in most districts. The analysis requires teacher and aide salaries and stipends, course activity schedules, teacher and aide

TABLE 3.1

To obtain cost per course, assign salaries to courses and divide by enrollment

Teacher	Course/activity	Minutes/ week	Enroll	Salary	Stipend	Salary per activity	Cost per student
	Algebra I, Sec 1	300	24			$10,000	$417
	Algebra I, Sec 2	300	22			$10,000	$455
#1	Algebra II, Sec 3	300	23	$50,000	N/A	$10,000	$435
	Geometry, Sec 6	300	22			$10,000	$455
	Geometry, Sec 7	300	21			$10,000	$476
	Art, Sec 2	300	18			$11,250	$625
#2	Art, Sec 3	300	16	$45,000	N/A	$11,250	$703
	Health, Sec 5	300	29			$11,250	$388
	Health, Sec 6	300	26			$11,250	$432
#3	Volleyball	540	12	N/A	$10,000	$5,000	$417

assignments, and course and activity enrollment/participation totals.[7] As table 3.1 demonstrates, each teacher's salary (and aide's salary, if relevant) is then allocated across her course sections proportionately. In our example, high school Teacher No. 1 earns $50,000 and teaches five sections of math, such that $10,000 is attributed to each section. The per-section salary costs are then divided across the enrollment to get a per-student cost. Weighted averages can be used to convey the per-pupil costs for groups of sections or courses (e.g., all math classes).

If, after comparing the costs of different courses or groups of courses, district leaders find routinely higher costs for some courses, the district might then pursue cost savings with any of the following options:

- *Consider consolidating some courses, perhaps for high-cost electives.* For example, offering one less art course (thereby raising class size in all art courses) could free up $11,250 in the above analysis. Clearly, realizing savings would require that current staffing would shrink proportionately—a difficult assumption in many districts where sticky commitments (e.g., via contractual obligations to existing full time staff) to staff make shrinking the workforce a challenge.

- *Rethink the schedule for electives.* Imagine, for instance, that electives met for 60 percent of the time allocated for a core course. If course time for electives shrank by, say, two periods per week, and staffing for those classes was also proportionately reduced, then spending on those courses would shrink proportionately. For those districts looking to cut funds from electives but not wanting to eliminate them altogether, scaling them back in this way could be an option.
- *Investigate offering a high-cost course in a different way.* For example, a district might replace a specialized course with a digital online course or via a contract provider. Offering access to photography, for instance, through a community college or community center might yield savings. Similarly, an AP German class for just a handful of students might be more efficiently offered via an online program that charges a per-student fee.
- *Rethink salaries to better align funds with offerings.* We could imagine that a district leader uncovers persistently high salaries for physical education and health teachers and the opposite in math and science, where high turnover is keeping average salaries low. One option would be to concentrate funds for salary raises on those teachers where raises are needed to stem turnover, using fewer funds for those where retention has historically been high and average salaries are higher.

USE PER-UNIT COSTS AS A WAY TO CONSIDER TRADE-OFFS

District leaders know how difficult it is to make budget cuts. They must weigh the value and cost of different programs, compare options, and ultimately make decisions about which cuts inflict the least harm on children, staff, and the system. Clearly, not all stakeholders can objectively consider the larger picture in this same way. Rather, they understandably worry that their programs will be cut, their jobs will be eliminated, or their students will lose out.

Explaining trade-offs in per-unit terms is one way to engage stakeholders and interest groups who may have something at stake in such decisions.

By moving the dialogue away from one about whether or not to eliminate a particular program to one centered on a range of options for cuts, district leaders may be better able to share the trade-offs at stake.

The cheerleading example in the preceding section validates the power of per-unit cost figures. Students, parents, and citizens who care both about cheerleading and about the efficient and effective management of that school district might understand the superintendent's action. She kept the cheerleading program but at a reduced cost and, in the bargain, liberated funds for other priority education purposes. Armed with such per-unit cost figures, the superintendent could persuasively communicate to all interested parties the reasoning behind her decision.

An obvious stakeholder group to engage when discussing trade-offs is that of teachers, and with teacher salaries being the largest single expenditure in all district budgets, most proposed budget cuts will affect teachers in some way. And when district leaders propose cuts that raise class sizes, limit wage increases, or cut teacher aides, we should expect that teachers will not be thrilled. But what most districts do not do is lay out a range of cost-cutting options in equivalent per-teacher or per-student terms as a way to help communicate what is at stake.

By way of illustration, table 3.2 lists four cost-equivalent cuts in *per-teacher* terms that have been computed using nationally representative salary data from urban districts.[8] Each of the options presented in table 3.2 would individually save the district approximately 3 percent of the operat-

TABLE 3.2
Considering tradeoffs: how a $4,500 cost cut stacks up per teacher

	Cost Equivalent Cut
Teacher salary	$4,500 pay cut
Pupils per class	2 added
Teacher aides	1/6 eliminated
Preparation time per week	2.5 hours added

ing budget. Faced with information like this, teachers could readily recognize how a range of cost-equivalent options might affect them and express preferences on a relative basis.

In fact, we already know something about teachers' preferences on the cost-equivalent options listed in table 3.2. Michael DeArmond and Dan Goldhaber, with the Center on Reinventing Public Education, surveyed teachers on their preferences regarding similar cost-equivalent options (though they posed the options as new spending, not reductions in spending).[9] They found that the majority of Washington State teachers valued their salaries at higher rates than they valued smaller class sizes, more planning time, and more help from teacher aides.

Considering trade-offs can also be helpful when layoffs are on the table. Because of such unexpected budget gaps in 2009, many districts across the country just recently faced decisions on teacher layoffs. But rather than examine a set of cost-equivalent trade-offs, many proceeded as though layoffs were the only option. In truth, layoffs are rarely the only option. Total teacher expenditures are comprised of not just the number of teachers employed but also days worked, wage levels, and mix of staff, among other factors. Thus, one analysis used nationally representative data to compare options for districts to save on teacher wages, examining potential implications for the average teacher salary, for layoffs per thousand teachers, and ultimately for class size.[10] The analysis created a hypothetical situation in which a district must cut spending by 5 percent and then spelled out a set of cost-equivalent options and their implications. Table 3.3 demonstrates the real tradeoff between layoffs and class size, on the one hand, and teacher wages on the other. As wages increase, teacher layoffs increase, and so does average class size.

In Option 1, a 2 percent across-the-board increase is applied to the entire teacher salary schedule, meaning that each cell on the pay scale is increased by the same 2 percent. Teachers continue to move from cell to cell each year as they gain experience and education credits, but the 2 percent also means each cell also increases. In this simulation, the potential impact on teacher layoffs is 14.3 percent of the workforce, or 143 for every

TABLE 3.3

Salary decisions can determine layoffs and class sizes

	Balancing salary changes and layoffs to meet a 5 percent reduction in teacher salary expenditures (after attrition)		
Options re: Teacher salaries	For continuing teachers, average change in salary	Layoffs per 1000 teachers	Percentage increase in class size
1. Continue with "modest" increases to overall salary schedule (2% across-the-board increase in addition to an average 3.16% increase in step change)	5.16%	143	16.7%
2. Freeze current salary schedule (teachers still get the average 3.16% step change)	3.16%	119	13.5%
3. Freeze all current salaries (teachers are paid what they were paid last year, with no step changes)	0%	75	8.1%
4. Roll back salary schedule by 5% (but allow teachers to continue to earn step changes averaging 3.16%)	-1.84%	47	4.9%
5. Roll back salary schedule enough to avert layoffs while allowing for step changes (entire schedule would roll back by 8.16% = 5% plus 3.16% to allow step changes)	-5%	0	0.0%

thousand teachers, causing class sizes to rise by almost 17 percent. For an average class of twenty-five students, this would translate into roughly four additional students for a total of twenty-nine students per class.

In Options 2 and 3, different decisions around wages work to mitigate the effect on layoffs and class size. The second simulation "freezes the schedule," allowing teachers to continue to receive their step increases, averaging 3.16 percent, creating the need to lay off 12 percent of teachers to achieve the targeted 5 percent reduction in teacher salary expenditures. Resulting class sizes would increase by 13.5 percent. In the third simulation, teachers' salaries are frozen (with no step increases), forcing a change in class size of just over 8 percent. In Options 4 and 5, layoffs are reduced further and class sizes are protected as teacher wages are reduced.

With this kind of information, a district leader could weigh several options, all of which are cost equivalent, and select the optimal, least painful, or perhaps most popular route to save 5 percent of the budget. Presented with these options, important stakeholder groups can better understand the trade-offs and, one hopes, recognize that budget reduction decisions typically must move beyond the question of *whether or not* to make cuts and focus instead on *where* to make them. If a district chooses to forego one considered budget cut, there will be one made in another area.

In the spring of 2009, many districts did just the opposite. Instead of communicating their decisions as a selection of trade-offs, they announced layoffs as though there were no other options. Teachers and parents, in many cases, vigorously opposed the layoffs. In many districts, including Seattle Public Schools, teachers picketed layoff decisions at the district's headquarters. The teachers' union in the Los Angeles Unified District planned a one-day walk-out of school to protest layoffs, a move ultimately blocked by L.A. superior court judge James Chalfant.

A few districts, however, did indeed enact layoffs as one of several trade-offs. And other districts made different decisions. For example, teachers in the William Floyd District in Long Island traded portions of their salaries to avert layoffs of nineteen district employees.[11] Facing a similar trade-off, the opposite decision was made in Ridgewood, New Jersey, where wage reductions were considered but ultimately rejected. In both cases, presenting options helped stakeholders understand that if the district were to forego a reduction in one area, the result would be to shift to a reduction in another area.

Sick days are another significant expense, since districts hire substitute teachers at roughly $100 per day. Some districts, including Marietta City

Schools in Georgia, have asked teachers to cover for each other as a way to minimize these costs.[12] With the average teacher taking just over nine sick or personal days per school year, the total cost to the district is over $900 per teacher in substitute fees alone. If they put it in terms of the cost per teacher, district leaders working to contain these expenditures might offer their teachers some monetary incentive to reduce absenteeism. For instance, a teacher might earn a portion of the savings incurred for those teachers with lower absenteeism. Using these substitute teacher rates, a district could consider paying out some portion of the savings, say $70, for each day not taken.

This idea, while seemingly bold, was hatched out of a conversation with a Colorado district's director of substitutes. As he put it, "If it is snowing at dinner time and is forecast to be sunny tomorrow, I might as well start calling in subs 'cause people live here to ski."[13] He added that a lift ticket is about $15 less during the week than on the weekends, so teachers use their sick and personal days to head to the slopes. We wondered what might happen if the district offered the $70 for each sick or personal day not taken. It certainly seems plausible that at least some teachers, once the $70 bonus was factored in, might think twice and opt to wait for the weekend.

While we have not yet put the notion to the test in any experimental way, the idea could make sense even without the lure of fresh powder. Imagine a dual working couple where one parent is a teacher. What happens when the couple's own child is sick and requires a parent to stay home? If the decision about which parent stays home is partially dependent on which parent is impacted financially, it makes sense that the costs of the teacher's substitute be factored in. Right now, if the teacher opts to head to work, the district saves money. The decision about which parent should stay home might be different if the district shared a portion of the savings with the person making the calculation. This kind of option not only computes a trade-off (this time in per-teacher terms) but also puts control of the trade-off directly in the hands of those teachers affected by it.

EXAMINE PER-STUDENT COSTS ACROSS SCHOOLS AS THE BASIS OF SCHOOL BUDGETS

One way to think about the district budget is as a collection of the school budgets. Figuring out where to squeeze the district budget, then, can pit schools against each other as each vies for its share of the overall pie. These kinds of battles can take numerous forms, many of which play out in school board meetings. In one district, plans to cut music teachers prompted a demonstration at the school board meeting by a high school jazz band in an attempt to save that school's award-winning jazz program. It worked, and the board made an exception for that school. Other principals noticed and argued for exceptions to other cuts in the name of fairness. In another district, a principal at Apple Lake school argued that her school should be spared since her programs were already less costly than those of the magnet, option, and alternative schools.[14]

There are districts that can sidestep some of these politics by using pupil-based formulas to pass along funds to schools. This weighted student funding practice uses a formula to allocate the dollars to schools based on student types and encourages school leaders to build their own budgets with the funds they receive. When revenues are constrained, so is the formula. Cuts are essentially passed on to schools in proportion to the number of students (weighted by their need) enrolled at each. Decisions about which schools get to save a counselor or music teacher are not made by district officials but made by each school (ideally factoring in the needs of students and the local context).

Most districts, however, still rely on a staffing-based allocation model where staff full-time equivalents (FTEs) are allocated to schools. Staff are allocated largely according to a formula such that each school gets a teacher for every twenty-five students, a principal, a counselor, a reading coach, and maybe a vice principal (if the school's enrollment reaches four hundred), and so on. Additional staff are allocated to fund specific programs, such as a Montessori program, a gifted program, or a technology magnet school. In this more common model, applying cuts means district leaders often face decisions about whether to eliminate some part of the formula—the reading coaches or counselors, for example—or scrap the extra staffing for special programs, such as the Montessori program or the technology magnet.

These are difficult decisions. In one school the counselor may play a more critical role than the reading coach, but the opposite may be true in another. The Montessori school may prefer to keep the extra staffing to fund the Montessori magnet and sacrifice the counselor, but other schools may argue that they don't have this option. Were the district to ask all schools to surrender one staff position, the Apple Lake principal might rightly cry foul since her school already receives a smaller staffing allocation than many of the district's other schools. Then again, a school leader at a school heavily attended by at-risk students might counter that her school's higher spending is a function of the bilingual education program, not just enrollment.

Even in districts not using the weighted student funding model, the use of a per-student analysis of school spending can enable a comparison of spending across schools, even when the schools differ in enrollment and student demographics. The idea is to identify those allocations driven by each student type and compare them to the district average spending for that student type. For instance, the staff allocations across schools may average $5,100 per pupil for each regular education student, $6,200 for each poor student, $5,800 for each non-English-speaking student, and so on. Figure 3.2 displays the spending per regular education student across a set of schools relative to the $5,000 districtwide average. Ultimately, the technique allows the district to compare spending for each school against a student-weighted districtwide average spending figure that represents each school's unique mix of students.[15] In this example, such information would indeed illustrate that the mix of staff at Apple Lake comes at a lower relative per-student cost than the district average. Similarly, the extra staffing at the Montessori program puts its costs above the district average.

District leaders seeking more equity in applying cuts might start by working with those more pricey schools to get their costs in line with district averages. A more rational and formulaic approach may ultimately prove

FIGURE 3.2

Comparing each school's spending in per pupil terms can reveal deviations from the districtwide average of $5,000 per regular education student

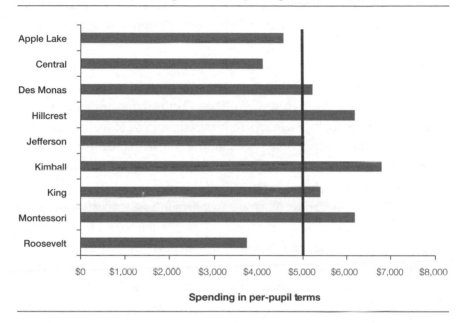

Spending in per-pupil terms

to counter political pressures, such as those faced by the district that made an exception for the award-winning jazz band. Converting budgets to per-pupil terms may, however, provide the equalizing tool for district leaders to resist such pressure.

PUT SPENDING IN PER-UNIT COSTS IN ORDER TO BETTER COMMUNICATE WITH THE PUBLIC

The foregoing sections describe how per-unit spending can work to define trade-offs and how districts can apply this to budget cuts. As districts face budget cuts, many district leaders will have little choice but to engage the public and explain the thinking behind seemingly unpopular decisions. The larger community can be made to understand that budget reductions are about deciding where to apply cuts and that deciding against a cut in one area means pursuing one in another area. For the examples above, presentation of the per-unit options can help district leaders garner support for proposed strategies, particularly those unpopular with a particular stakeholder group.

While the presentation of cost-equivalent trade-offs is still fairly uncommon, a few district leaders have recently used them to draw in the public around sensitive decisions. San Diego Unified, for instance, created a survey for community members to assess their preference among a set of potential 2009 budget cuts. By including dollar figures in the survey instrument, community members were able to consider the costs as they rank-ordered their preferred cuts.

While the examples above illustrate how per-unit costs clarify trade-offs, per-unit costs can also be used as a way to draw attention to inefficient or unproductive spending. An example from a report released in 2009 computes the per-pupil expenditures associated with the salary bump earned by teachers as they accumulate graduate credits and ultimately a master's degree.[16] Paying teachers more for educational credits is standard practice, despite the overwhelming evidence that indicates that additional degrees do not yield corresponding improvements in student learning outcomes.[17] The report calls attention to this problem by computing the per-pupil costs of master's bumps—$174 per pupil nationally, with a high of $416 per pupil in New York.

In a different example, analysis by the author computes the effect of one of the side effects of making layoff decisions based on seniority—namely, that the lower salaries of junior teachers mean that more layoffs are needed to achieve a desired budget reduction. For a district using layoffs to contain salary expenditures by, say, 5 percent, under a seniority-neutral policy, 5 percent of all teachers would receive pink slips. With seniority-based layoffs, however, a 5 percent savings in total salary expenditures would require laying off 7.5 percent of all teachers (50 percent more teachers laid off). If seniority-based layoffs were indeed applied nationally to reduce all public school salary expenditures by 5 percent, 154,000 more people would lose

TABLE 3.4
Personnel layoffs under seniority-neutral and seniority-based policies

| To reduce salary expenditures by: | Projected public education jobs reduced nationally | | | |
	Using seniority-neutral layoffs	Using seniority-based layoffs	Difference (extra layoffs attributed to seniority)	% attributed to seniority
2.0%	124,657	190,707	66,050	53.0%
5.0%	305,670	460,328	154,658	50.6%
10.0%	612,256	874,623	262,367	42.9%

their jobs than under a seniority-neutral layoff policy. This is a significant effect, one not otherwise obvious without such analysis. Table 3.4 shows how the number of teachers receiving pink slips under a seniority-neutral policy and a seniority-based policy would change if salary expenditures decreased by 2 percent, 5 percent, and 10 percent.

Data quantifying the effects of using seniority as the basis of layoff decisions have already affected policy. In Arizona, for instance, a new law disallows districts from making layoff decisions on the basis of seniority. In passing the law, policy makers hope to reduce the total overall layoff numbers.[18]

BUDGET IN PER-UNIT TERMS TO STABILIZE THE BUDGETING PROCESS

Each of the previous five sections provides tools to facilitate the budget-cutting process. And while the current fiscal climate certainly necessitates unprecedented cutting for many districts, a budget crisis is not an unprecedented event. In fact, a quick scan of education headlines from big city districts in the last decade shows dozens of districts buried in budget woes. Sometimes the stress is caused by fiscal mishaps; but more often cuts are needed in response to enrollment shifts, run-away cost growth, or other seemingly predictable factors. Regardless of the source of fiscal stress, the outcome is nearly always disruptive as district leaders find themselves focusing on little other than budget cuts.

This chapter suggests that budgeting in per-unit terms can be a tool used to stabilize the budgeting process, enabling budget expansion and contraction without the all-too-familiar upheaval we have now come to expect. Even more promising, managing budgets in per-unit terms might even be a way of containing costs and thereby averting one source of fiscal stress—that of built-in cost escalators.

As is typical in education, fixed costs and built-in cost escalators drive up spending from year to year, even without the addition of new staff or programs. Many districts faced this problem this year when, despite flat revenues (or even modest increases), balancing the budget meant making difficult cuts to avoid cost growth. In districts, unlike some other sectors, personnel expenditures act like fixed costs in that district leaders find it difficult to cut personnel except under dramatic circumstances. Escalating costs come in many different forms, but, in most cases, rising costs are prompted by rising employee salaries and pensions as well as by increases in utilities costs, prior obligations, and the like. In districts where revenues drop further as enrollments shrink, the budget challenges are magnified.

What is it about school districts that makes them unable to shrink as revenues are flat or decline? Obviously, there is not some magic expenditure level needed for fiscally viable district operation. A scan of the 14,000 or so districts in this country shows that they can and do operate on all different budgets, and many smaller districts manage to function on per-pupil revenue levels less than those of larger districts perpetually in fiscal crisis. Further, districts need only look back in time for examples of when they themselves operated at lower per-pupil expenditure levels.

For many districts, it is not that they cannot exist at a lower spending level; it is the shrinking itself that creates fiscal chaos. When district leaders sit down to revise their budgets, they start with last year's allocation showing the per-school staffing allocation and how much they spent on the athletic department, the American Indian heritage program, the energy-conservation unit, the college-readiness team, and others. Each department, program, or school summarizes its expenditures in terms of personnel counted as full-time equivalents (FTEs). FTEs are relatively bulky allocations that make it difficult to enact incremental or proportional cuts to departments or units. Inevitably, each unit has its own director and core administrative staff. None of these positions is linked in any meaningful way to revenues, and all of them fight for their lives during budget cuts. Districts rarely, if ever, merge or scale back programs. So for district leaders trying to make spending cuts, the only options are to eliminate an entire program (very unpopular) or make tiny, indistinguishable adjustments to each unit's budget.

Similarly, when facing the school staffing model, making an across-the-board cut to a staffing allocation (say, cutting a librarian FTE from all schools) means eliminating some key dimension of each school. For budget administrators, each program or staffing unit looks and feels like a fixed cost. And to make matters worse, these fixed costs have built-in cost escalators (via fixed salary schedules, pension obligations, rising health-care commitments, etc.) driving up spending even when no new budget items are added.

One strategy for redesigning budgets toward making them more flexible, nimble, and ultimately more responsive amid revenue fluctuations is to design them instead around per-unit costs. What this means is that instead of allocating a fixed number of FTEs to each budget unit, what is allocated are per-pupil amounts that are tied more directly to revenues.

As mentioned earlier, a variant of this approach, weighted-student funding, now exists in a handful of larger districts for some expenditures. With weighted-student funding, school resources are allocated per pupil (or pupil type) directly to schools as a way to achieve equity and/or enable decentralized control. In this case, when revenues drop, district leaders maintain the weights but vary the base allocation proportionately.

A much larger share of district resources could be allocated on the basis of units not only to schools but also to programs, departments, services, operations, administration, or other district functions. This kind of allocation model makes district-level budgeting inherently responsive to changes in revenues. As revenues decrease (or increase, for that matter), the per-unit allocations vary proportionately, and each unit contracts as needed to accommodate the new reality. Where high school literacy was a priority, it is still a priority. Where the district has made a commitment to summer programs or foreign languages, these programs continue, though perhaps with incremental adjustments in delivery.

Clearly, budget cuts to units may mean those units need to reorganize delivery, possibly by jointly providing the service with another district or contracting out for the service on a per-unit basis. But what does not happen is that budget cuts effectively hijack district leaders for months or more as officials go line item by line item through their budgets trying to apply cuts that wreak the least havoc on the system.

Redesigning district budgets in per-unit terms is not easy, as traditional budgeting practices are deeply rooted in district habits and even in local politics. School board members facing reelection have been known to make promises that wreak fiscal havoc in years to come, while clearly efforts to stabilize budgets ought to begin by discontinuing the practice of making long-term spending commitments unless they can be budgeted for in present-day dollars. But the benefits of budget reform are real, not only in terms of long-term fiscal stability but also in the sense that priorities can be articulated in district spending patterns. Perhaps most importantly, a stable financial infrastructure can set the stage for more stability in leadership, priorities, and strategies.

CONCLUSION

The goal of this chapter is to provide the reader with tools to look at expenditures in a different way toward uncovering implications for budget cuts. Rather than close by summarizing a list of suggested cuts, this chapter concludes with the reminder that the kinds of analyses suggested here are good practice for districts in any fiscal climate. As with any organization, thoughtful and strategic allocation decisions depend on clear understanding of how and where resources are deployed in the context of the organization's goals. These tools are intended to provide the reader with strategies needed to make better decisions about the allocation of scarce resources across competing priorities.

But, of course, we are in dire fiscal times. Districts are looking for answers to questions about what and where to cut. Many seek instructions from state or federal officials as to what programs or services can be discontinued. Some want instructions to raise class sizes, shorten the school year, or escape seat compliance regulations. But the examples here suggest that there may not be many easy, transferrable, clean cuts that will allow district leaders to escape the tough thinking that needs to be done about how to do more with less. Rather, replacing one spending scenario with an improved one will require more thought, effort, and courage to change spending so that funds are used differently. Rather than simply eliminating electives, sports, or afterschool programs, the goal implied here is to figure out how to allow students access to these services by spending money in different ways and at reduced costs. Rather than continue to staff all classrooms evenly—with all teachers paid off the same scale and all classes meeting for fifty-five minutes five days a week—doing more with less might mean changing some of our basic assumptions about how schooling is organized. The tools provided here for examining spending in per-unit terms suggest a means for taking apart spending, uncovering key cost drivers, and learning about trade-offs.

While the analysis requires some dedication, it is not impossible to do. Clearly, many of the numbers are not yet standard on finance documents. That said, the analysis can be done with relatively accessible data and basic math. The resulting analysis will differ from district to district and school to school, which means that the implied cuts or solutions will too.

While daunting, the promise of doing the hard work is innovation in education spending. For years researchers have been frustrated over the weak link between education spending and outcomes for students. Ultimately, finding new and better ways to apply funds to serve our students, even if prompted by recessionary budgets, is a positive outcome. Now more than ever, calculating the costs of education should not end at the cost of educating a student each year.

4

Managing for Results in America's Great City Schools

Michael Casserly

AMERICA'S GREAT CITY SCHOOLS are under enormous pressure to improve their academic performance, strengthen their leadership and management, and regain the public's confidence—maybe under more pressure than any institution or organization, public or private, in the nation.

We are being told to produce results or get out of the way. We are being told to improve or see the public go somewhere else. We are being told to be accountable for what we do or let someone else do it. Some of the criticism is justified. Some of it is not. Either way, we are being challenged in the court of public opinion and by history to improve in ways that we have never done before.

Many institutions might have folded under the pressure or sat passively by waiting for someone to save them. But urban school systems across the country are doing what a lot of people would not have expected. They are rising to the occasion, working to reshape their own destinies and striving to produce better results. This effort in urban education has been particularly evident on the academic side of the house, where big city schools have backed the development of national standards, originated urban school participation in the National Assessment of Education Progress (NAEP), published their annual state test scores, launched innovative research on effective system reforms, and provided hard-hitting technical assistance teams to help urban school districts improve student achievement.

These and other efforts are paying dividends. Between 2003 and 2009, the number of large central-city students scoring at or above proficiency on NAEP jumped 45 percent in math and 35 percent in reading—rates of gain that far outpace improvements nationwide.

While much remains to be done to improve student achievement in urban schools, urban education leaders finally have trend lines moving in the right direction. Now they are turning their attention to strengthening management, operations, and resource use. This chapter describes a broad national effort by America's Great City Schools to improve efficiencies, strengthen operations, save money, and deploy more scarce resources into our classrooms.

This effort could not have come at a more critical time. The current economic climate has forced many urban school systems to close gaping budget holes. New York City faced a revenue loss of more than $800 million, Los Angeles had to close a deficit of nearly $600 million, and Chicago had to close a deficit of almost $400 million. Even with federal stimulus dollars, urban school systems are floating in a sea of red ink that is forcing them to think more urgently and strategically about how they deploy their resources and spend their monies.

The Council of the Great City Schools and its member big city school districts are developing a unique system by which urban school districts can make this exercise more data driven and effective. The system involves a large series of key performance indicators that allow an urban school system to compare itself operationally and financially with other big city schools—in much the way they are now able to do academically—and save millions of dollars by improving their relative standing among their peers.

THE PURPOSES AND DESIGN OF THE PROJECT

The Council of the Great City Schools, the nation's primary coalition of large city public school districts, launched an initiative called the Performance Measurement and Benchmarking Project in order to build such a system. The project was based in part on lessons that the organization had learned in conducting scores of technical assistance projects for urban school districts to help them improve business and financial operations. It was also founded on the assumption that greater effectiveness and efficiency would depend on the ability of these districts to better measure their performance, compare themselves to each other and to other sectors, identify effective management and operational practices that produce top-of-the-line results, and make better decisions about where to put their human and financial capital. The organization also assumed that better data were the key to making this happen.

When the Council looked around for prototypes, however, it was surprised to find almost nothing either in education or in municipal government except for limited datasets in niche organizations that specialized in one business operation or another. The Council also knew from its technical assistance work that very few cities had benchmarks or targets by which they could gauge the performance of their finances and noninstructional operations. And there was nothing in place that would allow the cities to compare themselves operationally or financially with one another.

If a school district was interested in performance metrics it would have to contract with a private firm that could reanalyze that system's data or create dashboards or indicators for that system, but the outcomes were not uniform from one city to another and often reflected what the companies could do rather than what was needed by the districts. The result was that school systems have had little means to compare themselves with others or to know whether their operations were efficient and cost effective.

So in 2004, at the annual meetings of its COOs and CFOs, the Council of the Great City Schools began to develop a series of Key Performance Indicators (KPI). Council staff members were the first to float the idea based on work that the Los Angeles Unified School District was doing at the time, but the CFOs and COOs quickly agreed that their operations could be vastly improved with better and more comparable data. After much discussion, the two groups agreed to design and build a set of statistical indicators by which they could accomplish the following:

- Establish standardized performance measures for critical K–12 operational and financial functions in urban schools.
- Compare performance on these operational and financial functions from district to district.
- Document effective management practices used by top-performing urban school districts.
- Establish a clearinghouse of best practices so urban school districts could learn from one another.
- Improve decision making by urban schools by equipping them with better data on which to base policies.

An initial project framework was designed around identifying initial indicators, developing a common methodology for measuring the indicators, implementing a measurement strategy, gathering and analyzing comparative data, and documenting effective management practices. The initiative started with prototypes on a preliminary set of business-service KPIs. By the end of 2006, when the preliminary measures and prototypes were first laid out, urban superintendents and school board members greeted them with enormous enthusiasm because they held the promise of better decision making and less politicking.

The response prompted the Council late in 2006 to name a senior project team of COOs and CFOs to take the work forward. The COOs agreed to focus first on school business services, including procurement, transportation, food services, safety and security, and maintenance and operations. The CFOs agreed to focus initially on budgeting, financial management, general accounting, and compensation. Technical teams were selected from these operating groups, and they began brainstorming on potential indicators. The teams reviewed how each variable "added value" to the efficiency and effectiveness of the organization and developed a master list of indicators of the most important variables. The teams discussed potential measures of performance relating to each indicator and began developing methodologies for defining, quantifying, and aggregating each indicator.

Then, draft surveys were created to gather preliminary information on the draft indicators and to pilot-test the capacity of city school districts to report the necessary data. Results from these surveys were analyzed to determine the feasibility, range, and values of potential indicators using metric definition worksheets based on Six Sigma processes. Definitions, data sources, and equations were prepared on each indicator. Measures were fine-tuned, and the teams decided which items to modify or to drop. At that point, every numerator and denominator from the Six Sigma worksheets was used as the basis for every question on the surveys.

Districts were asked to provide raw data and not to perform their own calculations. This was done to ensure quality control in the calculation process. This approach allowed the teams to analyze the same data points across surveys and to calculate uniform performance rates. The process also helped ensure the uniformity, reliability, and validity of results across cities.

An initial report on business services was presented to the Council in March 2007. The technical teams reconvened at the April 2007 meeting of COOs to refine the measures further and to add others. The teams of COOs and CFOs subsequently developed a second survey that they used to gather and analyze data on new—and newly refined—measures. The results of this second round of surveying were presented to the Council in October 2007 and were well-received by superintendents and school board members.

In the meantime, two other Council groups began work in their areas of expertise: the human resources officers in February 2007 and the chief information officers (CIOs) in June 2007. The human resource officers chose to focus on human resource operations, recruiting, and staffing areas; the CIOs chose network operations, applications, and help desk support. And the CFOs met again in the fall of 2007 to define their original measures further and to add new ones, including grants management and risk management. Technical teams were chosen, measures were identified, and surveys were developed to gather and analyze data. Results were reported to the broader organization at the 2008 annual meeting.

This 2008 report was followed by an intensive effort in 2009 to expand data collection on the full range of indicators, increase the number of participating districts, and automate the results. This expansion was assisted by support from the Hewlett Foundation, the Microsoft Corporation, and TransACT Communications—all of which saw enormous potential in the initial work. Up to that point, major foundations and the U.S. Department of Education had refused to support the effort or had expressed no interest. The 2009 report includes data from sixty cities that returned 66 percent of 1,582 surveys on 227 indicators in four major operational functions (see table 4.1). The full list of 227 indicators, moreover, was winnowed down to seventy-seven "power indicators."

The reports produced from these surveys include a brief description of each indicator, a short discussion of why the measure is important, and a brief explanation of how each is calculated. The data also include brief descriptions of factors that influence the variables, response rates and ranges of results, and an explanation for why some variables are unusually high or low in some cities. These explanations and mitigating factors are important because unfavorable results do not always indicate inefficiency. For instance, it is possible for a district to have higher per-pupil transportation costs due not to inefficiency but to large numbers of one-way streets, bad weather, or extensive square mileage.

Indicators were also broken into three categories: Power Indicators, Essential Few, and Performance Measures. Power Indicators are those measures that school boards, superintendents, and other policy makers could use to assess broadly the performance of their districts in noninstructional areas and to establish priorities and policies. An example in the food service area would include overall meal participation rates. The Essential Few, which are yet to be fully delineated, involve indicators that senior school managers could use in reviewing district performance, creating project plans, and setting management directions. Examples in the food service

TABLE 4.1

Functions and numbers of indicators for each function

Function	Subfunction	Number of indicators	Number of power indicators[a]
Business operations		97	32
	Food services	18	4
	Maintenance and operations	10	5
	Procurement/supply chain	32	10
	Safety and security	16	9
	Transportation	21	4
Finance		57	19
	Accounts payable	13	6
	Cash management	7	
	Compensation	16	4
	Financial management	13	5
	Grants management	6	3
	Risk management	2	1
Human resources		46	16
	Employee relations and services	10	4
	Human resources development	12	
	Operations and school support	12	6
	Recruitment and staffing	12	6
Information technology		27	10
	Applications	5	1
	General technology information	4	3
	Help desk	7	2
	Network operations	9	3
	Information technology security	2	1
Total		**227**	**77**

[a] Power indicators were those measures that school boards, superintendents, and other policy makers could use to broadly assess the performance of their districts in noninstructional areas and to establish priorities and policies.

area would include elementary and secondary breakfasts and lunches and program fund balances. Thirdly, Performance Measures are indicators that technical staff can use to assess their respective department operations and to implement and execute priorities and policies. Examples in food service might include point-of-sale sites, vacant positions, and indirect costs.

INITIAL RESULTS

The results from the first three waves of data collection are proving to be both interesting and promising. Data on business services–transportation, procurement, maintenance and operations, food service, and security– finance and budget, human resources, and information technology are good examples. Data in the most recent 2009 report are presented on fiscal year 2008.

Business Services

The project collected information on some twenty-one transportation in- dicators, including: the total transportation cost per student; the number of district and contracted buses in use on any given day; the percentage of stu- dents enrolled receiving yellow bus transportation; the percentage of general fund expenditures devoted to transportation; the age of the bus fleet; average daily ride time per student; on-time arrivals; cost per mile and deadhead miles; the number of mechanics per bus; average miles between accidents; the number of runs per bus; and the average number of students per bus.

The number of buses in daily operation, for instance, is an important indi- cator of efficiency because it tells a school district something about whether it has a fleet that is too large for its needs or has a maintenance program that is not keeping pace with repairs. In this case, the results ranged from a high of 94.1 percent of buses in operation on the average day to a low of 69.0 percent. The median among the Great City Schools was 84.9 percent (see table 4.2). The numbers can be affected by enrollment projections, changes in transportation eligibility policies, the age of the fleet, and other factors.

TABLE 4.2
Power indicators for transportation with high, low, and median values

Indicators	Low	Median	High
Annual cost of transportation per student	$35	$839	$5,056
Percentage of all district and contracted buses used daily	69.0%	84.9%	94.1%
Percentage of students in district receiving home-to-school yellow bus service	8.8%	44.9%	99.9%
Percentage of general fund expenditures devoted to transportation	1.2%	4.9%	16.7%

Theoretically, if a district had 100 buses and only 69 were in operation on any given day, it could sell 16 seven-year-old vehicles in order to align with the median number of buses in use in the average district at their expected rate of depreciation and save $320,000 —enough to hire five extra teachers. Other options, of course, might be to lease the buses to other organizations for special events, increase the pool of eligible riders (thereby accessing a higher state reimbursement rate), or sit on the leases until the buses were fully depreciated. A district might not know that its fleet was in excess, however, unless it was able to compare itself against other cities.

Likewise, the project collected information on thirty-two procurement indicators, including the percentage of total purchases that were competitively bid, the costs per purchase order, total P-card (purchase cards that are similar to personal debit cards) transactions, warehouse inventory value, and the like.

The number of P-card transactions is an important procurement indicator because use of P-cards significantly improves cycle times for schools acquiring low-cost items, decreases procurement transaction costs, reduces the workload of accounts payable staff, and provides more flexibility for school staff while central office procurement staff members focus on more complex and strategic purchases.

P-card transactions can be affected by such factors as district policies on the possession of such cards, use of technology, internal controls, and accounts payable policies. The data from this project indicated that 46.5 percent of all procurement transactions were made with P-cards. Usage ranged from a high of 94.4 percent to a low of 0.0 percent. P-cards, moreover, save money. Suppose a district that did not use P-cards completed one thousand transactions at an average purchase order cost of $88.95 per transaction. By moving 46.5 percent of the transactions to P-cards at $19.49 per transaction, the district could save $79,487.

A school district with approximately 36,000 students, 5,500 full-time employees, and an annual budget of $387 million could easily have between three and four thousand purchase orders per year, so the potential annual savings from moving to P-cards could run as high as $318,000 per year for a district this size and much more in a larger district. A district with about 250,000 students could easily have forty-five thousand purchase orders a year to outside vendors, not including internal warehouse purchase orders and P-card transactions.

In the area of maintenance and operations, ten indicators were created including custodial cost per square foot, custodial workload, percentage of general fund expenditures devoted to maintenance and operations, maintenance costs per square foot, work order completion time, and utility usage per square foot.

One of these maintenance and operations indicators assesses custodial workload in square footage. The measure is important because it allows districts to evaluate the relative efficiency of custodial employees. The values ranged from a high of 76,995 square feet to a low of 14,792 square feet. The median was 25,536 square feet (see table 4.3). A low value could indicate that custodians have other assigned duties or that there are opportunities for efficiencies. A high number could indicate that the custodial program is well managed, that some housekeeping responsibilities are assigned to other employees, or that the facilities are not well kept. A district with 10 million square feet and an assigned custodial workload of 14,792

TABLE 4.3

Power indicators for maintenance and operations with high, low, and median values

Maintenance and operations indicators	Low	Median	High
Custodial costs per square foot	$0.01	$1.57	$4.46
Custodial workload or district square footage *divided by* number of custodians	14,792	25,536	803,437
Maintenance spending as a percentage of general fund spending	0.9%	9.7%	57.9%
Maintenance cost per square foot	$0.61	$1.71	$10.02
Work order completion time (in days)	1	17	131

square feet per custodian could save approximately $5 million by increasing the workload to the median of 25,536 square feet.

Again, a district with about thirty-five elementary schools, nine middle schools, and five high schools serving 36,000 students could easily have 5.5 million square feet of floor space, including mobile units. Larger districts could have at least ten times that much floor space with the potential of savings in excess of $50 million.

In the area of food services, the project developed eighteen indicators that included such information as free and reduced-price eligibility and participation rates, total costs as a percentage of revenue, food costs, labor costs, fund balance, point-of-sale sites, and compliance with federal nutritional standards. Food costs per total nutritional revenue is important because food costs are the second largest expenditures in food service programs after labor, but they are more controllable.

The results of the data collection on food costs showed that districts devoted a high of 60.9 percent of food service revenue to food and a low of 24.1 percent. The median was 36.3 percent. The values can fluctuate with USDA menu requirements, purchasing practices, use of commodities, and other factors. One district in the survey allocated 52.1 percent of its nutritional budget to food costs. If it were able to move to the 36.3 percent median—by more careful menu planning, more competitive bidding and commodities use, and more consistent and standardized production practices—it could save $3.9 million annually.

Finally, the project has developed a series of safety and security indicators to measure such variables as the presence of safety and security plans, annual training for security staff members, requirements for staff and visitors to wear identification badges in schools, general fund expenditures devoted to safety and security, weapons incidents per one thousand, students and the like. Specific data in this area are included in the reports prepared by the Council but are not presented here because they have less to do with cost savings than do most other variables presented.

Finance and Budget

Some fifty-seven indicators were developed in the area of finance, including thirteen in accounts payable. These encompassed such measures as invoice costs, number of days to process vendor payments, number of invoices processed per person per month, voided checks, automation, positive payrolls, and invoice payment methods. One finance measure involved the average cost of processing invoices. The Institute of Management indicates that this measure is the second most commonly used metric in benchmarking accounts payable operations in the private sector.

The results of the KPI data collection effort indicated that districts ranged from a high of $65.39 per invoice to a low of $1.70. The median was $5.19. The values are sometimes affected by levels of automation, the number of staff in the accounts payable department, organizational structure, and district policies. A district with an average cost per invoice of $18.70 could save $136,000 for every 10,000 invoices processed at the median rate of $5.19 per invoice. Likewise, a district that increased the total number of invoices processed per person per month from 210.7 to the median of 711.7 could generate annual savings of $245,000 (see table 4.4). A district with 36,000 students could easily have 11,500–15,000 invoices per year. Larger districts will have many more. A district with about 250,000 students could easily have 315,000 invoices a year.

TABLE 4.4

Power indicators for finance and budget with high, low, and median values

Indicators	Low	Median	High
Finance—Accounts payable			
Cost per invoice	$1.70	$5.19	$65.39
Number on non-PO invoices processed per FTE per month	19.4	428.4	1,960.4
Number of days to process vendor payments	0	15	80
Number of PO invoices processed per FTE per month	11.9	366.9	1,961.1
Total number of invoices processed per FTE per month	61.2	711.7	2,992.6
Percentage of total non-salary checks voided or reversed	0.0%	1.0%	5.2%
Finance—Cash management			
Presence of a districtwide investment policy		83.7%	
District assesses return on investment against external benchmarks		70.8%	
Finance—Compensation			
Cost per pay check	$0.47	$7.18	$236.38
Percentage of all payroll checks produced off-cycle	0.1%	2.8%	50.0%
Percentage of all W2s that have to be corrected annually	0.0%	0.1%	7.2%
Percentage of total checks made by direct deposit	0.0%	85.7%	99.8%
Finance—Financial management			
Percentage of general fund expenditures in actual unreserved general fund balance	-10.6%	8%	35.5%
Percentage of approved budget actually spent or encumbered	75.4%	96.9%	116.9%
Percentage of approved revenue actually received	95.0%	100.9%	116.3%
Percentage of prior-year's audit findings resolved	0.0%	66.7%	100.0%
Districts with unqualified audit opinions		95.2%	
Finance—Grants management			
Percentage of operating budget targeted for grant funding	0.0%	14.4%	20.3%
Number of business days for budget approval and access to grant funds	5	30	110
Percentage of unspent grant funds lost	0.0%	9.0%	30.0%
Finance—Risk management			
Percentage of total operating funds devoted to general liability claims	.04%	0.44%	1.15%

The project, moreover, collected a large amount of budget data. One of the most important indicators involves fund balance. This assesses the fiscal health of a school district—and other organizations—by examining the organization's ability to meet unexpected demands. A higher percentage often means greater fiscal health, while a low value signals risk. The Government Finance Officers' Association (GFOA) typically recommends that large government entities maintain unreserved fund balances in their general funds of between 5 and 15 percent, or between one and two months of general operating expenses. The districts on which data were collected ranged from a high of 35.5 percent to a low of -10.6 percent. The median was 8 percent, well within the recommended levels. These values can depend on such factors as district policies, state or municipal requirements, spending volatility, and revenue variances.

One school district in the survey had a general operating fund balance of 9.1 percent. If it reduced that balance to the median of 8 percent, it could redirect some $6.8 million into the instructional budget. In another case, a district reported a fund balance of 35.5 percent. By reducing that balance to the median, the district could redirect some $79.2 million into instruction.

Human Resources and Personnel Operations

The project also developed forty-six indicators in the area of human resources, including such personnel and organizational measures as the numbers of staff members handling benefits, compensation, employee relations, employee services, information, labor relations, recruitment, payroll, risk management, and training. These indicators are important benchmarks by which city school systems can compare themselves on how they staff and structure their human resource departments.

Other human resource indicators are more operational in nature. These include such items as approved workers compensation claims, average time to complete personnel transfers, payroll transaction accuracy, response times on personnel information requests, insurance programming, professional development on operational procedures, risk management, and investigations on alleged employee misconduct. These indicators give districts a sense of operational smoothness and timeliness.

A third category of human resource indicators relates to overall customer satisfaction with human resource operations and overall district functioning. These include items such as grievance rates and settlements, surveys of employee satisfaction, perceptions of union-administration collaboration, EEO charges filed, workers compensation days, employee turnover rates, and terminations.

A final category of human resource indicators was more directly related to instructional performance and academic achievement—some of which also have cost implications. For instance, the project measures the percentage of instructional days lost due to teacher absences. This bears directly on the quality of instruction, working conditions, teacher supports, and overall school climate. But it also means that the district has to spend money to hire and train substitute teachers while paying the daily rate of the absent teacher (see table 4.5).

The results of the KPI data collection effort indicated that the median teacher absenteeism rate among the districts was about 6 percent. Districts ranged from a low of almost zero absenteeism to a high of 11.1 percent. A district with ten thousand full-time equivalent teachers and an absenteeism rate of 11.1 percent could save $229,500 each year by lowering its rate to the median, 6 percent. This would include savings on the average teacher daily rate and costs of the substitute teacher. A district with 50,000 employees might be expected to save $1.1 million or more.

Other human resource indicators developed by the project, like teacher position vacancies on the first day of school, are more a gauge of the effectiveness of a district's recruiting, selecting, hiring, and staffing processes than of cost. Still, these vacancies mean some lost instructional time, costs to fill the positions temporarily, and weakened public confidence.

The same is also true for indicators the team has developed related to teacher retention over one to five years, an indicator that answers recurring questions about the staying power of new teachers over their first five

TABLE 4.5

Power indicators for human resources and personnel operations with high, low, and median values

Human resources—Recruitment and staffing	Low	Median	High
Percentage of teacher positions that are vacant on the first day of school	0.0%	1.7%	11.2%
Numbers of days required to fill teacher vacancies	0	15	58
Percentage of newly hired teachers retained after one year	58.7%	92.5%	100.0
Percentage of newly hired teachers retained after two years	51.1%	77.8%	100.0%
Percentage of newly hired teachers retained after three years	35.1%	65.8%	100.0%
Percentage of newly hired teachers retained after four years	33.7%	63.0%	100.0%
Percentage of newly hired teachers retained after five years	28.7%	58.3%	100.0%

Human resources—Operations and school support	Low	Median	High
Length of time to complete personnel transfers in days	0	2	9
Length of time to complete displacements in days	0	1.5	10
Length of time to complete promotions or demotions in days	0	3.0	10
Length of time to complete pay-rate changes in days	0	1.5	9
Length of time to complete medical leaves in days	0	2.5	20
Length of time to complete non-medical leaves in days	0	2.0	10

Human resources—Employee relations and services	Low	Median	High
Percentage of all grievances filed by employees resolved in the district's favor	0.0%	42.9%	100.0%
Percentage of all grievances filed by employees that were settled	0.0%	25.7%	94.4%
Percentage of all grievances resolved in favor of the complainant	0.0%	10.3%	47.4%
Percentage of employees involved in formal investigations of misconduct	0.0%	0.5%	7.2%

years. The data on the teacher retention indicator show that the Great City Schools enjoy a median retention rate of 92.5 percent of their new teachers after their first year on the job, but the retention rate ranged from a high of 100 percent to a low of 58.7 percent. After the second year, however, the median retention rate of the new teachers had dropped to 77.8 percent. By the end of the third year, the median retention rate of the original new teachers had dropped to 65.8 percent, with the lowest rate at 35.1 percent. Interestingly, the retention rate did not change much between the end of the third year and the end of the fourth year; nor did the range. But by the end of the fifth year, the retention rate of the original cohort had dropped to a median level of 58.3 percent, and the weakest district had retained only 28.7 percent of those teachers.

These data are powerful because they tell the districts about their ability to hold on to their talent. The research is clear that the effectiveness of teachers is particularly high between their third and fifth years—about the time half of them leave. The data have tactical cost implications, as well, in that newer teachers have to be recruited, trained, placed, and mentored as they replace the original new teachers, all at substantial cost to the districts and schools. And the data have particular relevance in that they can identify cities where the retention rates have been particularly strong. This means that it should be possible to find out what these cities are doing that other cities with high loss rates are not doing.

These organizational, operational, customer satisfaction, and teacher data provide school districts strong measures of whether their functions compare well with other cities. Most of these indicators have cost implications, but the project has not yet fully articulated or quantified all of them. For instance, the number of grievances filed relates to any number of factors, including relations with the unions, professional development on procedures, and legal talent. But there are also financial costs associated with the amount of administrative time devoted to handling claims and with lost productivity among employees involved. The Council of the Great City Schools is working on methodologies for estimating financial costs and savings opportunities behind these organizational, operational, and satisfaction indicators.

Information Technology

Finally, the project has developed twenty-seven indicators in the area of information technology. These indicators include variables measuring such general information as a district's average age of computers, technology spending per pupil, student-to-networked-computer ratio, various computer security variables, and help desk information, including problem resolution rates, network operation costs per student, bandwidth per student, telecommunications cost per student, and annual personnel costs per number of help tickets created.

One information technology indicator relates to first contact resolution rates (FCRR), which measure the ability of local help desks to resolve technology problems on a first call and are important because they appraise a caller's ability to get back to productive work sooner. Districts with low resolution rates may need to investigate the types and patterns of tickets not resolved, help desk staffing and training, the technology itself that staff members complain about, or the automation used to track and report tickets.

The results of the KPI data collection effort indicate that the median district has an FCRR rate of 45.7 percent. Districts range from a low of 6.2 percent to a high of 95.0 percent. A typical help desk staff member takes 20 to 30 calls per day on average, and the average cost per ticket is $15.91 for a tier-1 call, a first-time call. If the call requires travel to a site or needs to be handled by a functional expert, then the average cost jumps to $100 per ticket. A district with three help desk staff members could save $448,410 per year by raising its FCRR rate from 6.2 percent to the median level of 45.7 percent. In the process, it would also increase customer satisfaction and productivity.

Return on Investment

The kinds of analyses, cost savings, and potential efficiencies described in the previous section are now increasingly possible with the KPI data that the city school systems have designed. As the districts face increasingly difficult economic challenges, the data and the return on investment (ROI) analyses that are being done with them are also being used more and more. A good example is found in Los Angeles, which is home to the KPI initiative. Historically, the Los Angeles Unified School District cut budgets the same way many of its school district counterparts across the country did: it made across-the-board reductions without much thought to core mission or ROI analyses. However, the district has begun to move away from this traditional approach by assessing each prospective budget cut in two ways: How does the activity and cuts to it affect the core mission of the district? What is the ROI of the cut compared to the district's risk in making it?

In Los Angeles, every potential cut was subject to a quadrant analysis and received an index score based on its core mission-to-ROI ranking. The relationship to core mission was scored on a four-point scale ranging from "this is the reason for our existence" to "this is an activity that we might have conducted historically but has little relation to our mission." The risk-to-ROI ratio ran from high-risk/low return—meaning, implementing the cut is complex, may not be achievable, has considerable political ramifications and/or could jeopardize credibility, and the dollar savings are minimal—to low-risk/high return, meaning that implementing the cut is viable and achievable, has limited political ramifications, and will result in high dollar savings. Staff members from the district estimate that about three-quarters of the 2008 budget cuts were subjected to this process before political considerations finally became paramount. Still, the methodology offered a rational way of budget cutting for a time.

The measures are also beginning to be used to improve operations and performance. Los Angeles now uses the KPI system as part of its annual performance management reports on each of its business services. The district also used the indicator on the age of the bus fleets, compared with other cities, to deploy $75 million in bond funds for vehicle replacements. Columbus used the transportation indicators in much the same way as Los Angeles and allocated $22 million for bus replacement. Boston used the transportation indicators with its city council during budget hearings. In Los Angeles, the data on secondary student participation in school lunch programs resulted in an increase in the amount of time that high school students were given to eat. Philadelphia is building the food services indicators into its districtwide report cards. Albuquerque has used the Information Technology indicators to better track monthly performance of their customer call center. These examples illustrate the potential of these Key Performance Indicators to help urban school systems save money and deploy resources into activities that might enhance the instructional program.

In addition, the first fledgling steps are being taken to track trend lines on the indicators. For instance, one of the indicators mentioned previously—custodial workload—shows that the average square footage covered by custodians increased from 23,501 in fiscal year 2005 (FY05) to 24,164 in FY06 to 24,554 in FY07 to 25,536 in FY08. The average age of the bus fleets dropped from 7.7 years in FY05 to 7 years in FY08, meaning lower repair costs. Food costs as a percentage of all food service costs dropped from 39.3 percent in FY05 to 36.3 percent in FY08. Work order completion times dropped from a median 21 days in FY06 to 17 days in FY08. Electricity usage dropped from 58.3 units per square foot in FY05 to 53.7 units in FY08. Median general fund balance also improved from 7.2 percent in FY06 to 7.5 percent in FY07 to 8 percent in FY08. Work on these trend lines has only just begun, but the ability to create them has been demonstrated. Over time, the capacity to track these indicators will give the cities and the public a much better sense of whether and how cost savings are being realized as operational efficiencies are being put into place.

Theoretically, a district serving about thirty-six thousand students that was consistently in the bottom quartile on most of the "power indicators" we have described could save between $20 and $50 million a year by moving closer to the median performance of their urban peers. Larger cities that are consistently weak performers on the critical metrics might be able to divert more than $100 million a year into the classroom by adopting practices that their peers have already implemented.

NEXT-GENERATION INDICATORS

Although the project is now in its fifth year, in many ways it is only just beginning. The effort has demonstrated that it is possible to identify and define a set of operational and performance indicators for the nation's big city school districts. The initiative has also shown that it is feasible to collect comparable data from a substantial number of cities and to produce multiyear trend lines on that data. And the project has established that city school leaders and others find value in the data and will use them to improve operations and redeploy resources. But the Council knows that more needs to be done in order for the initiative to realize its full potential.

Power Indicators

The Council and its members have now demonstrated proof-of-concept in developing 227 Key Performance Indicators in four broad functional areas. The project team has also taken the first steps in winnowing down the larger set of KPIs to seventy-seven preliminary "power indicators." The Council now is setting up cross-functional teams to review the first draft of the power indicators and to determine if others are needed. The project also wants to make sure that these power indicators can be viably translated into data dashboards at the district level and regularly monitored. More importantly, however, the team wants to make sure that the best indicators are included not only to ensure operational effectiveness and resource efficiency but also to improve policy making at the local level.

There is considerable discussion, moreover, about extending the concepts behind the project into areas of academic attainment and instructional processes. The project envisions including special education, early childhood programming, afterschool programming, out-of-field teaching, ninth-grade course failure rates, NAEP data, and other measures that would provide urban school systems with an unprecedented level of data to drive reform.

Finally, the development teams are looking at the possibility of articulating which of the measures might be thought of as "leading" indicators or predictors and which might be considered "lagging" indicators. The team has already been differentiating between outcome-oriented rather than operational or process indicators.

Performance Standard

The initiative is also beginning to examine standards of performance for each of the indicators, particularly the power indicators. Currently, the project is able to tell each district whether its performance in a particular area is above or below the norm among the participating districts, but a district cannot tell whether the median itself is above or below an agreed-on standard of performance.

The project team is considering the use of external standards from other fields if they do not exist in education or developing a consensus-building process to define them if they do not exist at all. The team has already begun to identify some existing standards. For example, as mentioned previously, the GFOA has standards for general operating fund balances. The National Institute of Governmental Purchasing (NIGB) has standards for initiating and completing formal competitive bid processes. The National Association of Purchasing Card Professionals has standards for the average cost of processing purchase orders. And there are national standards for on-time bus arrivals and custodian costs per square foot of building space. The teams are scouring these and other sources to determine operational standards in as many areas as is feasible so that the cities can compare themselves against more than each other's averages.

In addition to these standards, the team envisions examining performance criteria in other sectors, such as the military, health care, airlines, manufacturing, insurance, energy and telecommunications companies, commercial services, government, and other large-scale organizations. An initial pilot of this concept in Los Angeles showed that the school district had lower payroll costs as a percentage of revenue than the vast majority of 164 other private-sector companies but a considerably higher payroll processing error rate.

Automation of Indicators

The Council and its development team are spending considerable time automating the Key Performance Indicators. This is being done for two reasons: to allow data on the KPIs to be gathered electronically and automatically aggregated as the data come in and to allow districts to ask how they would perform relative to other districts if they changed certain variables or practices. For instance, a district might ask whether the cost of paycheck preparation would rise or fall compared with other cities if online deposits were increased. Or a district might ask if drive time and expense would rise or fall with regional garaging of buses versus centralized garaging. The system is being designed to allow districts to analyze their own data and compare themselves to cities of similar size or to other characteristics. And the new electronic system is currently being designed to allow districts to compare themselves with similar cities and to create their own Web-based data dashboards with easy-to-use gauges, charts, and tables that would keep plans, budgets, and performance measures on target with a series of triggers.

Analyses of Best Practices Behind the Results

It is already clear that some urban school districts have more consistently positive indicators, or KPIs, than other districts. For example, Wichita, Buffalo, Columbus, Omaha, and Rochester consistently rated higher on both participation and operational indicators in the area of food services than did other major city school districts; Milwaukee, Columbus, and Atlanta consistently rated higher than other cities in the area of maintenance and operation; Anchorage, Broward County, and Buffalo consistently performed well on indicators of financial management; and Baton Rouge and Norfolk did particularly well on procurement indicators. What we do not yet know is why some districts consistently do better in some areas than in others and why some cities do better than other cities across the board. What are the best practices, policies, and procedures underlying these indicators that appear to produce positive performance, and how are they different from those in districts where the indicators are consistently low?

To determine the factors behind the results, the Council and its development team are now planning to conduct a series of case studies of high-performing and low-performing districts in each of the major functional areas. The findings could then be used to produce a set of best practices to guide the technical assistance that the Council delivers to its members.

Cross-Functional and Policy Analyses

Finally, the Council and its development team are working on how to modify and shape the next generation of indicators so that they will allow a district not only to ask itself questions about how its practices might affect its relative standing among other cities on each KPI but also to "war game" various operational scenarios and ask *What/if?* about how the indicators inform outcomes. These indicators allow districts to ask what the service/cost drivers are, how changes in practice influence numbers of students served or level and cost of services, and what the relative trade-offs are of one set of practices versus another. These tools would allow a school district to simulate or model management decisions before putting them into practice. We envision questions being aligned at both policy and leadership levels and management, operational, and process levels. Finally, the development team is looking at the possibility of linking the operational indicators together with the instructional and academic ones to create a more comprehensive look at how these systems perform in tandem.

LOOKING TO THE FUTURE

The nation's major urban public school districts are initiating an extensive array of efforts to improve academic achievement, enhance operations, and improve efficiency. They know that many more years of rigorous work are needed to strengthen outcomes and gain the public's confidence. But there is growing confidence among city school leaders that both goals are attainable and that the districts generally are on the right track. A critical component in the districts' strategy to improve involves this Performance Measurement and Benchmarking Project.

It has taken a number of years to get the project to its current point. Still, a considerable amount of architecture remains to be designed, particularly at the policy level, to move the effort forward. Improving the efficiency and cost effectiveness of these school districts will require more than squeezing operational waste out of the system. To be sure, districts are tightening their belts, and that process will be improved by the Key Performance Indicators described in this chapter. But the overall effort will also require addressing larger strategic questions about how the school systems are structured and how they use their resources broadly.

For instance, the project currently collects data on the number and percent of satisfactory job evaluations of administrators and some classified staff, but the Council is aware that such data on teacher evaluations may soon be part of the U.S. Department of Education's data collection efforts nationwide. This project can easily gather such data and better determine the need to overhaul staff evaluation procedures. In addition, the project has collected data on the costs of staff benefits but has not collected detailed information on teacher compensation systems.

Generally, huge questions remain about how the systems use their resources to compensate teachers and how current practices relate to instructional quality. Issues surrounding pay-for-performance and other results-based compensation systems are just the tip of the iceberg. New challenges are emerging about the whole "step and lane" structure of teacher pay and the back-end loading of compensation that may be benefiting older teachers to the detriment of younger teachers who may be just as effective and who their districts are trying to retain.

Fresh questions are also being asked about the degree of increased compensation received by teachers over their careers and how it relates to increased responsibility or performance versus longevity. There are emerging concerns that the practice of back-end loading teacher compensation to reward tenure is short-sheeting the compensation of new teachers when it is not always clear that the more highly compensated teachers are that much more effective. How do districts use their resources in ways that provide incentives to new teachers, reward performance, and retain the most effective teachers? What criteria other than seniority should districts use to lay off teachers and staff when budget cuts are needed? How should districts redeploy resources during bad economic times such as the present? How does a district align teacher salary increases with district priorities and student needs?

New challenges have also been raised about the return-on-investment of lowering class sizes beyond the point where they produce measurable results. Have we devoted more resources than necessary to lower class sizes at the expense of teacher quality? How do we balance effective teaching across schools?

Moreover, issues are emerging about how equitably resources are distributed across states, districts, schools, and classrooms—and how those resources match up with the academic and social needs of students. How are resources added or cut from schools with differing student needs? What is an appropriate pattern of staffing in schools where students bring widely varying challenges? How should district leaders decide on closing schools and redeploying resources when there are limited options for where the children can go? How should resources best be used to turn around chronically low-performing schools versus how resources are used in other schools? How do the lowest-performing schools currently deploy their resources?

Finally, the existence of these Key Performance Indicators raises new issues about who should be accountable for ensuring that progress is made on them and how they align with the goals and priorities of the school systems. A district could easily focus considerable attention on demonstrating progress on the KPIs without fitting its broader vision of how to better align resources and strategic goals to produce a better outcome for the same resources or less. For instance, it is not unusual for school districts to tie up large amounts of resources on activities that sound productive but don't show much efficacy in raising student achievement—like K–8 schools, supplemental educational services, and master's degrees for teachers or professional development units. It is also not unusual for districts to underinvest in activities that could work if done well—like better aligned formative assessments, preschool programs, or collaborative teacher planning time. And it is not atypical for districts to devote considerable resources to things that could work but are done too unstrategically to be effective, like undifferentiated, generic, districtwide professional development. Finally, there is no end to the amount of money that is invested in one positive activity but results in little benefit because of poor investment in or lack of attention to another activity—like spending lots of money on designing and building data systems but not training anyone to use them.

The alignment of resources with strategic priorities is just as important as the ability to squeeze operational efficiencies out of program administration. Are there better ways for districts—particularly large ones—to use economies of scale to reduce costs? Can more cohesive programming result in cost savings, as compared with programming that is more fractured? Can costs be offloaded through more outsourcing or contracting, or does the strategy actually increase costs over the long run? Would multiyear budgeting help more districts think strategically about their resources, or is it an exercise in pretension and speculation? What resource reallocations would have the greatest impact on student achievement and how feasible are they? Can new revenue streams be created or existing ones be enhanced? Unfortunately, this type of alignment work takes careful assessment and analysis, target setting, prioritizing, planning, confidence building, and time, something an impatient public isn't always inclined to grant. But the task is highly complex and will require patience as schools struggle to get this right.

It is clear that the present economic condition of the country has spurred fresh questions about how school districts use their resources. These questions now involve public education's very organization, funding, infrastructure, human capital, programming, technology, and other features.

But before critics assume that the enterprise is not capable of innovation, of learning from others, or of borrowing ideas and practices from other sectors, they should consider this effort by the nation's urban public schools to create a whole new mechanism—through both the urban NAEP on the instructional side and these KPIs on the noninstructional side—by which they can analyze their performance, assess their efficiencies, streamline their operations, and save precious dollars. These new tools are not fully developed yet and are not as widely in use as they will be, but the leadership of city schools and their growing participation in their own handiwork holds enormous promise for them and for public education in general.

5

The Efficient Use
of Teachers

Steven F. Wilson

THIS BOOK ASKS, *In a time of recession, how can schools cut costs while boosting outcomes?* Any serious appraisal of the question must begin with teachers, for spending on teachers represents a school district's single largest expense—in 2006, 45 percent of total expenditures in public education.[1] While other sectors have increased productivity, improving outcomes while reducing labor costs, schools have done the reverse. From 1980 to 2006, student enrollment grew by 17.9 percent while total school employment grew by 47.9 percent.[2] In 1955 there was one teacher for every twenty-seven students; by 1997 there was one for every sixteen.[3]

Yet, achievement results have remained flat. American seventeen-year-olds, at the end of their public education, performed barely better on the National Assessment of Educational Progress (NAEP) tests in reading and math in 2008 than in the early 1970s.[4] In international comparisons of student achievement, even though the United States spent more per student than any other country, the performance of the oldest students continues to be undistinguished.[5] American fifteen-year-olds performed worse than their peers from all but five of the thirty Organisation for Economic Cooperation and Development (OECD) countries in the most recent Trends in Mathematics and Science Study (TIMSS) math assessment; in science they performed worse than students from all but nine nations.[6]

Could teachers be deployed more effectively in U.S. schools, boosting achievement while lowering costs? In this chapter, I consider reform initiatives that would decrease teacher compensation cost—the overwhelming expense in any district—while improving academic outcomes. By better deploying faculty, ensuring that all students in a class have mastered precursor skills, judiciously substituting instructional technology for labor, equipping teachers with intellectual property that provides detailed and coherent designs for teaching and learning, and launching a comprehensive human capital initiative, districts cannot only cope with punishing revenue declines but can emerge as leaner and higher-performing organizations.

Belleview Public Schools is an urban school system in the Northwest that educates 29,500 students in thirty-seven elementary schools, eleven middle schools, five high schools, and six alternative programs.[7] Fifty-nine percent of its students are from low-income families. It employs 1,944 teachers, who account for 74 percent of the district's total of 2,637 employees. Total salaries and benefits account for 84 percent of the district's total spending of $326 million.

At its September 2008 board meeting, the district's superintendent said he would not make extensive cuts to school programs; instead he would wait to see how the state legislature "fully funds basic education." If the legislature does not bail out the district, it will need to cut spending in the face of declining state and local revenues by 7 percent over two years, or $22.8 million.

Deployment of instructional staff and technology initiatives

Initiative	Annual savings
1. Increase class size	$17.6 million

By increasing student-teacher ratios, with a commensurate increase in class size, from 15.3 students to 17.3 (from 13.2 to 15.2 in kindergarten through fifth grade and from 17.5 to 19.5 in grades six through twelve), the district could save $17.6 million annually in teacher salaries and benefits. Additional savings would accrue from reduction in facility costs, utilities, and other noncompensation costs. The savings from this modest increase in class size (on average, two students per class) would alone provide for more than three-quarters of the required savings.

The reform may seem heretical, since Belleview, like many other districts, has spent heavily over the last quarter-century in class size reduction and since smaller classes are popular with parents and students alike. But the drive to reduce class size has been extraordinarily costly. From 1955 to 2005, the student-teacher ratio in public schools nationally tumbled from 26.9 to 15.6.[7] During the 1970s and 1980s, this decline alone accounted for an astonishing 85 percent of the $25 billion increase in annual instructional spending over the same period.[8]

Does the evidence justify sustaining this investment?

Class Size Reduction

Throughout the 1990s and continuing today, the American education establishment has pressed for smaller class sizes in public schools, promising achievement gains. The National Education Association (NEA), for example, "recommends an optimum class size of 15 students in regular programs, especially in the early grades, and a proportionately lower number in programs for students with exceptional needs." The American Federation of Teachers (AFT) concurs: "Compelling evidence demonstrates that reducing class size, particularly for younger children, will have a positive effect on student achievement overall and an especially significant impact on the education of poor children."[9] The American Educational Research Association (AERA), the professional association of educational researchers, stated in 2003 that "small classes rank near the top of the list in the stockpile of educational policy initiatives that are worth finding resources for."[10]

Smaller classes made intuitive sense: with fewer children to handle, teachers would be able to devote more attention to individual students. The public was persuaded, and reducing class size became the most popular education reform strategy. A 1998 poll found that 88 percent of parents favored further class size reduction in K–3.[11] Class size reduction, as Douglas Harris has noted, is popular with parents because it is tangible, immediate, and intuitively attractive.[12] President Clinton proposed to decrease class size in the early grades to an average of eighteen students.[13]

Advocates of small classes cite the Project STAR (student-teacher achievement ratio) experiment conducted in Tennessee in the mid-1980s. K–3 students were randomly assigned to three types of classes, one of a typical size (twenty-two to twenty-five students) with a single teacher, a second of the same size but with a teacher aide, and the third with only thirteen to seventeen students. While students in regular-sized classes with an aide performed no better than those without, students in the smaller classes for three years posted tests scores of up to 0.22 standard deviations (depending on the subject) higher than students in regular-sized classes.[14] This effect is the equivalent of a student who begins at the fiftieth percentile on a nationally normed test moving up 8 percentile points to the fifty-eighth percentile. The effect was considerably greater for black and low-income students, which may be due to the greater impact of additional resources in schools serving children from poverty.[15] Students who were taught in small classes were also slightly more likely, later research found, to take college entrance tests and state that they planned to go to college. Nearly 44 percent of students who were educated in smaller classes sat for the SAT or ACT test, compared with 40 percent of students in regular classes.[16]

But even these modest gains have been questioned. Because no baseline tests of students in the three groups were performed, it is impossible to confirm that class assignments were truly done at random. Parents strongly prefer smaller classes for their children, and in each school in the experiment students in large classes were educated across the hall from students in small classes. If parents of more capable students were able even occasionally to have their child assigned to the more advantaged setting, it would fully account for the effect. That the benefit of small classes was one-time—the gap in performance between the two groups did not increase as students remained in small classes—supports this concern.[17]

Indeed, later critiques of STAR found that sorting of students within and between schools obscured any causal relationship between class size and achievement effects. Moreover, other studies contradict the STAR findings. In her research on class size and achievement, Harvard economist Caroline Hoxby selected an experimental design that permitted the effects of smaller classes to be examined apart from other factors that may infect explicit experiments like STAR, including the assignment of particular teachers or students to the smaller classes, the "Hawthorne effect" (where individuals temporarily increase their productivity when they are being evaluated), and the existence of incentives to obtain results that might not exist if the policy were broadly enacted. (The schools may perceive that a class size reduction policy would not be enacted if the experiment fails to demonstrate gains.) Examining natural variations in class size—in the range of ten to thirty students per class—in 649 Connecticut elementary schools, where teachers were unaware of the experiment, Hoxby found no statistically significant effect of class size on student achievement.[18]

In 1996, after California's fourth graders tied for last place in reading among thirty-nine states participating in the NAEP, the state enacted legislation that gave districts a financial incentive to reduce class sizes in grades K–3 to twenty students.[19] The state's student-teacher ratio had been calculated prior to 1996 at 29:1. From 1998 through June 2003, 99 percent of districts participated in the reform. The cost in 2003 was $906 for every full-day K–3 student in the program.[20] The cost to the state exceeded $1.6 billion for the 2002–2003 school year.[21] Yet a major study of the class size reduction (CSR) initiative, conducted over four years for the California Department of Education, reported that although parents of children in reduced-size classes had "far higher" levels of satisfaction, researchers found "only limited evidence" linking gains in student achievement to the smaller classes.[22] In fact, urban districts had been damaged by the hiring of thousands of unqualified teachers to staff new classrooms. A "school-level analysis finds no relationship between CSR exposure and student achievement," the report concludes flatly. "For many people, the lack of a clear relationship between CSR and student achievement will be disappointing."[23] The report notes the failure of California to duplicate the gains of the STAR experiment but also points out that California's goal was a class size of twenty, substantially larger than those studied in STAR.[24]

A recent analysis of the STAR initiative by Christopher Jepsen and Steven Rivkin finds fault with the research designs of Hoxby and other CSR skeptics and finds modest achievements gain from the California initiative. Jepsen and Rivkin attempt to isolate statistically the effects of teachers who entered the workforce as a result of the dramatic increase in teaching jobs from the California mandate (many of whom lacked experience and were less effective) from the effects of an approximately ten-student drop in class size. In a simulation exercise, the authors estimate that the long-term benefits of CSR are 0.167 standard deviations in mathematics and 0.099 standard deviations in reading.[25] These findings are not dissimilar from those of other researchers, who report positive achievement effects from small classes. (Angrist and Lavy found a ten-student reduction in class size would yield 0.17 standard deviations in the fifth grade in Israel; Krueger reported gains in test scores of 0.20 standard deviations in Tennessee's kindergarten classrooms; and Rivkin, Hanushek, and Kain estimate an increase in fourth-grade scores in Texas of approximately 0.1 standard deviations from a reduction of ten students per class.[26]) But Jepsen and Rivkin acknowledge that the statewide implementation of CSR makes its effects difficult to isolate from other major policy changes, including the imposition of performance standards and accountability, test score inflation, and the advent of charter schools.[27] They also recognize the extraordinary price tag of CSR, concluding that "an important question is whether the benefits justify the substantial cost."[28]

Consider just how expensive smaller classes are. Not only must vast numbers of new teachers be hired (California increased its teacher workforce from 62,226 to 91,112 in three years, between 1995–1996 to 1998–1999),[29] but additional classrooms must be built, equipped, and maintained. Hoxby has estimated the cost of a 10 percent reduction in class size at $615 per pupil, in 2001 dollars, when average spending was $8,157.[30] To achieve a reduction in class size commensurate with the STAR program would require a 37.5 percent decrease, or $2,306 per pupil, or nearly 30 percent of total educational spending.[31]

These conclusions are just as apposite to districts wrestling with spending cuts as to policy makers evaluating increased investments in education. Courageous district leaders will ask whether the benefits of small classes justify their extraordinary costs. As teachers are the single largest expense in schools, class size and teacher assignments are far and away the most powerful lever for controlling costs and increasing productivity.

Even the largest increases in average class size that a district might consider would be a fraction of the STAR experiment and would therefore yield, as we have seen, an indiscernible effect on student achievement. In fact, implemented in conjunction with other delivery reforms that it would fuel, class size increases could have a strongly *positive* effect on student attainment.

Certainly a look at the performance of school systems internationally lends little support to an American reform strategy based on smaller classes and high teacher-student ratios. In an analysis of class size and student achievement in eighteen countries, using data from the 1994-95 Third International Mathematics and Science Study, the largest international study of student performance, Ludger Wössmann and Martin West found little support for reducing class size. That three of the five highest-performing countries (Singapore, Korea, and Japan) had average class sizes greater than thirty students (Korea's averaged more than fifty) might alone give one pause. The study aimed to look deeper by examining the relationship between class size and performance within the countries themselves. There were statistically significant benefits in student performance from smaller classes in only two countries, Greece and Iceland. In these two nations, average student performance is low (much lower than Singapore, Korea, and Japan, despite much smaller classes), and school spending is substantially below the average of countries without class size effects. Teacher salaries are also low. From salary and teacher education data, the authors speculate that these countries' teachers are less skilled and better able to manage smaller classes than larger ones.

> Thus, the evidence on class-size effects presented in this paper suggests the interpretation that capable teachers are able to promote student learning equally well regardless of class size (at least within the range of variation that occurs naturally between grades). In other words, they are capable enough to teach well in large classes ... It may be better policy to devote the limited resources available for education to employing more capable teachers rather than to reducing class sizes.[32]

Further evidence that the nearly universal drive to reduce class size is misguided comes from top-performing charter schools. The first ten years of the charter school experiment, launched in Minnesota in 1991, fostered a broad range of designs that, perhaps unsurprisingly, performed on the whole little better than the traditional district schools. But then emerged a particular model of schooling that posted striking results. The Knowledge Is Power Program began with two schools serving students from low-income families in Houston and the Bronx and now counts eighty-two small schools in nineteen states and the District of Columbia, with a total enrollment of some 21,000 students.[33] Nearly 95 percent of Knowledge is Power Program (KIPP) eighth graders matriculated to college preparatory high schools in 2008, according to the organization.[34] On national norm-referenced tests, KIPP fifth graders began on average at the forty-first percentile in math and the thirty-first percentile in reading; after four years these students are performing on average at the eightieth percentile in math and the fifty-eighth percentile in reading.[35] Two other fast-growing networks, Achievement First and Uncommon Schools, are also posting achievement–gap closing results. The educational methods of the three organizations are strikingly similar. Highly educated, driven, and generally young teachers lead their students in a rigorous academic program, tightly aligned with state standards, that aims to set every child on the path to college. The approach has been dubbed "no excuses" schooling because founders and staff steadfastly reject explanations from any quarter for low achievement, whether a district apologist's appeals to demographic destiny or a child's excuse for failing to complete an assignment. Small classes are not a feature of the "no excuses" approach. In fact, KIPP believes its focus on rigorous academics and orderly environment permits large classes (occasionally with as many as forty-five students) to be effective. KIPP cofounder David Levin explains, "Class size is not an issue if teachers know how to manage kids."[36]

Initiative	Annual savings
2. Eliminate teacher aides above first grade	$6.4 million

By eliminating teacher aides in all classes above first grade, Belleview could save $6.4 million annually. Eliminating teacher aides (except in special education, kindergarten, and first grade, where they play an important role in helping students adapt to formal instruction) is a sensible additional savings initiative. The STAR experiment found only minimal achievement benefits from placing aides in classes; above the first grade, any effect was statistically insignificant.[37]

Class Formation

A principal reason districts cite increasing staffing ratios—whether by adding teacher aides, instituting team teaching, or lowering class size—is the challenge of "differentiating instruction" to meet the needs of an educationally heterogeneous population in each class. But a far more effective—and less costly—solution is to change how classes are formed.

While much attention has been given to the size of classes, almost none has been directed to how they are formed. Classes are not chance aggregations of pupils; at least in principle, they are composed of students who have mastered the prerequisite skills and knowledge to function in the class. But in most American schools students are assigned to classes based on age—regardless of whether they have demonstrated such mastery. As students move up the grades, their teachers confront an increasingly unmanageable array of undiagnosed knowledge gaps among their students; these gaps impede the acquisition of new skills and explain the dismaying fall-off in student performance in the middle and high schools grades that is a hallmark of American schools. Exhorting teachers to address these gaps through "individual attention" or, to use the current buzzword, "differentiated instruction" is a fool's errand.

The Sabis model of class formation proposes an alternative. The Sabis International Charter School in Springfield, Massachusetts, enrolls 1,574 students in kindergarten through twelfth grade and has the largest waiting list of any Massachusetts charter school, nearly 2,700 students. Tenth graders from low-income families outperform their peers in the Springfield district schools by 45 percentage points on the state's respected Massachusetts Comprehensive Assessment System MCAS test (92 percent versus 46 percent proficient or advanced) in English and 50 percentage points in math (83 percent versus 33 percent proficient or advanced), and for the past seven years every SABIS Springfield high school graduate has been admitted to an institution of higher learning.[38] The school has literally closed the achievement gap by race and income; tenth graders in the low-income and African American No Child Left Behind (NCLB) subgroups outperform the average student statewide. In 2008, *Newsweek* named the school one of only three urban "top U.S. high schools" in Massachusetts.[39]

Students are placed in grades by skills level, not age. From phonics in kindergarten through AP classes in high school, students are taught each learning objective to mastery. Through electronic assessment tightly keyed to the curriculum, their teachers are alerted immediately when they fail to demonstrate mastery of a skill they have just been taught. Rather than move forward, their teacher reteaches the concept or arranges for tutoring of individual students by their peers so that knowledge gaps do not form that undermine later learning. A schoolteacher can no more successfully introduce algebra to students who have not mastered division than a college professor can teach an advanced chemistry class to students who have not completed basic courses in the subject.

So equipped, SABIS teachers routinely succeed with classes of thirty students. Ralph Bistany, SABIS's founder, sees it is as SABIS's mission to demonstrate that a world-class education can be delivered affordably and scoffs at those who claim thirty children cannot be effectively taught in one classroom. "First, we need to define the word 'class,'" he says. "Every course has a prerequisite—concepts that the course is going to use but not explain. That list of concepts determines who belongs in the class and who doesn't." If the course is German, and one student is fluent and others cannot speak a word of the language, the students obviously should not be taught together, he explains. At SABIS, students in a class have the same background but neither, he hastens to say, "the same ability nor the same knowledge." So formed, it doesn't matter whether the class has ten students or fifty. "In fact, fifty is better," he adds. "We have worked with classes of seventy in countries where it is allowed, and it has worked like a charm." Students have a responsibility to their classmates to pose questions pertinent to the concepts being taught, not material that the class has already mastered. "Anybody who asks a question that is not legitimate is wasting the rest of the class's time," says Bistany.

The often-promised "individual attention" of small classes is doomed to fail, Bistany says. "In a class of twenty, it means five minutes for every child. And before you can help him, you have to find out what his problem is. That is not teaching. That is a study hall." Conversely, large classes do not impede the progress of the brightest students. A yearlong course might encompass four hundred concepts; usually some one hundred of these are "essential concepts" that all students must master. "The weaker students must know the 'essentials.' The brightest will know 90 percent of the others" by the end of the course, Bistany explained.[40]

Were he speaking of higher education, and not of primary and secondary education, Bistany's description of class structure would be familiar and his argument self-evident. There, no one would think it practical—let alone normative—to educate a classroom of students with widely diverse preparation and precursor skills. Students would be expected to master fundamental skills before being instructed in more advanced ones. But as applied to K–12 education in the United States, his plan seems radical, even repellent. SABIS's approach may encounter initial resistance from parents but is a far more rational way of organizing schools to produce high levels of student achievement than reducing class size.

Initiative	Annual savings
3. Complement teacher-led instruction with instructional technology	$16.2 million

By allocating one quarter of instructional time to independent learning with instructional technology, the district would save $16.2 million. In a hybrid instructional model, students at every level of school—elementary, middle, and high—would spend one quarter of their time in a learning lab using select, state-of-the-art instructional technology. At each of the district's schools, this would result, on average, in an eight full-time employee reduction in teachers, which would be offset by the hiring of two full-time learning lab specialist teachers, annual debt service on amortized technology and software acquisition costs ($390,000 per school), and professional development expenses (including vendor-delivered training and district professional development coordinators).

In the learning lab, students focus on their individual learning needs. Online and client-server software is rigorously curated by central district staff and includes educational Web sites, computerized assessment, and research-validated learning software. Special software manages each student's skill deficits and their portfolio of software applications; each time a student logs into the lab, the software steers students to the appropriate content.

Independent Learning and Instructional Technology

The productivity of American schools has steadily declined as per-pupil costs have soared, ratios of teachers to pupils have increased, and educational outcomes have remained flat or modestly increased. In nearly every other sector of the economy, the substitution of technology for labor, made possible through technological advances, has steadily increased productivity. Education has been an exception. For four decades, entrepreneurs and educational technology enthusiasts have promised that technological innovations would imminently transform schooling. Educators have every reason to be skeptical of the industry's latest claims. But today's commercial learning products are less fanciful than in the past and the technology more advanced. Focused deployments of current technology can now yield, in concert with other reforms, demonstrable learning gains.

Rocketship Education, a nonprofit school network, has posted impressive early results from a hybrid model of conventional instruction and independent learning. Every student spends one hundred minutes each day in a learning lab addressing specific skill deficits. The lab combines computerized curriculum, independent learning, and enrichment programs. The approach saves each school $500,000 a year, which the schools then invest in higher teacher pay, individualized tutoring, a full-time academic dean, and a full year of training for principals.[41] At the Rocketship Mateo Sheedy Elementary School in San Jose, California, 78 percent of students are from low-income families and 73 percent are English language learners. In 2009 the school posted the highest scores among schools the state classifies as serving primarily low-income students in San Jose and Santa Clara and the third highest of all such schools in California.[42]

For more on the cost savings from the substitution of technology for labor, see John Chubb's chapter in this volume.

TEACHER QUALITY AND COMPENSATION INITIATIVES

At Belleview, as at most districts where the supply of strong teachers is limited, CSR initiatives by districts and states exacerbated the scarcity of good teachers in schools. To fill the new teaching slots from the pool of available teachers, districts had to be less selective about whom they hired. Yet virtually every study of class size has found that effects of class size reduction are dwarfed by variations in teacher quality.[43]

Studies have documented the dramatically different trajectories of students who are taught by capable teachers and those who are not. One of the most noted involved students in Tennessee, where all students in the state in grades two through eight were tested annually. Teacher value-added effects could be calculated from these data. Teachers were categorized into five quintiles of effectiveness. Eighth graders who had benefited from a progression of teachers over three years who were all in the top quintile of teacher effectiveness performed, on average, more than 50 percentiles higher than students who were educated by a progression of teachers who were in the lowest quartile of effectiveness. This is in contrast to the benefits of smaller class sizes, which, as noted above, resulted in an 8 percentile point advantage at the very most. Other studies reach similarly dramatic conclusions. The achievement penalty of having a low-performing teacher is especially severe for primary school students, for their educational losses are rarely later overcome. Third-grade results are a powerful predictor of later achievement, including obtaining a college diploma.[44]

If the quality of teachers is paramount, what can districts do to elevate it? School districts, like any other organization pressured to improve performance with dwindling resources, should engage all four levers to improve the talent pool: dispense with their poorest performing teachers, improve the instructional performance of those who remain, attract the most capable new talent, and retain their star teachers. For skilled leaders, fiscal austerity does not inhibit reform; it begets urgency.

Four actions are indicated. Some generate savings and others carry a cost. But these investments would consume only a fraction of the savings that would be generated by disinvesting in failed strategies like class size reduction.

Initiative	Annual savings
4. Terminate chronically ineffective teachers	$6.4 million

Like most medium-to-large districts, Belleview continues to employ a significant number of teachers no school wants. Some lack basic work discipline and are manifestly uncommitted to their jobs; others are demonstrably incompetent teachers; and a few have a pattern of physically or emotionally abusing their students. Cowed by the cost and expense of attempting to terminate these teachers, the central office instead meticulously rotates these approximately eighty teachers (5 percent of teachers, after class size increase) among the schools each year so that no one school is unduly burdened. Terminating these teachers would save the district $6.4 million.

Over the last twenty years, much attention has been given to the consequences of policies that make it virtually impossible for districts to terminate chronically low-performing teachers. In many states, districts are constrained by both statutory tenure laws and collective bargaining agreements that make terminating a teacher for poor performance impracticable. For decades districts have reported that it takes two years and $100,000–200,000 in legal fees to rid themselves of a chronically incompetent teacher. Instead, districts either assign them to "rubber rooms," where they have no teaching responsibilities but continue to draw their full salaries, or to schools in a planned rotation. Fortunately, recent lurid accounts of such policies have alienated even long-standing union supporters, and, for the first time in half a century, leaders at both the district and state levels finally have a chance to reform them.[45]

Districts could seize this period of scarce resources to devise a thoughtful, modern, and rigorous annual evaluation system in which the academic progress of students is the foremost criterion. (The task is well suited to a major management consulting firm, many of which are eager to work with districts on either a paid or pro bono basis.) Today, most evaluation systems are farcical; virtually all teachers are rated "superior" or "excellent" by their principals and hardly any are deemed "unsatisfactory"—in part, because principals know that nothing is to be gained in granting low marks to their weakest teachers (they cannot be terminated) and much is to be lost (the action breeds resentment and invites union grievances). Each year in Chicago, only 0.3 percent of teachers are rated "unsatisfactory," and over a four-year period 88 percent of the city's six hundred schools had not awarded a single "unsatisfactory" rating to teachers.[46]

Superintendents should consider budgeting a substantial sum to prosecute a series of high-profile terminations that embolden principals and demonstrate that the district is newly serious about ridding itself of staff who are incompetent or worse. Meanwhile, superintendents need to work in association toward fundamental tenure reform, including eliminating prohibitions in some jurisdictions on the use of test data in evaluating whether or not to grant tenure. If this remains politically impossible, superintendents might consider an alternative approach proposed (but not realized) by Chancellor Michelle Rhee in the District of Columbia schools. Under Rhee's plan, teachers could elect to either remain within the tenure-protected system, with its overriding promise of job security, or to forgo such protections (including tenure and seniority rights that allow them to bump more junior teachers out of their job) in exchange for the opportunity to make substantially more money ($100,000 annually, instead of $62,000, funded through philanthropy) and assume greater responsibility for the performance of their students. Teachers who chose the new track would retain their jobs only if they improved their students' scores and passed an annual evaluation.[47] It is probable that many ambitious and confident teachers will choose the latter, to both their and the district's benefit.

Initiative	Annual savings
5. Invest in codified skill professional development	$1.9 million

Typical of districts nationally, Belleview spends approximately 3 percent, or $9.8 million, of its budget on professional development.[48] As with most districts, professional development programs are a hodgepodge of brief and facile trainings for which there is no evidence of improvements in teacher skill or student outcomes. The district would save $4.9 million by reducing spending on such legacy training programs by 50 percent and then could reinvest $3 million, or the majority of these savings, in a new centrally coordinated training program designed to equip every Belleview teacher with exemplary classroom culture and pedagogical practices. Over the next four years, one-fourth of the faculty could participate each year in the program. Based on the path-breaking program of Teacher U at Hunter College in New York City, developed in association with KIPP, Achievement First, and Uncommon Schools, the program codifies and imparts the specific techniques of exemplary teachers. This program would cost $3,600 per trainee annually; each trainee would also receive a $5,000 stipend for the extended hours required by the program.

Professional Development

The professional development programs of most districts are disjointed, poorly linked to the curriculum, and of little or no demonstrable value in improving teacher proficiency or student outcomes.[49] In the rare case that a district holds a coherent theory of effective instructional practice, it is unwilling to assert it, since this would be seen as an incursion on teacher discretion and autonomy. With curricular decisions largely left to individual schools, instructional approaches are scattershot. It is no accident that professional development dollars are dissipated on topics at the periphery of instruction, like team building, enrichment programs, or the latest education school vogues, like "differentiated instruction" or "multiple intelligences."

Districts should take advantage of fiscal pressures to insist that professional development be devoted entirely to improving the core skills of teachers: their ability to control their classroom, build an effective culture, minimize lost time, devise well-crafted lessons, and deliver engaging and effective instruction. So-called "no excuses" schools that are beginning to close the achievement gap, such as those run by KIPP, Uncommon Schools, and Achievement First, intensively train their staff not in the education school canon of Piaget, Vygotsky, and other theorists but, rather, in the nuts and bolts of instructional technique: discrete classroom management and instructional skills that, strangely, are neglected by teacher training programs yet are consistently practiced by the best teachers. Classroom management and culture-building skills include teaching students how to pass out and collect papers efficiently (the minutes saved add up to days of instruction over the course of a year), "least invasive interventions" (how to avoid issuing verbal corrections to individual students and instead progress through a specific sequence of less disruptive alternatives, beginning with nonverbal signals), and "narrating the positive" (where the "teacher talk" builds a joyful momentum in the classroom by constantly describing what is going well and what the class is together accomplishing). Instructional techniques include the effective use of cold calling, "right is right" (teachers break the ubiquitous habit, when calling on students, of endorsing incorrect answers), and "stretch it" (where teachers reward "right" answers by asking follow-up questions that extend student knowledge). Each of these skills can be taught and practiced; together, they can lift a classroom from mediocrity to excellence. By codifying these techniques, perhaps for the first time, Doug Lemov, Norman Atkins, and David Steiner (newly appointed commissioner of education for New York State) are reinventing teacher preparation at Teacher U. Tuition and fees for the two-year, part-time master's program is $14,670 as of 2010; a school district could expect to devise an in-service program with similar objectives for a quarter of this cost.

Initiative	Annual (cost)
6. Establish a teaching fellows program	($5.0 million)

Recognizing that teacher quality is paramount, Belleview should contract with the New Teachers Project to establish a teaching fellows program modeled after those in New York City, Chicago, and Boston. The program could be expected to cost $5 million annually and identify one-third of the district's new hires. The highly selective program could combine nine weeks of preservice training in the summer, in partnership with an area university, and ongoing training and mentoring during the first two years, during which the fellows earn a master's degree.

Recruiting and Teacher Training

America's education system sources its teachers from its least successful students. The problem has worsened over the decade; in the period from 1964 to 1971, 20–25 percent of female teachers scored in the top decile of high school achievement tests; by 2000, less than 13 percent did.[50] By contrast, countries that consistently score at the top of the two respected international assessments, TIMSS and Programme for International Student Assessment (PISA), such as Finland, South Korea, Singapore, and Hong Kong, draw their teachers not from the bottom third of their high school classes, as in the United States, but from the top 5 to 30 percent, depending on the country.[51]

Nearly every country requires teachers to embark on their careers with a period of formal teacher training. Most nations, including the United States, do little to restrict access to these programs; teacher training is an option for those students who lack others. Because the quality of students is low, so is the quality of courses; professors at schools of education are famously the least respected faculty at universities. Teaching becomes a low-status profession, and far more students earn education degrees than are employed as teachers. Top-performing countries, in contrast, restrict access upfront to teacher training programs. In Singapore, for every one hundred applicants for teacher training programs, only twenty are selected, and of these eighteen are employed as teachers.[52] Money devoted to training is spread over a much smaller pool; so far more is spent developing each teacher. Subject teachers also receive vastly more content-area training than in the United States, and teachers are less likely to teach outside of their content area.[53] Training programs are prestigious and teaching is a high-status profession.

District leaders in the United States cannot affect selection policies at teacher colleges, but the most innovative have created alternative paths to teaching that emulate the practices of top-performing countries. The New York City Teaching Fellows program, Chicago Teaching Fellows, and the Boston Teacher Residency all aim to recruit top graduates and experienced individuals who want to teach, and they guarantee teaching positions to those who enter the training program. The New York program drew 2,100 applicants in its first year and selected 325.[54] Seventy percent of fellows attended a "more" or "most" selective undergraduate institution.[55] By 2008 there were 17,000 applicants for the program, and fellows accounted for one-third of the district's new math teachers.[56] The 2009 class was the most selective ever, with only one in ten applicants selected.[57] Rather than being required to obtain a degree in education, which deters many gifted prospective teachers, teachers receive brief but intensive preservice training and work toward their certification while teaching. Other school districts can readily emulate these programs while working with lawmakers to eliminate the requirement for coursework at schools of education altogether.

Initiative	Annual (cost)
7. Raise teacher pay and institute differential and merit pay	($13.8 million)

Belleview could invest $13.8 million of the savings from staffing initiatives to fund compensation reforms. Teachers in the top quintile of effectiveness of the district's faculty who agree to extend their reach to a larger number of students will receive a 50 percent salary premium, for a cost of $8.8 million. Another $5 million will fund a differential pay plan (paying more for teachers in short supply, such as high school math and science teachers, teachers of distinguished academic backgrounds and verbal skills, and those who commit to work in the most challenging schools) for newly recruited teachers who agree to forgo traditional job protections in exchange for higher compensation.

Compensation Reform

Better teacher deployment policies would result in a smaller workforce, which in turn would permit the district to increase teacher salaries and better recruit and retain star talent. But rather than raising salaries across the board, districts should undertake a wholesale redesign of compensation policies. The "step and lane" compensation system is obsolete. For decades, districts have paid teachers strictly in proportion to two attributes, neither of which has any demonstrable relationship to teacher quality or student achievement: degrees and education credits, generally earned from schools of education (the "lane") and seniority (the "step"). There is little to no evidence that teachers with master's degrees perform better than those without, or that a teacher with a doctorate in education is a better instructor than one with a baccalaureate from a selective college. On average, master's degrees in education bear no relationship to student achievement. Yet, according to a 2007 study, the "master's bump" in compensation amounted to 2.1 percent of all education expenses, or $174 per student annually.[58] The rationale for paying for seniority is equally deficient. The evidence shows that although a fourth-year teacher is on average more effective than a novice teacher, there are no benefits, as a statistical matter, from additional experience.[59]

In Harrison School District No. 2, in Colorado Springs, Colorado, Superintendent Mike Miles eliminated entirely the district's promotion of teachers based on years of service and hours of college coursework. "While these factors are objective and easy to measure, they are not the best measures of teacher effectiveness . . . The teacher salary schedule at its core is not designed to promote teachers' competency or to support student academic proficiency, but to provide for automatic salary increases and to reward longevity in the system," the district's Web site explains.[60] In their place, Miles substituted teacher performance measures and student results. Teachers progress through nine levels, or "grades," from "novice" to "master" with correspondingly higher salaries. Teachers move to the next grade based on both their evaluations (using a sophisticated evaluation instrument and process) and the academic performance of their students. In transitioning to the new plan, each existing teacher was placed in one of the nine levels; if the teacher's salary at that level was less than what he or she currently earned, his or her present salary was maintained.

If the goal is to improve productivity, districts should invest in what they actually need: teachers of subjects and grades who are scarce and in demand and teachers who demonstrably produce results. As Frederick M. Hess and Martin R. West have argued, "Teacher pay should reflect the scarcity and value of teachers' skills, the difficulty of their assignments, the extent of their responsibilities, and the caliber of their work."[61]

Once again, we have much to learn from countries with superior education systems. High-performing nations not only recruit capable people to the profession, they attract them with a high starting salary. The average starting salary in South Korea, as a percent of GDP per capita, is 74 percent higher than that in the United States. Hong Kong's is 20 percent higher, and Finland's and Singapore's are both 17 percent higher.[62] In exchange for a longer school day and year (similar to those of nearly all gap-closing "no excuses" charter schools), more planning time (for grade-level team meetings and the development of high-quality, detailed lesson plans), more professional development time (at least three weeks of rigorous training in August), and freedom from debilitating work rules (to permit greater flexibility in assignments and duties), districts should award higher starting salaries. Without these reforms, increasing starting pay would be unwarranted, as current compensation levels, adjusted for the contractual work day (six hours and twenty minutes in New York City) and summers off, are competitive with that of other professions.[63]

Differential Pay

Administrators, especially in urban schools with low-income student populations, are much more likely to report difficulty in filling math or physical science positions than in filling elementary positions.[64] College graduates majoring in math, science, and technology are in great demand outside of schools, and nonteaching jobs pay them much more than teaching jobs would. The problem is getting worse, for recent growth in teaching salaries has been no match for that of highly skilled nonteaching professions. The pay scales of current collective bargaining agreements tie principals' hands in making salary offers to scarce qualified candidates.

Districts should adopt "differential pay plans" that pay teachers in short supply—such as high school math and science teachers—a premium. Higher pay, bonuses, tuition assistance, tax credits, housing subsidies, and loan forgiveness have all been used by states and districts to attract teachers in high-need subject areas. Similarly, districts should pay teachers in the most challenging schools more than those in less demanding and more affluent schools.[65]

Schools should also pay more for teachers whose education at a selective college, high grade point average, verbal skills, and other objective attributes are in demand by academically ambitious schools. Unionization flattened teacher pay, and today graduates of selective admission colleges make no more than graduates of the lowest-tier schools. Prior to the spread of collective bargaining, districts sensibly paid more to teachers from prestigious universities. As schools drive to develop in their students not only literacy and numeracy but also critical thinking skills, principals may find that their scarcest resource is intellectually agile individuals, whom pay policies drive away to other professions.[66] Pedagogies that foster comprehension and critical thinking, like "guided reading" in elementary school and "inquiry learning" in high school, depend on teachers as interlocutors, devising searching questions in real time.

Merit Pay

The case for merit pay is clear: Paying bad teachers as much as good ones makes it harder to attract and retain good teachers, which in turn penalizes students by saddling them with inferior instructors.[67] The idea is not new, as Thomas Toch has noted. A 1955 commission to President Eisenhower urged that "every effort . . . be made to devise ways to reward teachers according to their ability without opening the school door to unfair personnel practices."[68] Unions have portrayed pay-for-performance plans as an assault on teachers, but survey results suggest teachers feel otherwise.[69] A 2003 Public Agenda survey of teachers found that substantial majorities believed that "it is easy to spot who the truly great teachers are," thought that the teachers in their building "could pretty much agree on who . . . [they] are," supported giving additional pay to their peers "who consistently work harder . . . than other teachers" and those "who consistently receive outstanding evaluations from their principals."[70]

Yet getting merit pay right is notoriously difficult. Poorly designed plans can seem to teachers capricious and unfair, and small bonuses broadly awarded do nothing to boost performance. Merit pay developers have learned from past mistakes, and emerging evidence points to significant student gains in well-conceived plans that are predictably implemented from one year to the next. One of the most-watched performance pay initiatives is the Achievement Challenge Pilot Project in Little Rock, Arkansas, where early evidence points to seven percentile point gains on standard-ized tests. Unlike in other merit pay designs, the study found no damage to the school climate or rise in counterproductive competition between teachers; teachers reported that their work environment was more posi-tive than those reported by comparison teachers.[71] As with any incentive system, its architects must take utmost care to make sure it rewards what the organization wants, as financial rewards can powerfully affect staff ef-forts. As James Guthrie and Patrick Schuermann have noted, teachers may work hard to achieve the goals that are rewarded but slight others that are equally vital. Plans must balance the need for transparency, on which acceptance by teachers rests, but also accuracy and fairness in measures of student performance, which may necessitate complexity. Teachers must be engaged in the development of plans and a far-reaching effort must be made to explain the plan and gain their support. Lastly, fluctuations in an-nual appropriations cannot result in fluctuating incentives.[72]

"3X" Teachers

This approach, proposed by Emily Hassel and Bryan Hassel of Public Im-pact, begins with the recognition that teachers in the top quintile of effec-tiveness produce on average three times the learning gains of bottom quin-tile teachers. It ought to be the district's urgent goal to identify such "3X" teachers and to extend their reach through initiatives like those described in these pages. 3X teachers should be relieved of nonteaching duties, focus on concept exposition (rather than leading students through practice), be responsible for the learning of a large number of students, and extend their reach through technology. In recognition of their exceptional impact and the number of students they affect, districts should pay 3X teachers sub-stantially more money—I suggest 50 percent more.[73]

Initiative	Annual savings
8. Align benefits with private-sector standards	$7.6 million

The cost of Belleview's employee benefits plan, like those of other dis-tricts, is unsustainable. Bringing the district's total current contributions to employee benefits in line with private-sector employers will save at least $7.6 million annually.

Employee Benefits

While reforming teacher pay, districts should also tackle the debilitating costs of employee benefits and teacher absenteeism. Pension costs, in particular, are unsustainable. Retirement benefits afforded teachers are exceptionally generous compared to those of private-sector professionals. Whereas most sectors now offer "defined contributions" plans, where the employee makes a fixed contribution per year to the employee's retirement account, public-sector employees continue to participate in "defined benefit" plans, fully funded by the employer, which pay a fixed amount (approaching full salary for a fully vested employee) for life. Michael Podgursky has noted that as of 1995, the average age of retirement for teachers was fifty-nine; for new retirees collecting Social Security it was sixty-four.[74] In 2008, private employers contributed 10.4 percent of employee earnings to retirement benefits; school districts contributed 14.6 percent.[75]

Health-care costs also make up a larger share of districts' total compensation costs than of private-sector employers' costs. Both sectors have seen the cost of coverage more than quadruple over the last three decades, but rising costs have hit school districts especially hard because districts are locked into unsustainably lavish plans. While most private-sector plans require employees to pay 15 percent or more of their health coverage costs, school district plans rarely do. Most districts also pay the entire cost of retirees' health benefits, while private-sector employers do not.[76]

Initiative	Annual savings
9. Reduce teacher absenteeism	$2.9 million

Through a combination of policy changes and financial incentives for exceptional attendance, Belleview can close 75 percent of the gap between the district's rate of absenteeism by teachers and aides and the rate of employers nationally. After the cost of incentives, the district would save $2.9 million annually.

Teacher Absenteeism

The high cost of teacher absenteeism has gone largely unnoticed. According to the Bureau of Labor Statistics, professional and managerial employees in the private sector are absent for 1.7 percent of annual hours. By contrast, in 2001 the New York City schools reported that teachers were out on average 11.3 days a year, or 6.3 percent of the school year.[77] Many of these absences are discretionary, and changes in policy, such as requiring teachers to report their absences directly to their principal or offering financial incentives (rewards for exceptional attendance or buy-back of unused sick days) would reduce them. Were absenteeism reduced to private-sector levels, the savings on substitute teachers would be dramatic, and students would lose fewer days of learning.[78]

PROGRAM INITIATIVES

Initiative	Annual savings
10. Establish robust pre-referral programs to special education	$2.5 million

By bolstering pre-referral programs to special education, strengthening regular education, and improving remedial interventions, Belleview would reduce special education enrollment from 13.3 percent to 11.3 percent, for an annual savings of $2.5 million.

Special Education

In many urban districts, schooling defects—a weak school culture and poor instruction, especially in the early grades—cause some students to be referred to special education who could be educated successfully in the regular classroom. Some are labeled as "learning disabled" or "emotionally disturbed" when their failure to progress in regular education is not the result of an innate disability. African American students in particular are overrepresented in categories of special education, such as specific learning disabilities, where diagnostic criteria are not consistently applied and it is possible to identify almost any underachieving child as learning disabled.[79] Black students are 50 percent more likely to be identified as emotionally disturbed as well; schools fail to distinguish between behavioral characteristics associated with the cultural context in which the children are raised and an actual disability.[80] Managing behavior explicitly in the early grades toward developing self-management skills in students and offering effective instruction to students who arc "at risk" in regular education will obviate many referrals.

By tightening pre-referral policies (required under the federal special education law) and ensuring that effective remediation is available to students prior to evaluation, districts would gradually reduce the number of students who are enrolled in special education programs. A modest drop in special education enrollment—15 percent, for instance—is a realistic target for many urban districts.

CONCLUSION

Districts coping with fiscal pressures from the recession would be wise to consider disinvesting in class size reduction, the primary and staggeringly expensive reform of the last several decades. Districts should instead attend to how classes are formed and student skills gaps are identified and filled and to equipping teachers with effective instructional systems. CSR's promised returns in student performance will prove chimerical. Other monies can be freed up by eliminating general education instructional aides above kindergarten, adopting a hybrid educational model that complements teacher-led instruction with instructional technology, cutting wasteful professional development costs, terminating chronically ineffective teachers, aligning employee benefits with industry averages, reducing faculty absenteeism, and strengthening referral programs to special education.

These savings, if achieved, would more than compensate for declining revenues. The remaining savings should be allocated to strengthening the capacity of regular education teachers to achieve exceptional results even with the addition of two students to their classrooms. The two categories of essential investments are human capital initiatives (to boost the capacity of the faculty) and acquisition of carefully chosen intellectual property (that equips teachers of average skill to achieve exceptional learning outcomes for their students).

The impact of these savings initiatives for the Belleview district is summarized in table 5.1. When fully implemented, they would result in annual savings of $42.7 million, nearly twice that required by the anticipated 7 percent reduction in district revenues. Embarking on these actions now would not only address the district's fiscal challenges in fiscal year 2011, it would deliver the savings required for fiscal year 2012, when revenues are likely to tumble further.

As districts struggle to cope with steep declines in revenues, states should remove constraints in laws that restrict districts from forming larger, educationally effective classes. Such constraints include both class size limits and class size reduction incentives that deny state funding streams to districts with larger classes. Runaway retirement and benefits costs also require leadership at the state level. In many states, districts are powerless to tame spiraling pension costs without legislative action.

TABLE 5.1
Summary of Belleview Savings initiatives

Initiative		Savings/(Cost)
	Target savings	$22,835,600
1	Increase class size	$17,607,483
2	Eliminate teacher aides above first grade	$6,369,644
3	Complement teacher-led instruction with instructional technology	$16,246,348
4	Terminate chronically ineffective teachers	$6,437,322
5	Invest in skill-based professional development	$1,883,289
6	Establish a teaching fellowship program	($5,000,000)
7	Raise teacher pay and institute differential and merit pay	($13,800,814)
8	Align employee benefits with industry averages	$7,573,641
9	Reduce faculty absenteeism	$2,924,313
10	Establish robust prereferral programs to special education	$2,501,106
	Total savings	**$42,742,331**

While there is a reasonable disagreement about the proper role of the federal government in K–12 education, few dispute its vital role in providing rigorous evidence on which to ground education practice and policy. After decades of investment by the states in increasing teacher-to-student ratios, it's the responsibility of the Institute of Education Sciences to provide a sober accounting of the educational returns from this investment.

The philanthropic community could be invaluable in assisting and emboldening districts to undertake these urgent reforms. Many district officials assume that labor contracts are far more restrictive than they actually are. A national center for specialized legal and technical support to districts could help districts to overcome apparent constraints in law or contract and to prevail in administrative hearings and courts when challenged. Such a center could also serve as a clearinghouse for districts to share broadly their expertise and successes as they implement these bold initiatives to more effectively deploy instructional staff, reduce costs, and bolster productivity.

6

More Productive Schools Through Online Learning

John E. Chubb

IN OCTOBER 2009 EVERY public school in the state of Hawai'i began closing on Fridays. For seventeen consecutive Fridays, stretching to nearly the end of the school year, Hawai'i's public school students would not be educated. For those same Fridays public school teachers would not be paid. For the school year, students would receive 163 days of instruction instead of the normal 180, a 10 percent cut in their opportunity to learn. Teachers, who are paid on a longer year, would lose nearly 8 percent of their annual earnings.[1]

Like every state, Hawai'i was hit hard by the economic recession of 2008–2009. Business contracted, unemployment rose, tax receipts fell, claims for public services increased, and states were left with yawning budget deficits that required extraordinary measures to fill. California issued IOUs to taxpayers entitled to income tax refunds; the state simply did not have the funds to meet its obligations.[2] Education is the largest obligation in state and local budgets by far. While policy makers certainly strive to cushion children against the harshest consequences of economic downturns, the latest recession—the worst since the Great Depression—forced policy makers to cut back in schools like never before.

The District of Columbia Public Schools laid off 6 percent of its instructional staff. Schools chancellor Michele Rhee made headlines by basing layoffs on performance rather than seniority—at least in part.[3] The departing teachers were alleged to be less effective than those who remained. The norm in public education systems, where employment practices are often reinforced by collective bargaining agreements, is to follow seniority. If cutbacks are necessary, the last hired are the first fired. The practice means that an energetic new teacher could be sacrificed for a burned-out veteran teacher. This is a stereotype, of course. Experienced teachers are often superior to inexperienced ones.[4] But blind adherence to seniority does not provide a school with the most effective mix of talent. Throughout the nation, school districts let go of thousands of teachers in order to weather the recession, and most reductions followed seniority.

Matters could have been much worse. The federal government sought to protect schools through the American Recovery and Renewal Act (ARRA) of 2009. Otherwise known as the "Stimulus Bill," ARRA provided public education nearly $100 billion in funds for 2009–2011, about four times the normal annual rate of federal funding. The funds enabled states to fill district budget gaps and limit layoffs. The results are still being tabulated; states are required to document every job saved. There is no question that the recession could have hurt public schools—and yes, children—even more than it did.[5]

The pain for students takes many forms. Instructional staff who are not in regular classrooms are the first to go. Guidance counselors are often early casualties—a tragedy at a time when the nation, as President Obama has vowed publicly, aims to regain world leadership in college attendance. Librarians are another early target, which then limits student access to books and other media—at a time when literacy is our greatest educational challenge. Then teachers depart. The consequence is larger classes taught by more senior teachers and fewer new teachers, none of which helps students learn.

And then there is Hawai'i. The state negotiated its response to the recession with the Hawai'i State Teachers Association. The teachers wanted to avoid layoffs, to keep good teachers on the island and available to help students when economic growth returns. They proposed, therefore, a furlough program in which teachers would not work for seventeen days and would not be paid. The state would save, along with other cuts, enough to close its more than $200 million budget gap. Unfortunately, teachers cannot all be furloughed without closing schools. Students then suffer the ultimate consequence: they do not get educated.[6]

LEARNING FROM HARD TIMES

A deep and prolonged economic downturn is bound to cause hardship and force sacrifices everywhere. Public education could hardly expect to escape untouched. But if all that comes of this crisis are temporary measures and short-lived compromises, a huge opportunity will have been missed. Many industries use economic crises as an opportunity to look more fundamentally at how they do their work. Problems encountered in tough times are often the result of long-standing issues that required genuine adversity to expose them.

The American auto industry produced too many similar models with too little quality at too high a cost for too long. It had been losing market share to more distinctive, better engineered, and more efficient imported cars since the mid-1970s. But good economic times allowed American automakers to pursue incremental improvements without calamity. Then the recession of 2008–2009 cost them nearly half of their sales. Facing bankruptcy, the industry sought government protection while it made long overdue and wrenching adjustments, including eliminating whole brands, dealer networks, and tens of thousands of jobs.[7]

Public education is arguably overdue for an overhaul as well. America spends more on public education than almost any nation in the world.[8] Whether measured as a share of Gross National Product or per-pupil expenditures, spending on public schools in the United States ranks among the highest on the planet. As James Guthrie and Arthur Peng note in chapter 1, spending has also increased steadily for years. Even controlling for inflation, per-pupil expenditures are double their levels of just twenty years ago. Total spending now far exceeds a half-trillion dollars a year, a sum that averages nearly $10,000 per student.[9]

For that investment, the United States obtains academic results that everyone agrees are not adequate. Achievement levels fall well below the top tier internationally. Only a third of American students, on average, achieve proficiency by our own national yardstick, the National Assessment of Education Progress. The achievement of African American and Hispanic children trails that of white and Asian children by three grade levels. Dropout rates exceed 40 percent in most inner cities. College completion rates hover around 30 percent, as they have for a generation, behind some fifteen nations with which we must compete economically.[10] One can quibble with any given statistic, but no one—Democrat or Republican, liberal or conservative—seriously disagrees with the overall picture: America's schools are not doing the job that the nation needs them to do.

They are also not doing well with the monies afforded them. This is not a point of agreement. But on its face, it is true. The United States spends more on public education that most any nation, but for that the nation gets results that are mediocre at best. One can argue that the United States faces unique challenges of size, diversity, and poverty, or that it invests more than most in special education and social equity. And for these and other reasons the country must spend more on education to begin with. But it is increasingly clear that the American taxpayers are not embracing more spending. They certainly did not endorse tax increases to bail the schools out during the recession, despite the warnings of dire consequences. Public support for the schools has been declining steadily for two decades.[11] Time will tell whether public schools are now at a crossroads, like the American auto industry. But the pressures for public education to reexamine its fundamentals have never been greater.

THE TECHNOLOGY OF TEACHING AND LEARNING

Seventy percent of school budgets are spent on instructional personnel. The bulk of that—half or so of the entire education budget—is spent on classroom teachers.[12] Schools systems, particularly large ones, employ lots of support staff who help classroom teachers. Special educators, teachers of English language learners, trainers, coaches, counselors, and various other experts help regular classroom teachers try to get the most out of their students. School budgets also include administrators in central offices as well as school facilities. It is easy to question the contributions of the "bureaucrats" or those educators who are not in the classroom. But the fact of the matter is that those personnel took on roles over time that were prescribed by policies or programs adopted by states, local boards of education, and sometimes the federal government to help regular classroom teachers succeed where they had not been succeeding before.

That's right. The regular classroom teacher was not succeeding. With twenty-five (give or take) students often of different abilities, sometimes with cognitive or language limitations, and all needing to master reading, writing, math, science and social studies, the elementary school teacher was easily overwhelmed. At the secondary level, where subject matter becomes far more sophisticated, teachers specialized in particular disciplines, but they taught six classes daily and a total of 150 students—again, students with a wide range of skills and challenges.

Every school in the world struggles with the traditional model of classroom instruction. It is simply daunting for one individual to try to teach a large and diverse group of children any subject to a truly high standard. Different nations have tackled the challenge in different ways—from using larger classes but better trained and compensated teachers, to employing smaller classes with more support personnel, to tracking students into more homogeneous classes of differing levels of difficulty. Each approach is constrained by public school budgets. No nation has unlimited resources to devote to education. Every solution is a compromise. While some nations have found better compromises than others,[13] every nation is trying to solve the same problem: how to enable, with finite resources, one teacher to help a large group of students learn.

This challenge has existed for as long as the technology of teaching and learning has been teacher-led large-group instruction. But what if the technology could be different? What if the default mode of schooling was not students grouped into classrooms led by teachers period after period all day long? That is the promise of computer-based technologies: to enable schools to break out of the mold that shapes current practice most fundamentally. Schools that take full advantage of modern technologies—employing the Internet, information systems, and computerized instruction, among others—can transform their core economics and performance. In such transformation lies the potential for radical improvements for students and for taxpayers.

ONLINE SCHOOLS

It is already possible for students to receive their entire education without setting foot in a traditional teacher-led classroom. For the last decade, private companies, working with boards of community leaders, have developed charter schools that provide instruction and other elements of a quality education exclusively over the Internet. Roughly 100,000 students attended online, or "cyber," charter schools full time in twenty-five states in 2009.[14] More than a million students took at least one course online that year as well.[15] Online education is hardly confined to charter schools. Three-quarters of all public school districts offer some instruction online.[16] But to appreciate the potential of teaching and learning through technology, it is useful to consider those schools where the traditional classroom is simply not part of the equation.

Students Online

The promise of online education begins with what students can learn through technology. In a traditional classroom led by an accomplished teacher, students learn through a regular cycle of instruction associated with each of a series of lessons. Consider the classic model.[17] Each lesson begins with some form of motivation. Teachers engage students by "activating prior knowledge": they connect the topic of the new lesson to an earlier lesson and, ideally, to something students can relate to in their lives outside of school or in current events. The teacher then explains the objective of the new lesson and proceeds to impart the new knowledge or skill using whatever resources are available in a classroom setting—an old-fashioned chalkboard or overhead projector or a contemporary LCD projector or interactive whiteboard.

Then it's the students' turn. The teacher first gives them a problem or question with which to grapple collectively and guides and challenges them to a solution. After that the teacher provides an assignment the students attempt to work through on their own, individually or in small groups, while the teacher supervises, coaches, and helps students as questions arise. Class ends with a summation of what should have been learned. Homework is then assigned so students can practice further independently. Homework is later reviewed in class, and after several lessons a test or assessment determines what students have mastered.

This classic cycle of whole-group instruction works well for many students but not so well for many others. Some students may not have comprehended prior lessons and therefore approach a new lesson with fear of failure. Some students may have struggled for years with fundamentals, such as reading comprehension, and look at every lesson as yet another frustration. No matter how cleverly the teacher tries to motivate interest in the lesson, students who are behind will not be very motivated. If students begin lessons unmotivated, they will simply not make the hard effort necessary to learn.

In the traditional classroom everyone must move at the same pace. But students who are already behind simply cannot keep up. If the teacher slows down for them, the others, especially the most able, become bored or frustrated themselves. While state-of-the-art presentation media can help teachers promote understanding of new concepts—better than a chalkboard—teachers will still struggle to find the right mix of media to reach every student.

Then there is the students' own work. Student practice is critical; it is when students actually make knowledge their own. But practice must be carefully guided by teachers if students are not to make the same mistakes over and over. And teachers do not have the time to customize coaching for all students. Practice, then, does not produce mastery for many students, and quizzes and exams yield low or failing grades. Which leads to what? Is the next lesson delayed so that struggling students can catch up? Is the next lesson narrowed for slow students so they only have to learn the "essentials?"[18] There are no good answers. With whole-group instruction, even extraordinary teachers will not be able to help every student succeed, especially if many students are underachieving. And we cannot expect all teachers to be extraordinary. The problem is just that stark.[19]

Technology offers a solution. It begins with motivation. Students today are accustomed to using technology nonstop outside of school. Cell phones (which are becoming more like computers), text messaging, computers, the Internet, social networks, Skype, Twitter, video games, iPods, infinite "apps"—the ever-changing tools of information technology—are embraced by young people as fast as they are invented. These tools are ubiquitous. Disadvantaged city teens are as inseparable from their iPods and cell phones as their more privileged suburban counterparts.[20] Much technology requires little or no teaching. It is intuitive by design, but especially so for children who have known nothing but technology their entire lives.

Kids love technology, a passion schools have largely ignored. School is the least technological time of a young person's day. Students power-down when they enter school—lest their cell phones be confiscated—and power back up when they leave. But technology can just as easily engage young people for educational purposes. The Internet is certainly a rich research tool, and schools generally do expect students to use it for the occasional paper or project. Yet this limited use only scratches the surface. The best new technologies can help students learn all the time. Instructional technologies mimic the technologies that students see outside of school. They include gaming environments, personal avatars to negotiate academic lessons, and social networks to connect students as they learn online. Familiar, easy-to-navigate interfaces allow students to get what they need to get—without raising their hand.

The best technologies are as captivating—and motivating—as the technologies that students use outside of school. Instructional software allows students to proceed at their own paces. It is able to present new knowledge and skills in multiple ways. Students can read lessons or have lessons read to them as they follow the highlighted text—a huge assist to students learning English or still mastering reading comprehension. Students can watch animations and videos that illuminate concepts or ideas—and as often as need be—surpassing what textbooks could ever do. Technology is interactive; students can manipulate mathematical equations, geometric objects, and the variables in scientific experiments for hands-on experiences. Technology provides students more opportunities to learn. And, bottom line, success in learning is motivating. Students who have struggled and lost motivation in traditional schools can regain confidence and motivation by moving online.

Instructional technology not only allows students to move at their own paces in particular lessons, but it allows students to get precisely the lessons that they need. In the critical area of literacy, for example, students at the same nominal grade level may have vastly different needs. Some fourth graders, who ought to be learning to appreciate the twists of story plots and the morals of timeless pieces of literature, are often still hung up on decoding words. Software now offers powerful programs that enable students to sound out letter blends and whole words while voice recognition technology responds with corrections. Other programs provide higher achieving fourth graders the chance to read literature and nonfiction, both on grade level and above, and to write essays that are graded by remote teachers online. A group of fourth-grade students whose diverse needs would otherwise be impossible for a teacher to meet, no matter how skilled at differentiation, could be satisfied simultaneously if all were able to work online.

Technology is superb at providing practice. The best software is not only able to supply students almost endless problems to solve, fiction and nonfiction to comprehend, and questions to answer, but it can provide quality feedback. Not merely the "good job" or "try again" of early instructional software, today's software offers explanations of why answers are wrong, how a distracter in a multiple choice question represents a common error, and how a problem or solution should be approached. The best software is also intelligent. It "knows," based on patterns of success or failure, what concept or skill to teach next. It can customize remediation or acceleration, giving students what they need, not what the standard curriculum prescribes. It's impractical for a regular classroom setting to provide the same opportunity for differentiated practice.

Further, what happens when the weekly quiz reveals that some students have not mastered the material? Online, students are not evaluated merely every week. Their progress can be gauged lesson by lesson, day by day. Assessments can evaluate progress continuously. If a single student fails a single assessment, the online program can prescribe an intervention, perhaps additional work with instructional technology or tutoring with a teacher online. Online assessment is not limited to closed-ended test items, such as multiple choice, true/false, and the like. Instructional technology makes full use of assessments requiring short answer, essays, and research projects. The work is evaluated by live teachers who are also working online. Through open-ended expression, online assessment thereby facilitates higher-order thinking as well as the acquisition of more basic skills.

Teachers Online

In the brick-and-mortar school, the teacher performs many roles. Teachers must plan, differentiate, and deliver lessons; write, administer, and evaluate assessments; analyze student performance; plan and offer interventions; and report grades. Teachers must take attendance, manage classrooms, establish relationships, serve as role models, communicate with parents, and otherwise attend to the social and emotional development of their students. They must attend faculty meetings, help plan team meetings, and contribute to the overall welfare of the school. No wonder teachers are often heard to complain that they barely have time to "just teach." The other tasks can overwhelm the primary one.

Technology can help with this. The benefits are clearest in online schools. A lot of technology use in traditional schools is supplementary, meeting needs for remediation or acceleration that whole-class instruction has not adequately served. In online schools technology must carry the weight of delivering the instructional core—teaching, not just supplementing, algebra I, physics, freshman English, and every other subject from kindergarten through high school graduation. Online technology must therefore be rich in content and strong in scaffolding to give students every chance to succeed with the software. The best online programs have every lesson crafted by professional curriculum writers and presented and tightly tied to state academic standards. Assessments evaluate accurately the skills that need to be mastered. Technology analyzes student performance and specifies interventions when students fail a lesson the first time. Of course, technology also does the mundane work of taking attendance, documenting student effort (down to the keystroke), and reporting grades. The best online systems are designed to allow students to work asynchronously, meaning at their own pace and not tied to the work of teachers.

But where does that leave the teachers? Arguably doing what teachers do best. First and foremost, teachers teach. They teach whole groups and they teach individual students. Online education systems give students the option of working asynchronously or synchronously. Students can take an entire course working through online lessons or they can participate in a live classroom watching and listening to a teacher remotely. Teachers are selected for this role (or select themselves) because of their skill at whole-group instruction. The lesson is not simply a performance by the teacher; a lecture could be videotaped and shown without the benefits of online technology. But in modern online schools, students can "raise their hand" electronically and ask questions, or the teacher can ask questions that students volunteer to answer individually or are required to answer collectively, as in a "clicker" session in a college lecture hall.

There is an important difference, however, in online whole-group instructors. Far fewer of them are needed. Experience shows that students are successful in online classes working more asynchronously than synchronously. Given the choice, students will complete three-fourths of their lessons without attending an online session with a teacher. Online classes can also be larger—roughly twice the size of traditional classes—because the teacher need not perform all of the traditional roles, such as classroom management, supervised practice, and assessment. Online schools, therefore, require far fewer whole-group instructors than brick-and-mortar schools and, importantly, can be very selective in who teaches in this capacity. All things being equal, online schools have a better chance of providing their students with effective teachers.

Whole-group instruction is not the most common role for teachers online. Most online instruction takes the form of one-on-one or small-group tutorials. As students hit bumps in the road asynchronously, online assessment systems can flag the issue. If online interventions do not remediate the students' problems, the system can refer the student for tutoring. Students can also simply request individual help or join ongoing small-group help sessions. While tutoring, the teacher can speak to the student online, exchange text messages (if the student is reticent), employ electronic whiteboards to illustrate concepts or solutions (just like in a classroom), or take the student back through the electronic instruction with explanation. Online teachers regularly report that what they like best about the new medium is the one-on-one attention that they can provide their students—something they could not do very well in the traditional classroom.

Teachers can also devote more time to student work. Online schools often employ teachers as professional graders. The role might be performed in addition to tutoring, or it might be a sole specialization. Graders become expert at evaluating open-ended student work, everything from brief explanations to short essays to major research papers. Their job is to provide consistent and constructive feedback, the kind that helps students make progress with revisions and subsequent assignments. Open-ended assessment is a notorious problem in traditional schools. Teachers are prone to subjectivity, setting standards relative to class or school norms, judging papers based on their knowledge of the student producing the work, and struggling to guide improvement. A-level work in the inner cities, for example, often fails to translate into proficient scores on state assessments. Online graders, however, have the training, time, and accountability to evaluate objectively the work of students from many different communities. And graders report satisfaction in being better able to provide useful feedback.

Teaching and learning are not only cognitive processes, of course. On-line schools recognize this. With students working remotely, and often from home, professional supervision of students can become a challenge. Some virtual schools have also handled this with a specialized teaching role. Students are assigned an adviser who speaks with the family every week, monitors the progress of students in the electronic curriculum, ensures that interventions are provided when needed, and encourages the student to persist with lessons and keep pace. Performing only the role of adviser, this individual can be trained in the work of academic counseling and guidance and can support students without the competing demands of teaching.

With technology doing much of the heavy lifting of planning, presentation, assessment, and reporting, teachers can focus on what they can do best. They help students with the nuanced issues that impede their understanding, one by one. They can carefully evaluate student work that demands higher-order thinking and guide real improvement. They can attend to individual student needs and counsel, with help from the family, thoughtful solutions. And, of course, they can just teach.

Online Performance

The potential of technology to enhance learning should be obvious. Technology can address all of the shortcomings of whole-group instruction. Technology enables every student to participate effectively in the classic model of instruction: activating background knowledge, engaging and motivating interest, setting learning objectives and presenting new skills and knowledge, guiding practice, providing individual practice and feedback, assessing, and, if necessary, reteaching. Technology provides students more mediums through which to learn. Technology allows teachers to take on more specialized and manageable roles online that take advantage of their unique skills.

The evidence thus far is that it is working. Asynchronous instructional technology is not new. Schools have employed it for nearly as long as the personal computer has been around. In the early 1980s, renowned Stanford University psychology professor Patrick Suppes developed one of the first intelligent tutoring programs. Commercialized by the Curriculum Computer Corporation, the program found wide use in schools serving Title I eligible students requiring remediation. Other programs quickly followed, developed and distributed by the major education publishers. As technology became more sophisticated, the programs added multimedia, simulations, voice recognition, and more customized instructional algorithms. These programs addressed the traditional academic skills but expanded to treat various learning disabilities that responded to technology-supported training.

With nearly three decades of experience, instructional software has been the subject of extensive research. The evidence is that instructional technology is effective in raising student achievement. Not every piece of software is, of course. But many programs have demonstrated significant effects on learning, and the overall approach to learning has been validated. But something has also been missing, and that is a tight connection between what students learn via technology and the skills that teachers try to impart in the classroom. Almost without fail, schools have asked students to go to computer labs to use reading, math, and other programs but have done little to help teachers incorporate that experience into regular class expectations. Likewise, the computer programs have been unable to build directly on what teachers are doing in the classroom. The result is weak "transfer" of skills learned using instructional software to the skills taught and assessed traditionally.

Until now. The breakthrough of modern online schools is the integration of quality software with live teaching and advising. The online school combines asynchronous learning using the latest generation of instructional technology with synchronous teacher-led instruction with educators in roles that complement the technology. Research has already demonstrated the educational potential of instructional software. Research is now beginning to address online education as well. The initial results are very encouraging, showing online courses to be just as effective as traditional courses in raising student achievement.[21] This is remarkable given that integrated online instruction is relatively new, only a decade in large-scale use, while traditional instruction has been around in current form for at least a century. Technology and its integration with live teachers will only continue to improve, as, inevitably, will technology.

Online Economics

As technology improves, it will not only become more effective education-ally, but it will also become more efficient. In schools, as in every other enterprise that technology has touched, schools will become more pro-ductive as they substitute technology for labor. Historically, schools have seemed almost immune to the technological innovations that benefited other industries. Indeed, efforts to make the schools better have steadily made them more labor intensive and more expensive on a per-student ba-sis. As long as the "technology" of instruction was whole group and teacher led, the favored ways to pursue improvement were through smaller class sizes and more specialists to assist when whole-group instruction came up short. Thus the frustrating economics of education: vastly more spending for barely better results.

This is about to change. Online schools are already demonstrating how. Online schools may use educators in multiple roles—adviser, synchronous teacher, synchronous tutor, asynchronous grader, to name only the obvi-ous—but they rely on technology to do much of the work that educators need not do but traditionally carry out in brick-and-mortar schools. The result is that online educators can and do support many more students in their respective roles than their in-person compatriots. Asynchronous grad-ers may assess two hundred or more students a semester and still turn around grades more quickly, in say forty-eight hours, than they could in traditional classrooms since grading is all that they have to do. Advisers can oversee the work of sixty students, including weekly contact with parents. (This ratio, by the way, is several times *lower* than the ratio of high school guidance counselors to students in traditional high schools.) Synchronous tutors can support 150 students, since the technology provides online interventions before teacher-led tutoring is required. Synchronous teachers can support more than two hundred students because only some students choose to take lessons directly from a teacher daily.

These ratios, which put students in touch with educators regularly in various ways, require far fewer teachers per pupil than do brick-and-mortar schools. Certainly, online schools use different configurations of educators, some with more differentiated roles, some with less. But however configured, online schools typically employ about one educator for every thirty-five students. Public schools employ one teacher for every 15.8 students and an even lower ratio if every instructional specialist in a school system is included in the total.[22] Conservatively, then, online schools employ about half the number of teachers per student as brick-and-mortar schools do.

Labor is the biggest savings that online schools bring to education, though not the only one. Full-time online schools require smaller facilities because they must house only the school administrators and teachers, not the students. And schools have some flexibility about even this cost, because teachers can perform all or most of their work from home. Schools ask teachers to come to a common facility largely to collaborate, learn from one another, acquire professional development and coaching, and receive some measure of direct supervision. But the work that teachers do with students does not necessarily require a facility.

Now, some online schools *are* required to bring students to a place for face-to-face instruction; a few states demand this. There is no evidence, however, that this is best practice; it is more a provision created by opponents of online schools to make them more difficult to operate.[23] Online schools that serve statewide populations, as most do, must then provide for student attendance at multiple sites throughout the state. This can be logistically onerous and can cut deeply into the facility savings that online education might yield. These provisions can also exclude many students—particularly rural ones—from access to online programs. Such requirements typically demand one day a week of physical student attendance. Assuming this as the maximum, online facility costs for educators and students attending part-time should not exceed about one-third of those of brick-and-mortar schools. This savings is complemented by transportation and food savings; if students only require a bus or meal one day a week, transportation (allowing for more sites and longer distances) and food service should cost no more than a fourth of the norm in traditional schools.

How do these savings add up? Traditional schools spend 52 percent of their budgets on teacher salaries and benefits.[24] Online schools should spend half that, or 26 percent of traditionally budgeted dollars. Brick-and-mortar schools spend approximately 15 percent of their budgets on facilities (capital and debt) and plant operations. So online schools should not exceed one-third of that, or 5 percent of traditional school revenues. Transportation and food average 7 percent of school budgets; in online schools those costs should amount to only 2 percent of a brick-and-mortar budget. In total, traditional schools spend 74 percent of their budgets on instruction, facilities, transportation, and food—all areas in which online schools yield savings. Online schools spend 33 percent this way, meaning an overall savings of 41 percent against the traditional school budget.

That is an enormous savings.[25] It is not, however, the bottom line. Online schools have expenses that traditional schools do not. Every student working online requires a computer and an Internet connection. Full-time online schools normally provide these. Traditional schools buy computers and wire classrooms too, but the student-computer ratio in public schools is 4:1, not 1:1, as in online schools. (And the federal government's E-Rate program has paid to get nearly 100 percent of America's public schools online.) Public schools spend about 2 percent of their budgets on computer hardware and connectivity, whereas online schools spend five times that amount.

Online schools have a vastly different instructional delivery system than traditional schools, which rely largely on textbooks, other physical assets, and software. Annual spending on such materials averages about 3 percent of school budgets. Online schools have some of these same costs. They frequently ship traditional instructional materials to student homes. (The largest online education company, K12, is notoriously diligent is this respect, even shipping families dirt for science experiments.) But online companies also have to provide, for example, robust technology platforms with learning management, assessment, and online tutoring systems; portals for families, teachers and students; and grade books and systems to report to multiple school districts. These systems are more complex and expensive than the more limited information systems employed by school districts. Truly unique, online schools must provide a comprehensive curriculum electronically. The online platform and curricula are licensed by online schools from companies that invest in their constant improvement. License fees run $2,000–3,000 per student per year, or roughly 25 percent of a traditional $10,000 per-student annual public school budget.

The additional costs of online schools are not small. Hardware, software, connectivity, and other instructional materials may total 35 percent of an online school budget. Brick-and-mortar schools will spend only 5 percent in the same categories. That is 30 percent in extra costs in a full-time online school. But that is covered, of course, by a 41 percent savings in teachers, facilities, transportation, and food.

This is a rough calculation; costs and comparisons will vary with the grade levels served, the composition of student populations, and many other factors. There is some evidence that students with special needs are especially attracted to online schools, with their self-pacing, privacy, and multimedia solutions. These students are more costly to serve than regular students. If online schools need to meet some of their needs through face-to-face instruction, the logistics can be more expensive than in traditional schools. Online schools have other unique costs, such as renting temporary facilities statewide to administer state standardized tests and marketing their services to families far and wide.

In the end, full-time online schools may be able to show a 10 percent savings over traditional schools. Many jurisdictions force online charter schools to operate with less than the full per-pupil allocation to traditional schools or even the allocation to brick-and-mortar charter schools. Online charter schools now manage to operate in twenty-five states with differing limits on revenue. If even a few percentage points of savings could be multiplied against a public education budget exceeding a half-trillion dollars, the total savings could run in the tens of billions. But the key point here is not the savings gained from full-time online schools. The key is the vastly different allocation of the schooling dollar between technology and the traditional costs of education and what that might mean for the productivity of public education.

HYBRID SCHOOLS

The future of technology and education is not one of students staying home to learn on computers supervised by parents. Full-time online schooling will work only for some families. The vast majority of families will want and need their children to be supervised and instructed outside the home. Most parents must work. Students also want to participate in group activities that the school provides easily—sports, the performing arts, clubs— and that community organizations can also provide. But schools also facilitate the social and emotional dimensions of learning—working in teams, debating, participating in public, and other forms of social growth not offered by community groups or duplicated by interaction online. Simply put, most families will want their children to attend a physical school, and children benefit from doing so.

But schools of the future can and will be different. As the full-time online schools demonstrate so completely, students can thrive academically working online with both software and educators. Traditional schools can take advantage of this—now. Students need not learn in whole-group, teacher-led classrooms, which does not work well for many students anyway. Students can take some or all of their instruction online in a school building. Schools can decide which students, at what age, and for which subjects instruction is best delivered face to face or online. Advanced high school students might take most of their courses online. Elementary students needing remediation might spend a part of their day being assisted online. Schools might decide that courses that absolutely must be mastered by all students—say algebra 1—will be offered online so that students receive consistent instruction and can proceed at their own pace until proficiency is achieved. Schools might decide to use online instruction in classes for which quality teachers cannot be found. Or schools might find that some students simply learn better online than traditionally, or vice versa, and assign classes on that basis. Classes can also be a mixture of online and face-to-face, a bit like college classes that include lectures and recitations. Technology offers the potential—*right now*—for schools to change the mix of traditional and online instruction to better meet the academic needs of students.

Student achievement must always be the goal. Yet, technology may also make schools more productive, getting more achievement for the same total expenditure or even a few dollars less. Here is how that can work in a hybrid environment. If students take courses online, they need not be supervised by a traditional teacher in a traditional classroom. Students can work on laptops in large open spaces like libraries/media centers, school atriums, cafeterias, or large computer labs. Spaces and supervision must be age appropriate, of course. On average, it is safe to assume that online instruction, where the school-based supervisor is *not* instructing, requires half to a third the number of teachers on site as traditional instruction. As schools adopt online instruction, they require fewer traditional teachers.

Consider a conservative model of what is now possible. Elementary students might work online one hour per day, middle school students two hours per day, and high school students three hours per day. Teachers might normally teach five hours daily and have one hour free (covered by another teacher in, say, music, art, or another elective). These work rules require that a six-hour student day be covered by seven teachers, whether in secondary schools, where students see different teachers each hour, or elementary schools, where students see the same teacher all day.[26] If online instruction is supervised in double-sized student groups in grades K–8 and triple-sized groups in high school, the teacher savings are, for elementary schools, 7 percent fewer teachers; for middle schools, 14 percent fewer teachers; and for high schools, 29 percent fewer teachers.[27] Given the different numbers of years that each school spans, the weighted potential teacher savings across all grade levels is 15.4 percent. With schools spending 52 percent of their total budgets on instructional salaries and benefits, the teacher savings from online courses could average nearly 8 percent annually—or $800 per student in a $10,000 per-year per-student school budget.

These savings come at a modest cost. Online course licenses average $200 per student per year-long course, and the cost is much less for instructional software programs. A twenty-five-student online class costs a school $5,000, versus the $13,000 total cost (teacher salary and benefits and instructional materials) of a traditional one-hour class. In round numbers, the $800 per student that schools can save in teacher costs from a hybrid model nets a savings of $500 per student after paying for software.[28]

The scenario mapped out here is a plan that public schools could implement right now. It requires no more computers or connectivity than schools have in place already. And it only begins to capture future savings. If students take more of their coursework outside of brick-and-mortar facilities, working part-time from home and part-time at their hybrid schools, other education costs drop as well. Facilities might become smaller, plant operations cheaper. Fewer teachers would be required to supervise instruction. And, over time, online schools are likely to become more efficient. As more students move on line, technology firms will invest more in improving delivery systems and content, and prices will likely drop through competition and experience. Market forces are at work in the online world; they are largely not at work in the world of public education. If full-time online education costs 10 percent less than brick-and-mortar education today, when the online industry is in its infancy, it is not unreasonable to conjecture a 20 percent differential as online education matures.

PRODUCTIVITY, STUDENT ACHIEVEMENT, AND TEACHERS

Online education and instructional technology can save public education money. To sum it up, a modest shift of schools from full-time whole-group instruction to part-time online instruction can save 5 percent from current public education expenditures. That is approximately $30 billion a year that the nation could save right now. Full-time online schools, which may cost 10 percent less than traditional schools, currently serve only 100,000 students, or 0.2 percent of all public education students. That number could increase rapidly if states lifted the restrictions on online schools, which nearly all operate as charters. States and school districts do offer individual courses online, but full-time, full-service online education is provided largely by charter schools, which most states restrict or prohibit outright. These limitations will diminish as online education builds its own constituency and learning through technology gains acceptance. As students shift from full-time traditional to part- or full-time online, public education will realize further savings.

But productivity is about more than obtaining the same results for less money. The history of productivity gains in other industries is one of both lower costs and higher quality, as technology substitutes for labor. The same will occur in education. Technology and online education have great academic promise because of the virtues of self-pacing, multimedia, instant assessment and intervention, and one-on-one attention from teachers. Working online should boost student achievement, even as it reduces costs.

The biggest boost in achievement may come the old-fashioned way. Online schools require half as many teachers as traditional schools. If the 100,000 students attending online schools today were to grow to one million students (2 percent of all students), the nation would require 1 percent fewer teachers overall. If all public schools were to adopt a hybrid model of instruction, their teacher requirements would plummet by another 15.6 percent. Take the two sectors together—full- and part-time online—and the public education system might require over 16 percent fewer teachers.

The importance of this savings cannot be overstated. Individual teachers are the single most important influence on student achievement, within the control of schools. (Home and family influences are also large, of course, but schools cannot easily affect them.) But with 3.3 million teachers in public education today and annual turnover rates of 10–20 percent, depending on location, public schools have a very difficult time finding and holding on to large numbers of high-quality teachers. If schools had to employ 16 percent fewer teachers, the challenge of finding mostly high-quality ones would be far less. Imagine if schools could use this reduced need selectively, hiring only the best and replacing the lowest quintile of current teachers, the truly unsuccessful ones, the benefits to students would be very large. Without putting too fine a point on it, if public schools required 600,000 fewer teachers than they do today—16 percent of the current total—schools could raise the overall quality of the teaching force substantially.

So technology has the clear potential to reduce costs, by 5 percent or more, without major investment or change in infrastructure. Technology also has the potential to improve achievement through the advantages of online instruction over traditional whole-group teacher-led instruction *and* by raising the overall quality of the teaching force. That's a clear productivity gain: more achievement at a lower cost. But there is even further potential if costs were not reduced but kept constant. Savings from reduced labor requirements could be used to make other productivity investments. We know, for example, that teachers are the most powerful influence on achievement. If technology reduces the need for teachers, the net savings after technology costs could be used to increase teacher compensation, offer performance pay incentives, and make the job more attractive financially. In these ways, society cannot only get more achievement for less expense, but it can enjoy even more achievement for the same investment as today.

This brings us full circle to the financial crisis in Hawai'i and many othere states being forced to make painful and often unprecedented cuts in public education to weather the historic economic recession. States would do well to use this crisis as an opportunity to learn and to look, fundamentally, at how education dollars are spent and at how students are educated. Public schools currently make little use of technology to provide instruction. Indeed, public education discourages technology with laws that, among other restrictions, do not permit or underfund cyber charter schools, that prohibit online teachers from teaching across state lines, that demand "seat-time" instead of proficiency to award credit for online classes, and that require online courses to be taken in whole or in part in brick-and-mortar facilities under the supervision of certified teachers. Public education should eliminate these anachronistic restrictions and prepare schools for the future. If schools embrace technology, they can reduce their operating costs, help their students, and minimize the deep cuts that now jeopardize the opportunities for student learning. Investing in technology is a sound investment, financially and academically, in the future of our students and our nation.

7

Large-Scale Cost Cutting and Reorganizing

Jill Corcoran, Reginald Gilyard,
Lane McBride, and Jamal Powell

THE BOSTON CONSULTING GROUP'S (BCG) work in public education spans federal, state, and local school systems as well as topic areas such as strategic planning, transformation, performance management, operations, and human capital.

In our work with public education clients, we endeavor to marry our experience in the education sector with our learning from more than forty years spent serving private-sector clients. In this chapter we present three examples of cost efficiency to illustrate such a marriage. In the first, we identify broad-based cost efficiencies for a statewide school system for the purposes of funding statewide reform. In the other examples, we identify narrower efficiencies in central office costs for two school districts—each with a different purpose. The examples include the following key insights: significant cost efficiencies can be gained from, for example, benchmark comparisons, a detailed teardown of historical practices, scale advantages, and the pooling of expenditures across entities; it is possible to break some traditionally held compromises that suggest that an organization must spend more to improve service or performance; and it is possible to both increase efficiency and decrease spending.

BROAD-BASED COST EFFICIENCY

In late 2005, a coalition of Delaware's education, business, and community leaders crafted an ambitious reform agenda to make Delaware's schools the best in the country. With the support of The Broad Foundation, the Rodel Foundation of Delaware, and a BCG team, a steering committee of twenty-eight state leaders set out to develop and implement a bold ten-year plan, Vision 2015 (later included in the state's Race to the Top application).

With fewer than 900,000 residents, about 125,000 public school students, and just over two hundred public schools, Delaware is a small state. However, in some ways it is a microcosm of the nation, with its mix of high-poverty urban areas, sprawling suburbs, and rural farmland. The population is about 20 percent African American and 75 percent Caucasian, and the Hispanic population is growing. Approximately 15 percent of children live in poverty. According to measures such as the National Assessment of Education Progress (NAEP), Delaware's education performance has been in the middle of the U.S. states, despite its being in the top ten in terms of spending per pupil.

The development of Vision 2015 was, in many ways, unique. Its coalition of stakeholders included representation from nearly every potential set of oppositional forces in education policy making: the Delaware Department of Education and local school districts, union and management, school boards and district leaders, government and business, as well as urban and rural interests. And beyond the twenty-eight members of the steering committee, hundreds of additional Delawareans—elementary school teachers, high school dropouts, university experts, early childhood education advocates—were consulted in the plan's creation.

Developing and agreeing to a bold and cohesive plan was not easy. However, the steering committee unanimously agreed to a plan that was released to the public in October 2006. The Vision 2015 recommendations include internationally benchmarked standards, expanded access to and improved quality in early childhood education, teacher career paths, school leader empowerment, and weighted student funding.

Although no specific numbers were released, the steering committee acknowledged that implementation would take "courage, dedication, resolve, and money."[1] Several elements of the plan would require substantial investment—for example, "expand the scope of state support for early childhood education by providing tuition subsidies for all three and four year olds from low-income families."[2] So the plan's authors included as one of its recommendations that the state should "engage in a careful analysis of how our current education dollars could be spent more effectively or allocated differently."[3]

The early implementation of Vision 2015 quickly met with the need for such an analysis. In late 2006, ominous clouds were gathering on the financial horizon. A haven for financial firms, Delaware sat poised at the leading edge of the recession that hit the United States in 2008. Gloomy state revenue forecasts meant decreasing likelihood of public investment in the Vision 2015 initiatives.

In this context, Governor Ruth Ann Minner created the Leadership for Education Achievement in Delaware (LEAD) Committee in mid-2007 and directed a study of spending efficiency in Delaware education similar to the one called for by Vision 2015. She called for the study to "make recommendations for improving the fiscal efficiency of the system and reallocating funds among education priorities, particularly supporting those that most directly impact student achievement."[4]

The LEAD Committee began its cost efficiency study in early fall 2007. With the financial support of the Delaware Business Roundtable, the committee engaged BCG to provide analytical support and to help manage the development of their report to the governor.

We've Been Down This Road Before

As we at BCG began to review education spending in Delaware, we were warned that we were following a well-trodden path. Reports on the topic had been released in 1987, 1993, 1995, 1997, 1999, 2000, 2001, 2002, 2004, 2005, and 2007. Architects of the earlier studies and those who had endured them told us—and we could see for ourselves—that few of the report recommendations had been implemented. Skeptics could be forgiven for thinking this was yet another study that would collect dust.

Does this sound like the setup for an unqualified success story? It's not. Some of the LEAD Committee's cost-efficiency recommendations have been implemented. Some have not. And some are in the vast in-between, where positive steps have been taken but the jury is still out.

Cost Efficiency from Many Angles

Given the four-month duration and scope of the Delaware effort—all state spending on education through the twelfth grade—some approaches were not pursued. The study was not an audit; spending data had to be taken more or less at face value. The team neither observed individuals doing their jobs nor timed activities with a stopwatch. Nor could it dig into every budget line item or spending transaction.

We used available information sources to prioritize opportunity areas and conducted targeted analyses to validate and provide an estimated "size of the prize" for each opportunity. The team had several factors in its favor that are not common in all states. First, Delaware has a common financial system across state agencies and school districts, making it relatively straightforward to identify total spending amounts in specific cost categories. Second, the past reports, and in some cases their authors, were readily available. Third, Delaware's education community is tightly knit and geographically concentrated, so the team was able to engage a range of experts and policy makers, many of whom were LEAD Committee members.

We quickly identified a set of cost-efficiency hypotheses that focused on opportunities from which a neutral or positive impact on student outcomes could reasonably be assumed, excluding instructional areas that were deemed out of scope for this effort (e.g., class size).

Given a set of hypotheses, the team used several approaches to validate and estimate the size of the state's cost-efficiency opportunities. Individually, each approach has its challenges. Together, however, the various approaches allow for a quick triangulation that can identify areas for further pursuit.

Comparison with Other States.   The U.S. Department of Education provides state data on education spending through the National Center for Education Statistics' Common Core of Data. These data, self-reported by state education agencies, are subject to the limitation that different states report the same costs in different categories. However, the information provides for a high-level comparison of total and per-pupil spending by category, indicating areas in which one state appears to be spending more than its peers.

Comparison of School Districts Within the State.   Delaware's financial system allowed spending comparisons at a granular level. For example, although comparisons across districts at the level of Supplies and Materials could be illuminating, the system allowed for even more nuanced comparisons. The Supplies and Materials category breaks down into subcategories such as Books and Publications and Vehicle Fuel. It is also important to note that comparisons sometimes reveal discrepancies that have an explanation other than a difference in efficiency. For example, each of Delaware's three high school districts that focus on career and technical education hosts extensive night programs for adults, who are not counted in per-student analyses. Thus, the baseline for energy expenditures may be justifiably different in these districts. That said, some differences across districts were often validated by further exploration that revealed best practices in one district that could be adopted by another.

Use of Scale Curves.   Per-student comparisons can sometimes be misleading because in many cost categories one should expect scale: the per-student cost of providing a given service should decrease as the size of the entity (the district or state) increases. For example, there is little reason to believe that administrative support functions in education should be different from those in private industry, where "economies of scale" is a long-established concept.

Expected scale varies by the type of task performed. Tasks that involve heavy repetition, such as processing financial transactions, tend to have the most scale. At least two approaches can be used to approximate expected scale. The first is to use benchmarks. Administrative support functions found in central offices such as finance, human resources (HR), and communications have close analogues in other industries. We compared these functions with the scale we have observed across industries in BCG's private-sector experience. The second approach is to look for existing scale and find outliers. For example, we found 90 percent scale in administrative and instructional support spending. That is, the average district's per-student spending in these categories was 90 percent of the per-student spending of a district half its size. However, some smaller districts spent less per student than larger districts that, according to scale, should have been more efficient. Thus, in cost categories where scale is observed or expected, a rough and conservative savings estimate assumes that districts or states not taking advantage of scale could reduce spending to fit the scale-adjusted norm.

There is at least one significant caution in looking for potential scale based on current education spending, and this caution increases with the level of aggregation of the spending analyzed. At the extreme, it is generally fruitless to look for scale in a district's or state's *total* per-student education spending; a graphical plot of per-student spending in the fifty U.S. states against student population proves this. In most cases, what is spent is what is budgeted, and what is budgeted is a function of several factors—politics, history, funding formulas, ability to raise tax revenue—that go beyond the cost of providing comparable service to other districts or states. If, as we believe, scale exists in education, large districts or states with high per-student spending are less efficient or are spending their money on a wider array of services. Often, both are the case.

Comparison with Best Practices in Other Industries. Scale in administrative support functions is one example in which private-sector benchmarks can demonstrate the potential cost savings opportunities in education. Another such area is procurement: the purchase of all goods and services accounts for a significant proportion of education spending. Most organizations—even those with sophisticated dedicated procurement organizations—can achieve substantial savings through the customized application of best practices. These include systematically managing relationships with suppliers, bundling (buying in bulk), standardization (buying and maintaining a single kind of widget instead of forty-seven kinds), and demand management (reducing waste and using only as much as is needed). Although some are more relevant than others in particular circumstances, these best practices are consistent across industries. To verify and roughly quantify the savings opportunity in procurement, we surveyed Delaware's district-level purchasing managers and compared current practices to best practice.

Comparison with Estimates from an Outsourced Provider.   Outsourcing in U.S. public education is well established. Charter schools provide the extreme case, since the entire education enterprise is outsourced. Short of that, many support functions—including food service, transportation, and janitorial and maintenance services—are outsourced in otherwise publicly managed schools. One way to estimate the potential for savings is to provide specifications to a vendor for an estimate (request for information) that can provide a benchmark for comparison with current public spending.

Analogous Cost-Savings Efforts.   In areas of education not easily compared with other industries, analogues can be found by looking to past efforts and other locations. We leveraged the results of an earlier procurement efficiency effort in state government. In assessing the potential savings associated with exempting schools from prevailing wage laws, we looked at Ohio, which exempted schools in 1997. Like other methods, this is not foolproof: the context of one cost-savings initiative is never perfectly replicable in another. However, this approach is based on achieved outcomes that incorporate real-world complications that no scale curve can capture.

Understanding the Incentives Inherent in Funding Formulas.   Spending in education often has more to do with budgets than with costs. There is a particular opportunity for inefficiency when funding formulas provide categorical dollars that, if saved in one cost category, cannot be spent elsewhere; there is no incentive for efficiency. Although one can imagine blatant excess, such inefficiency is rarely malicious. In fact, as one local education leader explained, in Delaware it is often the result of a strategic calculation. He said there are many things he could do that would benefit his students a lot more than trying to find ways to be more efficient with money he cannot reallocate.

It is difficult to quantify presumed inefficiency that results from the lack of incentives for efficiency. However, identifying budgetary areas with misaligned incentives leads to identifying specific quantifiable inefficiencies using other means described here.

Identification of Budget Items Inconsistent with Public Policy Objectives. Often the most politically delicate cost inefficiencies are those for which arguments are sometimes made that there should be no public spending at all. Depending on one's definition, these might not be considered inefficiencies but, rather, differences of opinion on the objective of public spending on education.

One example from Delaware is a transportation subsidy for private school students. At the time of the LEAD study, $3 million was distributed annually among the families of roughly 15,000 private school students as reimbursement for transportation costs. This subsidy was not correlated with transportation costs incurred by private schools or the families of the students; nor were the families required to spend it on transportation. Such a subsidy is not necessarily wrong. However, from an outsider's perspective, it seemed that the subsidy resided in a strange place.

Professional Judgment.   When all else fails, ask. Managers often have the best sense of what could be cut from their budgets and how processes could be more efficient. In purchasing, managers most likely know market prices that they cannot take advantage of because of legal or regulatory limitations. Although some managers have a vested interest in portraying the facts in a certain light, we found them a helpful source for triangulating data across several cost categories.

A Range of Cost-Efficiency Recommendations

Employing all the approaches described above and building on the ideas from past studies and expert interviews, the LEAD Committee, with the support of BCG, identified cost efficiency ideas valued at between $86 million and $158 million per year in steady-state savings. (Total education spending in Delaware for the base year studied was just over $1.6 billion.) These ideas, presented to the governor in January 2008 after roughly four months of discussion, prioritization, and targeted analysis, fell into six main categories: student transportation, purchasing, energy, benefits, construction, and administration and central support (including shared services).[5]

The resulting recommendations, like the Vision 2015 plan, represented an aspiration. Few of the LEAD Committee's recommendations represented "low-hanging fruit." Full realization of the estimated savings would require both operational know-how and political will. Many of the greatest opportunities would require not only broad support, but also sustained focus and expertise from those in key leadership roles. The report's recommendations follow.

Student Transportation.   At the time of the study, Delaware's per-student spending on transportation was the fourth highest in the nation. School bus routes were funded directly by the state on a per-route basis, and more than two hundred contractors operated bus routes. The funding formula, designed to support contractors with one or two routes, allowed large efficient contractors to capture the savings. Also, the direct state funding lessened the incentive for school districts and charter schools to save. In addition, Delaware was funding school bus replacement at seven years, half the national average bus retirement age. The LEAD Committee recommendations included redesigning the bus contracting process to align incentives for saving, increasing the age at which bus replacement would be funded by the state, and eliminating the subsidy nominally supporting transportation of private school students.

Purchasing.   Delaware's education procurement structure includes purchasing functions at the state level in each of the nineteen school districts and in each charter school. Purchasing is a distinct central office function in the largest districts, but it is one of many hats for managers in small districts. School districts could purchase on statewide contracts, but local purchasing off statewide contracts was variable and loosely coordinated. In some cases, districts secured better deals on their own, as the state's contracts lacked features that would allow lower prices, such as time constraints or volume guarantees. The LEAD Committee recommended creating a coordinated professional purchasing function across school districts, incorporating local input through a purchasing council, and providing coordination through a dedicated specialized statewide purchasing function.

Energy.   Unlike transportation, in procuring energy Delaware's local school districts can keep and reallocate their incremental dollar. There is incentive to save, and some districts have implemented demand management (conservation) programs. Analysis shows that their energy spending per square foot is among the lowest in the state. The LEAD Committee found a significant opportunity to institutionalize these districts' best practices for other districts. The committee also recommended statewide, pooled purchasing of natural gas, similar to a successful previous effort to pool electricity purchasing.

Benefits.   The subject of employee benefits is touchy in any context. Although it was closest to the LEAD Committee's self-imposed restriction from cost-savings opportunities that might have some impact on student achievement, the committee could not avoid this topic. Delaware's pension plan for educators was fully funded, but its future obligations for retiree health benefits were less than 1 percent funded. The employee benefits were generous: in the year studied, spending on educator benefits totaled 40 percent of spending on educator salaries—well above the national average of 31 percent. The committee recognized that benefits are a critical recruiting tool but also discussed the possibilities of a more flexible model. Based on the complexity and sensitivity of this issue, the committee recommended it for further study.

Construction.   In construction, the committee identified an opportunity for savings through a more coordinated statewide approach: standardization of building design and component specification coordinated by a lean, dedicated construction management function at the state level. In addition, the committee explored the potential savings achievable by exempting schools from prevailing wage laws. Prevailing wage laws, present in most states, require a minimum fixed wage for public construction projects, typically those above a certain dollar threshold. Ohio, however, had saved an estimated 11 percent on school construction since 1997 after exempting schools from prevailing wage laws.[6] The committee in Delaware recommended a trial exemption.

Administration and Central Support (Shared Services).   School district consolidation is also politically sensitive. Earlier studies explored the possibility of consolidation and came to different conclusions about its advisability and savings potential. One significant issue is the assumption that consolidation savings are offset by "leveling up" salaries to those of the highest-paying district. The LEAD Committee discussed consolidation, but its recommendation focused on capturing similar benefits through shared services while retaining the current governance structures. The committee did not specify which functions should be shared across school districts but did discuss including, for example, finance and budget, information technology, facilities, operations, maintenance, personnel and HR, and general administration. The creation of shared services across school districts has the potential for both increased efficiency and more focused, coordinated functions. Because shared services come in many flavors and do not guarantee efficiency, the LEAD Committee recommended a five-year study to assess the progress of implementation. Table 7.1 shows a breakdown of the cost-savings opportunities identified by category.

TABLE 7.1

Overview of cost efficiency opportunity areas

Opportunity area	Addressable spend ($ million)	Opportunity size ($ million)[a]	Summary of efficiency opportunities
① Student Transportation	80	9–12+	• Redesign bus contracting process • Increase minimum bus retirement age • Eliminate funding for nonpublic schools • Eliminate specific provisions in budget bill
② Purchasing	178	15–25	• Formalize statewide coordination of the education purchasing function
③ Energy	28	4–7	• Implement best practices in demand management • Explore statewide pooling of natural gas
④ Benefits	311	0–29	• Pool local benefits purchasing • Examine offering a more flexible compensation package of salary, health benefits, and pension
⑤ Construction	195	31–48	• Centralize construction purchasing and design • Exempt schools from prevailing wage requirements
⑥ Administrative and central support and system recommendations	85	25–34	• Increase magnitude of scale in funding formula • Create broad shared services • Evaluate impact of shared services and consider consolidation in year five of implementation
Department of Education (DOE)	50	2–3+	• Enhance purchasing efficiency at DOE
TOTAL	927	86–158+	

[a] Estimated annual savings after full and successful statewide implementation of recommendations. Construction savings would accrue to the capital budget.

Source: The Delaware chart is an adapted version of a chart at the link cited in endnote 5.

Results and Lessons Learned: A Work in Progress

Given the LEAD Committee's challenging recommendations, it is not surprising that the jury is still out on their full impact. Some recommendations have been implemented in whole or in part. The age at which the state pays for school bus replacement has been raised, the subsidy for private school transportation has been reduced, and pooled purchasing of natural gas has begun. There has also been progress in areas requiring longer lead times before savings are realized—notably purchasing and shared services—in which reforms consistent with the LEAD report were in the planning stages at the time of this writing.

The state's worsening economic conditions over the past few years have provided a platform for consideration of many of the recommended changes. Still, economic conditions have meant that the recommendations implemented so far were put in place to reduce overall spending rather than to free funds for Vision 2015 priorities. This is understandable, but it only increases the importance of spending decisions once the state budget begins to grow. We offer several lessons from the Delaware experience.

There Is No Single Formula for Cost Efficiency.   For every Delaware, there is a state with low per-pupil transportation costs, no prevailing wage law, and larger school districts with dedicated professional purchasing functions. However, even that hypothetical state has cost-efficiency opportunities. Through a range of moderately detailed analyses, leveraging available data and expertise, other states (and school districts) can identify their most significant efficiency opportunities.

Managing Centralization Is a Key Issue.   Central coordination, a theme running through the Delaware recommendations, provides opportunities for lower costs through scale and better leverages expertise in areas such as purchasing and transportation management. Still, unlike in the private sector, there is no strong research base to suggest that large school districts, which in theory should have such centralization, are more efficient or that school district consolidation increases efficiency. One reason for this?

What is funded is spent. If funding formulas do not provide incentives for efficiency, efficiency should not be expected. Fundamentally, there is no simple solution to questions of centralization. A balanced model in which decisions are made as close to the student as possible and services are provided by customer-oriented service functions is promising. However, striking this balance requires a thoughtful and well-managed approach.

Most Boundaries Were Not Drawn for Efficiency.   Delaware's school district boundaries have deep historical roots. If the district lines were drawn today, it is unlikely that the largest school district would have seventeen times the number of students as the smallest. In many cases, school district boundaries align with communities, and we do not want to discount the importance of community roles in public schools. However, creative and thoughtful management can keep local communities engaged in public schools while breaking down or working across historical boundaries wherever they hinder efficiency.

Expertise and Focus in Leadership Roles Are Critical Needs.   Like so many other factors in education, spending efficiency is linked to human capital. Many managers in the current system, consumed by their day-to-day work, spend little time focused on efficiency. Some lack expertise and support, and (particularly in small districts) managers wearing many hats are unlikely to be expert at each of their roles. BCG finds that even sophisticated, high-functioning Fortune 500 companies have opportunities to drive significant savings in purchasing. How much untapped potential, then, is likely across an education system in which a purchasing manager may have five other roles? It is critical that managers be trained in driving operational efficiencies, that there be a pipeline into education institutions for talented managers with expertise and previous experience in leading back-office functions, and that school district and state education leaders hold these managers accountable for efficiency.

Vigilance During the Coming Economic Recovery Will Be Critical.   The current economic climate has encouraged tough spending decisions that may have been politically infeasible during better times. Most likely, these tough decisions have supported budget cuts rather than reallocation to policy priorities. The economic downtown will not last forever, however, so it is critical that investments be made in forward-looking priorities.

CENTRAL OFFICE EFFICIENCY EXAMPLES: DELAYERING IN TWO LARGE SCHOOL DISTRICTS

In 2006, BCG worked with Chicago Public Schools (CPS) to reduce costs and increase organizational effectiveness at the district's central office. That same year BCG was engaged by a large urban school district in a Southwest state.

The work with CPS identified several opportunities to reduce role duplication and layers of management, to standardize job titles and salaries, and led to an annual savings of $25 million. Similarly, the project with the Southwestern school district led to cost savings ($9 million) and also more efficient, timely decisionmaking and support from the central office to the school sites.

Example 1: Delayering the Central Office at Chicago Public Schools

In October 2009, CPS was the third-largest public school district in the United States, with more than 400,000 students and 23,000 teachers across 666 schools. The district employs nearly 44,000 people, and its 2009–2010 operating budget of $5.3 billion would put it on the latest Fortune 500 list if it were a public company. Nearly 85 percent of CPS students are from low-income families.

In January 2006, CPS leadership faced a predicted $328 million budget deficit for the 2006–2007 school year. Though budget shortfalls had become the norm in Chicago and across Illinois, that year's predicted deficit was the highest since Mayor Richard M. Daley had taken over the school system in 1995. A large increase in the district's pension costs and declining student enrollment were two of several contributors to the predicted shortfall.

CPS explored options for filling the gap, including the possibility of $75 million in new federal and state funds, changes to the pension rules, and numerous cost-savings initiatives. Former CPS CEO Arne Duncan said, "This is the toughest budget year I've faced, due largely to this drastically increased pension obligation . . . Our goal is to minimize tough cuts— anything that would impact the classroom and hurt students. But we have to prepare. We have to look honestly at a range of possible scenarios."[7]

Specifically, CPS leadership sought to avoid further increases in class size. It was estimated that another increase at the high school level—from twenty-eight to thirty-one students—would save $25 million.

Having worked with CPS leadership in to develop a long-term strategy to improve CPS high schools, BCG considered the organizational effectiveness of CPS's central office, which includes a range of departments focused on education and business services (e.g., HR, finance, and technology services). CPS's "theory of change" saw the schools themselves as the units of change, charged with achieving a set of student outcomes. The role of the central office was to provide the schools with targeted support.

The central office's 2005–2006 budget of $207 million included $157 million in staff costs across more than 1,800 positions. CPS leadership and our BCG team saw an opportunity to restructure the central office for increased effectiveness and greater accountability. We agreed to work with CPS leadership to achieve two complementary objectives: improve the overall organizational effectiveness of the CPS central office; and improve overall efficiency of the central office by achieving a $25 million, or 12 percent, reduction in annual central office costs.

The senior team was determined to minimize negative impact on classrooms and students. Every dollar removed from the central office was one that would not have to be removed from the classroom: $25 million in central office savings would translate into about 350 teachers working with students in the upcoming school year. The lens of organizational effectiveness was also critical in evaluating the central office's role as a support to schools.

A Systematic and Collaborative Approach

Delayering is a tool and process BCG developed and uses to improve an entity's organization structure by optimizing both the number of reporting layers in the organization and the number of persons directly reporting to each manager (span of control). Delayering transforms an organization, making it more agile, with fewer layers and appropriately wide spans of control. BCG used the delayering tool, in close collaboration with CPS officials, to assess and implement opportunities to increase efficiency at CPS's central office. Delayering has five objectives:

1. Simplify how an organization operates by clearly defining and communicating roles, accountabilities, and performance expectations;
2. Achieve substantial cost savings;
3. Improve collaboration across the organization;
4. Empower people to create bigger and better jobs; and
5. Streamline communications to enable faster and smarter decision making.

Delayering CPS's central office began with several weeks of interviewing employees at all levels and compiling organization charts and data on costs, compensation, and positions and titles. We then established and agreed on design principles for restructuring and facilitated a process by which CPS restructured and staffed its central office organization. Delayering uses a "cascading" method to do so, whereby each layer of management takes charge of redesigning the layer of administrators immediately below it. This method ensured that central office managers would take ownership of the design process and use their intimate knowledge of the organization's needs and staff to make the best redesign decisions.

Two to three weeks were allotted for reconfiguration of each management layer by the layer above it—including design, staffing, and articulation of clear role descriptions at the department level. BCG tracked progress using a rigorous methodology to ensure that each layer met the design principles.

Both Structure and Effectiveness Needed Change

The diagnostic work that preceded the redesign identified four key findings related to organization structure and three related to organizational effectiveness. The following are related to organization structure.

The Central Office Was Supported by Too Many Managers.   As part of the delayering process, we focused on the span of control for central office managers—the number of direct reports per manager—in the first four layers of the organization: Layer 1 is the CEO, Layer 2 includes the CEO's direct reports, and so forth. Benchmarks of comparable private sector organizations suggested that the target span of control in these layers should be eight—that is, each manager manages eight people.

The span of control for CPS central office managers in the first four layers was small, averaging 4.7 direct reports per manager. Our estimates suggested that increasing spans of control to eight could yield $20–28 million in cost savings. As a result of the low spans of control, personnel were spread across more than eight discrete layers in the organization; the appropriate benchmark target for organizations of similar size is four to five layers from the CEO to the front line.

Across all departments, only twelve of the seventy-nine managers in the organization had spans of control of eight or more. Some departments were well below the target. One department had eleven managers for just thirty full-time employees (FTEs), yielding a span of control of about 2.5; and other departments had average spans of control of fewer than four.

The staff provided a host of reasons for the low spans of control, many of which reflected issues of organizational effectiveness. The following are the top four reasons:

- Lots of managers were "player coaches" in the central office. They had day jobs in addition to their management role, making managing another eight people difficult or impractical.
- Manager titles were sometimes used as a reward or retention tool, along with the opportunity to manage a small number of staff.

- Managers in training needed to transition into the manager's role with a smaller span of control.
- Manager time was often focused on dotted-line, or secondary, responsibilities for both staff and projects—a symptom of a broader lack of clarity about roles and responsibilities.

Management Ranks Included a Large Number of Senior-Level Individual Contributors.   A corollary to the small spans of control was the large number of individual contributors—relatively senior staff with no direct staff-management responsibility. In the top four layers of the organization there were seventy-seven individual contributors, including seven of the CEO's fifteen direct reports. In Layer 3 there were twenty-one individual contributors, with another forty-nine in Layer 4—meaming that 40–50 percent of the organization's staff was in those two layers. The cumulative salary and benefits cost for individual contributors was between $9 million and $10 million.

Selected Key Functions Were Being Duplicated Across the Organization. Over time, the central office had developed redundant positions and departments that duplicated functions, including research and evaluation, technology services, budgeting, and grant writing. Senior staff said that as principals and other internal customers became frustrated with the ability of a certain department to support them or respond to a question or request, duplicate positions would be established. Several departments had established research and evaluation functions, multiple departments had their own grant writers, and the curriculum department had a budget person for every subject area. While there were hard costs associated with this phenomenon, staff also perceived reduced effectiveness. Several worried about the ability to maintain consistent information and data. In addition, the lack of coherence across the functional areas could sometimes be confusing for the field.

Job Titles Were Not Standardized and Compensation Was Not Always Calibrated.   We analyzed the titles of the nonadministrative staff and found 342 unique job titles among 1,650 FTEs. Also, some common titles, such as "manager" or "coordinator," had wide compensation bands and a wide range of levels of responsibility. For titles and roles that were comparable to industry standards, benchmarking research showed that some CPS staff were paid a premium to the market rate while others were paid at a discount.

Overall, the analysis suggested a real cost-savings opportunity to be realized by aligning salaries with industry standards. Specifically, we estimated a net benefit of $700,000: $1.1 million in savings from releveling salaries downward and a $400,000 cost from releveling salaries upward. A larger benefit could be achieved in the longer term by creating a set of consistent job titles and pay bands.

Some findings that relate to organization structure and organizational efficiency point to challenges of the central office organization as a whole. Our interviews during the diagnostic phase uncovered a desire for greater discipline and clarity around decision rights, organization structure, and performance management. The following are three of the most relevant findings:

• Ownership of strategic decisions was unclear
• The organization structure itself was unclear to many
• Performance management was limited, and compensation was not based on merit

Ownership of Strategic Decisions Was Unclear.   Because processes and "decision rights" were not clearly defined or communicated, decision making was seen as slow and suboptimal. It was rarely clear who was responsible for a given decision, who was accountable for its results, who needed to be consulted, and who should simply be informed. Too many people could weigh in on decisions, which were rarely final and too often escalated to the leadership ranks. "Decision shopping" was common: if a person did not like the first answer, he would appeal to someone more senior. Several people commended the top leaders on their accessibility, but some said that unclear ownership meant that those leaders were distracted by issues that should have been resolved one or two layers lower in the organization.

The Organization Structure Itself Was Unclear to Many.   Staff reported that organization charts were incomplete and that it was difficult to determine who reported to whom. This was exacerbated by the central office's use of individual consultants, contractors, and miscellaneous payroll (sometimes former CPS) employees. Total spending in this professional services category was roughly $32 million.

Performance Management Was Limited and Compensation Was Not Based on Merit.   Interviews and analysis pointed to limited department-level accountability for results and to what some described as a lack of a "service" mentality. Senior staff said that performance management for individuals was limited and uneven. One middle manager had not had a performance discussion with his supervisor in years.

Compensation and raises were determined not by merit but by "step and scale" compensation tables dictating tenure-based increases. Some senior staff believed this contributed to diminished initiative and that eliminating the seniority-based pay system for nonunion staff and replacing it with merit-based rewards could help improve performance, encourage innovation, and increase retention of high-performing staff.

Getting to Outcomes

As CPS continued to manage the budget crisis on other fronts, the organization achieved three critical outcomes for the central office's redesign.

First, CPS committed to, achieved, and sustained a $25 million cost reduction. This allowed the district to keep roughly 350 teachers without increasing class size. The fiscal year 2007 budget of the central office was reduced by 12 percent, from $217 million to $192 million. Three years earlier, the central office represented 6.3 percent of total district costs; the target was 4.2 percent in fiscal year 2007.

Figure 7.1 illustrates the primary areas of targeted cost reduction. A major source of the cost savings (more than $10 million) came directly from position reductions through the delayering process, made largely by increasing the spans of control across the organization. In fiscal year 2007, CPS eliminated more than 60 positions and planned the outplacement of 80–110 central office employees. Spending on consultants and contractors was reduced by $6 million. In addition, salaries were releveled: a pay freeze was put in place for 1,300 central office employees earning more than $40,000, and a set of vacant positions was eliminated (or releveled).

Second, CPS began to implement HR and budget policies to broaden the impact of the effort in future years. With the pay freeze in place, the organization piloted a system of individual performance evaluations and merit-based raises to replace the seniority-based pay system for nonunion central office staff. CPS reduced the number of job titles from 342 unique job titles to eighteen functional job titles (e.g., officer, senior manager, and

FIGURE 7.1
More than $25 million in targeted cost savings through redesign

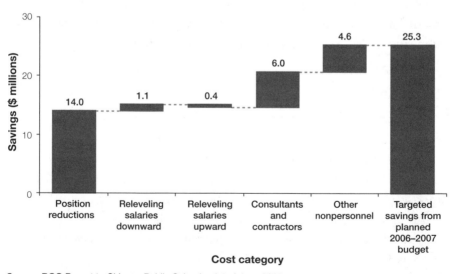

Source: BCG Report to Chicago Public Schools, dated June 2006.

manager). Each title was defined with clear criteria, and there were now eleven specific pay bands.

Third, the organization itself was streamlined. The average span of control for each manager increased from five to eight, resulting in a reduction of layers between the CEO and frontline staff. Direct reports to the CEO were reduced from fifteen to ten, and there were fewer individual contributors.

Describing the 2006 effort, the district's former chief administrative officer, David Vitale, said, "Some of this was literally just changing the way we did work, the way work was done. It was inefficient, ineffective. And we really didn't need to do all the handoffs we were doing. We are streamlining the process and automating the process."[8] The redesign and streamlining of CPS's central office is a work in progress, with state officials continuing to look for opportunities to improve effectiveness while reducing costs amid budget woes.

EXAMPLE 2: DELAYERING THE CENTRAL OFFICE—A DIFFERENT DISTRICT, A DIFFERENT PURPOSE

In contrast to the CPS example, whose primary objective was to address a projected budget deficit, this project was done as part of a larger plan to transform the school district. The primary objectives were to create a more customer-centric and efficient central office, simultaneously freeing up resources to fund other transformation priorities.

This particular district serves more than 150,000 students and has a significant minority population of African Americans and Hispanics. Like many other urban school districts across the United States, this district faced challenges related to student achievement, particularly college readiness, graduation rates, and proficiency. Graduation rates were just above 50 percent, and student proficiency—based on state standards—hovered around 80 percent for reading and 60 percent for math. But many students who met the state's proficiency standards needed remediation at the college level. Furthermore, white students from the district were twice as likely as African Americans and five times as likely as Hispanics to graduate from a two- or four-year college.

Facing these and several other challenges, the superintendent organized a commission comprising diverse representatives of business, government, and civic and faith-based organizations. The commission's objective was to produce recommendations—based on a data-driven approach and study of best practices—to enable true transformation of the district. A local foundation funded the commission's work. The commission hired BCG to support the development of the specific recommendations and facilitate commission meetings along with the foundation leadership.

One Hundred Recommendations—Where Do You Start?

The commission's transformation plan consisted of approximately one hundred recommendations centered on high-achieving and engaged students and included recommendations related to teachers, principals, parents and guardians, and the surrounding community. One critical need was a truly service-oriented central office. "Campus-focused central services" as a theme comprised five major recommendations to improve the operational efficiency of the central office and focus district funds where they could have the greatest impact on student achievement.

One key recommendation within the campus-focused central services theme was to "reduce management layers to improve efficiency and effectiveness" of the central office. The superintendent and commission recognized how important it was both to realize savings to fund other recommendations and to make changes to improve the central office before asking for changes from the campuses. They therefore decided that reducing management layers would be the first recommendation implemented. With the superintendent's desire for the plan's recommendations to be grounded in best practices from school districts across the country, be representative of practices in the best-performing for-profit and not-for-profit organizations, and be grounded in data unique to the school district, there was considerable work that led to justifying this as a critical recommendation. Figure 7.2 illustrates how we developed hypotheses before actually using tools and processes to fix the core issues.

FIGURE 7.2

Reporting chain for the maintenance function

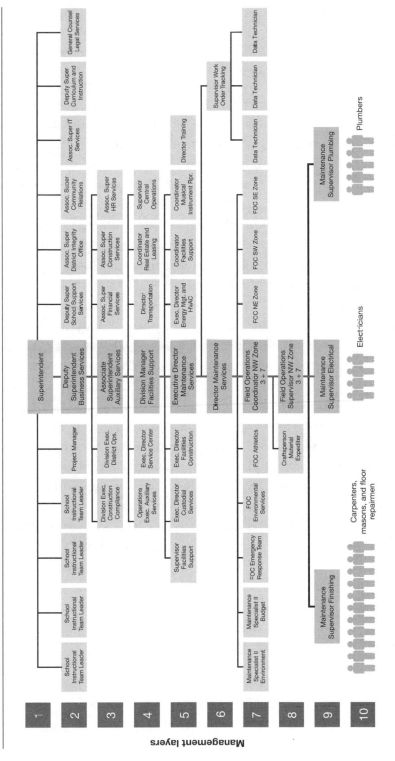

Source: BCG report to client, dated January 2007.

Eight management layers existed between the superintendent and school maintenance personnel. In highly bureaucratic organizations, the need to make major decisions through eight layers can mean slow response time, poor communication, and an inability to address the true problem. We found that much of this held true in the district's maintenance department. In fact, it was one of the departments that received high numbers of complaints from campus-based personnel. This was one of several areas suggesting inefficiency within the central office. Aiming to improve efficiency and realize savings that could be invested in programs that further academic achievement, the superintendent and commission engaged BCG to assist in conducting the delayering process.

A most significant step in the process was the design and completion of an offsite meeting at which the superintendent and his leadership team designed the organization of the future to provide the greatest opportunity for enhancing service levels and improving student achievement. The all-day off-site meeting, facilitated by BCG, provided the opportunity for the entire leadership team to openly discuss the successes and failures of the current organization model, debate the shape of a future state organization model, and identify the challenges of transitioning to the optimal future state. This discussion took place after the superintendent had identified his direct reports. As a result, everyone in the room was safe. Working with the superintendent, BCG created an atmosphere in which people felt comfortable challenging historical norms concerning which departments should be responsible for which functions. BCG spurred the group's thinking with examples of organization structures used in other districts and the private sector. The intent was to set the stage for individual sessions in which one or two BCG team members would work with one direct report to design the major functions within the entire organization and identify individuals to fill their direct reporting roles.

The follow-up sessions with each of the superintendent's direct reports began with an assessment of the current design and challenges. In designing the new organization, the key constraint was that each individual should have five to seven direct reports. The stronger the individual, the more likely he or she would have seven direct reports. Individuals who ended up with only two to four direct reports needed to present a strong rationale for their smaller teams to the entire executive leadership team. Those whose functions lacked adequate justification for small groups would either be combined with or distributed among other departments. At the conclusion of these sessions, the entire executive leadership team reconvened. Each person presented the design of his or her new organization and received feedback from other team members, allowing the superintendent to make sure that elements most important to improving efficiency and advancing student achievement received proper amounts of oversight from the right individuals.

Because the Teaching and Learning function was critical to advancing student achievement, a disproportionate number of the district's high performers were assigned to it, and any activities not directly related to the function were shifted to other departments. By the conclusion of the session, the leadership team had designed most of the organization. The design was then presented to, modified by, and finalized with each subsequent layer of direct reports as they were selected. If an appropriate individual could not be identified to occupy a position and subsequently staff those reporting to their position, the immediate supervisor would be responsible for staffing the department until an individual was identified.

Realizing the Objectives

This process helped the district to fundamentally rethink how it was structured and to improve both service levels and the focus on student achievement. Although it was a huge undertaking for the leadership team, members embraced the process and significantly changed the way the organization was structured. Numerous departments were eliminated; others were restructured, giving up some functions and taking on new ones. For example, the chief of staff role was expanded to incorporate functions previously led by the chief academic officer, so that this person could focus more time on student achievement. Many upper and middle managers embraced the changes, feeling that they made sense.

The tangible benefits realized by this district were significant. Overall, the district reduced the number of middle managers, removed duplication and inefficiency, and improved decision making by eliminating layers in the organization. In addition, the process resulted in improved focus on students and learning. Departments such as Teaching and Learning and Food and Child Nutrition were aligned against Learning Communities to provide one focal point of contact. Increased staffing of Human Development allowed more timely support to campus employees. And related functions were grouped into natural clusters. For example, Compensation and Benefits was transferred to the Human Development Organization; Evaluation and Accountability was transferred from Teaching and Learning to the Chief of Staff. Finally, the central office head count was cut by approximately 5 percent, saving about $9 million on an annual basis—savings that could be directed to implementing additional commission recommendations and supporting academic programs to improve student achievement.

Success Was Not Easy

One can only imagine the amount of resistance from the organization when it was announced that the district would go through yet another organization restructuring effort. Historically, reorganizations had been conducted in the district with no significant savings from central office head count reductions. This time, the superintendent made it clear through meetings with district executives and memorandums to central office staff, that all positions were being evaluated and everyone had to be selected for a position. In other words, no one was safe. Through proactive communication to all district employees—in addition to out-front leadership of the district's senior team, who first embraced the change themselves—the district executed the reorganization successfully.

Several other factors helped the district succeed. First, there was significant momentum around the larger transformation effort and the recommendations from the commission. Second, the superintendent and team recognized that for the transformation to succeed, they had to rethink how the organization was structured. In short, the ability to address the needs of the campuses quickly was an important outcome of the transformation process. Third, there was strong leadership: The setting and achieving of targets was no simple task. Managers can always justify the need for more positions and more people.

Without strong leadership to enforce the design parameters, the process can result in an entirely new organization with no financial benefits from the process. This district was able to preserve the value of the process by not letting skeptics prevail. Ultimately, the district's students will be the winners. It is often said that districts fail to put students before the adults. However, this process is an example of students' concerns coming before adults' issues.

IN CLOSING

The examples in this chapter point to areas for large potential cost savings and efficiencies, but identification and realization of these savings is far from easy. These savings opportunities are most pronounced in purchasing costs and personnel costs associated with small spans of control and multiple layers of management and decision making.

Also, the examples share some themes related to creating the right conditions for success in pursuing and achieving cost and efficiency gains for the purpose of improving student achievement and outcomes. The following conditions were evident during the course of our work: strong leadership; close collaboration among the consulting team, client team, and key stakeholders; and rigorous attention to implementation details, including a detailed plan (with commitments to tasks, timelines, and capable initiative owners) and active change management.

Strong leadership is a necessary condition for success, given the emotional response that often comes with cost efficiency and reduction initiatives. Leaders and their direct reports must clearly and frequently communicate the case for change to the organization. They must stand firm by decisions in the face of multiple debates not supported by facts. Last, they must be able to guide and motivate the organization through difficult periods that have the potential for very sharp declines in morale.

Moreover, close collaboration between the BCG and client teams—as well as the multitude of presentations, group meetings, and surveys to engage key stakeholders—was critical to success. The development of targets and plans could lead to significant impact with minimal disruption only when constructed collaboratively with those driving the changes and with input from those affected by the changes.

In addition, rigorous attention to implementation details led to the realization of savings. For such efforts, BCG is typically engaged to develop a detailed implementation road map and to structure and lead a program management office (PMO) to ensure that rigorous tracking is followed and course corrections are made in a timely manner when necessary. Implementation rigor also includes active change management, which is necessary to be sure that cost and efficiency improvements do not regress to historical conditions over time. In our work, we focus on specific steps designed to ensure that necessary change is embedded in the organization to achieve sustainable results. These steps include routinely collecting and acting on feedback from those driving and impacted by the changes; aligning budgets, evaluations, and incentive plans to the core change objectives (e.g., cost-savings targets); and coaching managers and change agents to be effective communicators of the change effort throughout implementation. With these elements in place, the identification, planning, and realization of cost efficiencies and savings are well within reach.

8

Investing in Improvement— Strategy and Resource Allocation in Public School Districts

Stacey Childress

IN A CLASSIC *Harvard Business Review* article in 1963, Peter Drucker proposed that the job of effective managers has three components: analyzing available opportunities to produce results and developing an understanding of their costs; committing resources to pursue the most promising opportunities; and, when some activities lead to results and others do not, deciding which should receive more resources and which should be abandoned altogether.[1] Drucker described the third component as the "most painful step."

Leaders of public school districts face challenges that make it difficult for them to follow Drucker's advice. Their operating environments are largely void of the market forces that reward a company's success with more capital and exert pressure on it to eventually abandon unproductive activities. Instead, district leaders must raise investment capital and increase revenue through a political process that requires them to convince taxpayers, the majority of whom do not have children currently in the schools, to vote for higher property taxes and approve the issuance of municipal bonds. This process is complicated by the fact that their various stakeholders disagree about the purpose of education and how to define and measure success. State accountability systems have helped but not solved this problem.

Stakeholders also wield political power that shapes internal decisions about how money is spent. Unions, parents groups, and state and local politicians can all influence decisions about which activities will be funded and at what level. As a result, district leaders often make decisions based on political considerations rather than organizational effectiveness. District leaders have plenty of ideas for improving performance, but when they launch these new initiatives, they often leave the old ones in place. This practice is financially possible as long as revenue grows faster than inflation and negotiated increases in compensation. The net effect is layer upon layer of activities, many of which have little going for them but the fact that they exist. Shutting them down would require releasing or reassigning employees and changing the services received by some students whose parents are strong advocates for the existing arrangements. Rather than jeopardize support for their initiatives by antagonizing powerful stakeholders, superintendents invest in their new ideas without disrupting existing programs. They rarely take Drucker's most painful step.

But what happens when the growth of annual revenue decelerates even as compensation and benefits costs increase? After years of increased spending, the rate of growth in many district budgets began to slow in 2006.[2] By 2009, with a global recession in full swing, most districts faced actual reductions in year-over-year spending, many of them for the first time in two decades. Since there was no longer enough money to go around for the layers of activities that could exist when budgets were growing, districts could no longer avoid decisions about which activities to abandon.

Because district leaders have not developed a habit of weighing the relative impact of various activities so that they can starve ineffective ones in order to feed promising ones, many of them simply reduce every line item by the same percentage in order to be "fair." Another popular approach is to make deep cuts to centralized support services so that schools can maintain spending levels, but without rigorous analysis to support these cuts as the most effective way to drive results while reducing spending. The magnitude of the current shortfalls makes it impossible to continue on this path.

This chapter describes the strategic resource decisions in three of the twenty public school districts that colleagues and I have studied through the Public Education Leadership Project at Harvard University (PELP).[3] The stories in San Francisco, New York City, and Montgomery County, Maryland, took place largely before the districts faced dramatic decreases in revenues, though they do show the superintendents facing budget concerns near the end of the narratives. Even so, the situations share common principles that superintendents and their leadership teams can use to make differentiated resource decisions: reducing spending in some areas and increasing it in others with a clear rationale for why these decisions will produce results for students. As a frame for the cases, the next section provides an overview of a stream of resource allocation research from the management literature that highlights some of the challenges present in the three cases as well as in many other districts.

RESOURCE ALLOCATION IN THE MANAGEMENT LITERATURE

For more than fifteen years, some education advocates have pushed for the wholesale decentralization of resource decisions to school principals and away from central offices. Their arguments have been bolstered by a number of researchers, most notably William Ouchi.[4] Ouchi studied subsets of schools in ten districts that were attempting different versions of decentralization. He found a positive correlation between how much control principals had over their budgets and how much their student performance improved. He did not compare the rate of improvement in these districts to a sample of similar schools in other more centralized districts; nor did he address whether this approach led to a reduction in the persistent gaps in performance between higher- and lower-performing schools or between student groups. Nonetheless, Ouchi and other advocates use the findings to frame a binary choice about who should control spending: out-of-touch central bureaucrats who inefficiently squander resources or entrepreneurial instructional leaders who make optimal decisions for their students. This starkly drawn caricature fails to capture the realities of resource allocation in a complex organization, a topic researchers have been studying in other industries for forty years.

In the late 1960s, management scholar Joseph Bower conducted a two-year study of National Products to understand how the company committed resources to support its strategy. In 1970 he published his findings in his seminal book *Managing the Resource Allocation Process*.[5] The conventional wisdom at the time was that senior executives developed strategy at the top and then implemented it by calculating the net present value of major projects proposed by field managers, only approving the projects that promised the highest returns on investment. Bower found something quite different at National Products. The company's strategy was actually shaped organically when frontline and middle managers used their own authority to commit resources to various small and medium-sized projects. These managers' decisions were more dependent on their individual motives, the systems of rewards and consequences that affected them, and the company's prior commitments than on the CEO's proclamations about the corporate strategy. As a result, the company had trouble implementing its intended strategy and meeting firmwide performance targets. Bower described this as a problem that could not be solved with a formula in the corporate financial office or by frontline managers acting independently. His findings were replicated by management scholars across three decades in domestic and international firms of various types (integrated, multibusiness, product, service, public agency, etc.).[6] In 2005, Bower said that these subsequent studies confirmed that "the problem of shaping a bottom-up pattern of committing scarce capital to a purpose formulated by top management [taxes] the leadership of private and public organizations of all shapes and forms."[7]

This literature is focused primarily on capital investments aimed at increasing the productive capacity of the firm, such as building a new manufacturing plant. The strategic resource decisions in the school districts we studied in PELP were largely programmatic operating expenses rather than capital investments, but their general intent was the same: to increase the capacity of the system to produce results. These districts faced the same tensions discussed in the resource allocation literature. Superintendents and their leadership teams developed strategies to improve performance, usually with the support of their school boards. Some strategies were quite ambitious, and some even included performance goals, but they were rarely concrete and usually did not specify interim benchmarks. Resources seldom lined up with the aggressive plans and vague goals. Decisions about staffing and other expenses were distributed across multiple schools, regions, and central office departments, making it difficult to mobilize concerted action to implement the strategy and reach objectives.

In many districts, this distributed approach to resource allocation was deliberate, based on the assumption that professionals closest to the action would make the best spending decisions. Even so, superintendents and their senior teams continued to control the majority of spending, even in districts that Ouchi touts as most decentralized. For example, New York City principals controlled 85 percent of their school-level budgets in 2008, by far the largest percentage of any big city district in the United States. However, only half of all New York City spending resides at the school level. Various central office and school support functions control the other half. As budgets shrink, it is imperative that the decisions about centralized resources become more strategic in order to drive performance. The resource allocation literature identifies at least three situations in which top-down decisions about resources can add value to an organization, even when field managers have significant budget autonomy:[8]

1. The cost of an opportunity that will benefit the whole organization is larger than the budget authority of frontline or middle managers.[9]
2. Current investors and customers like things as they are and therefore have few incentives to provide additional resources for new activities.[10]
3. Disinvestment from existing activities is required, but meaningful incentives exist for decentralized decision makers to continue funding them.[11]

In the remainder of this chapter I describe attempts in three districts to align resource allocation with a strategic direction by employing a mix of school-level decisions and centralized action consistent with these three circumstances.

STRATEGY AND RESOURCE ALLOCATION IN THREE DISTRICTS

The cases that follow describe three superintendents' efforts to improve performance at scale in San Francisco, Montgomery County, and New York City. The stories highlight changes in district resource allocation processes and the activist role each superintendent played in funding strategic activities while cutting off resources to others.

San Francisco STAR Schools Initiative

In the summer of 2000, the San Francisco Unified School District's (SFUSD) board of education appointed Arlene Ackerman superintendent of schools.[12] SFUSD had operated under a consent decree managed by a federal judge since 1983, which required the district to meet educational equity targets for all students. And so on her arrival, Ackerman appointed an educational equity committee to advise her on how to meet the requirements of the consent decree. The committee found that the achievement gaps between African American and Latino students and their white and Chinese counterparts were widening. After controlling for student and school characteristics in ten years of standardized test data, the committee demonstrated that African American and Latino students as a group scored lower than other ethnic groups regardless of poverty levels. The educational equity committee also reported that many schools used a "dumbed-down" curriculum for these students. The committee put forth recommendations to address these findings, which Ackerman incorporated into a districtwide strategy for improvement dubbed Excellence for All. The strategy eliminated attendance zones in favor of citywide school choice and gave principals and school teams budget autonomy in exchange for greater accountability for results.

To implement Excellence for All at the school level, SFUSD developed a weighted student formula (WSF) that attached a variable dollar amount to every student based on his or her learning needs. Before the WSF schools received resources in the form of staff head counts based on projected student enrollment. Under the new model, principals received revenue allocations based on the students who actually enrolled and created their own academic plans to use those resources to serve their particular students. In other words, they would get money instead of bodies.

Even though Excellence for All was a comprehensive strategy, Ackerman and her team believed that the district needed to adapt it to the needs of chronically underperforming schools. The team created a program called Students and Teachers Achieving Results (STAR) with a goal to increase student achievement at underperforming schools by providing targeted interventions at the school sites. STAR had a broad set of criteria that qualified schools for entry, and thirty-nine elementary, middle, and high schools entered the program in fall of 2001. The goal of STAR was to increase school, principal, parent, student, and teacher capacity simultaneously. The team created a concept model that mapped the cause-and-effect links between each part of the intervention and improved outcomes (see figure 8.1).

By mapping the links between the proposed design features of the STAR strategy and expected outputs and outcomes, the team got a better handle on where resources would be best deployed. They funded six additional full- and part-time positions at each STAR school: an instructional reform facilitator (IRF), a long-term substitute, a parent liaison, a student behavior adviser in elementary and middle schools, a nurse, and a learning support consultant (coach). The overall cost of the STAR intervention carried by the central office was approximately $9.5 million. Approximately 70 percent of the total was paid for out of state categorical funds, with nearly $4.7 million coming from consent decree money and $1.9 million from a state initiative called Economic Impact Aid. The remaining 30 percent, around

FIGURE 8.1

STAR schools initiative concept model

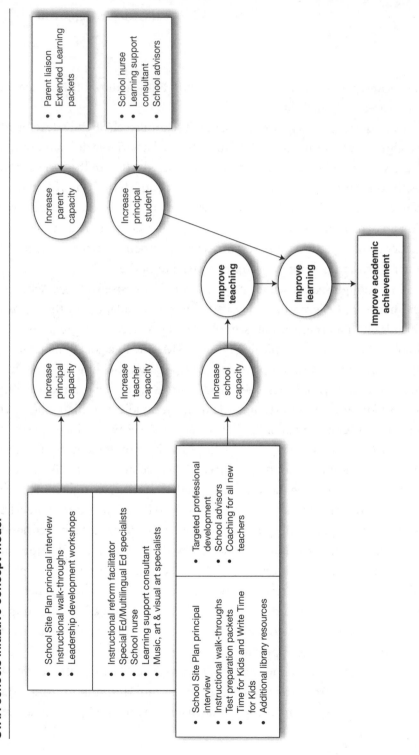

Source: Adapted from "The STAR Schools Initiative at San Francisco Unified School District," PEL–039 (Harvard Business School Publishing, 2006), Exhibit 5, p. 22.

$2.8 million, was funded through creative use of existing federal Title I dollars. The district raised no new funds for the strategy. Rather, it cut spending on other activities, such as outside program providers, curricular materials, professional development tied to previous interventions in low-income schools, as well as a number of administrative positions at central office focused on compliance functions. Resources freed by these cuts were used to fund the STAR strategy. On top of the standard revenue allocation that all schools received through the WSF, the thirty-nine schools that qualified received a WSF STAR Bonus that totaled $431 per student. All other STAR expenses were carried on the central office budget. Table 8.1 provides three representative examples of the scale of the resource increase at STAR schools.

As table 8.1 shows, schools saw significant percentage increases through the WSF STAR Bonus and expenses carried at central office. But why mix resource allocation methods so soon after winning approval to shift from the old staffing ratios method to the weighted student formula? Why not load all of the extra resources into the WSF STAR Bonus and send unrestricted dollars to schools based on their student enrollments?

The theory of action that drove the Excellence for All strategy was based on the assumption that adults closest to students could and would make the best instructional and resource decisions *if* they had the proper supports. Ackerman often said, "If low-performing schools knew how to fix themselves, they would do it." Because she and her team had developed a role-driven theory about how to improve their worst schools, they believed that it was best to mandate those roles and for the central office to take on the expenses they represented. Even if individual principals could make good decisions about how to deploy their WSF revenues in their own schools, they were not well-positioned to learn from what their colleagues were doing in other schools. Because the IRF position resided in the school but was funded and supported centrally, district leaders believed the central office was better positioned to learn from all thirty-nine IRFs and spread the practices across other schools to foster more rapid improvement.

TABLE 8.1

Representative impact of STAR Initiative on school resources, 2006

	Glen Park K–5	Sheridan K–5	Galileo 9–12
School-level revenue			
Student enrollment	294	216	2,100
Regular wsf allocation	$1,306,691	$964,647	$7,673,139
Wsf star bonus ($431/student)	$126,714	$93,096	$905,100
Total wsf allocation	$1,433,405	$1,057,743	$8,578,239
	–	–	–
Star expenses carried at central office			
Instructional reform facilitator	$74,217	$74,217	$74,217
Site support sub(s)	$40,017	$40,017	$80,034
Parent liaision (0.5 FTE)	$26,130	$26,130	$26,130
Elementary/middle school advisor	$13,780	$13,780	$0
Art/music/planning time for 4th and 5th grade	$37,109	$37,109	$0
Learning support consultant	$43,349	$36,125	$0
School nurse	$34,466	$34,466	$0
Test prep. packets	$588	$432	$10,010
Monthly library books	$935	$935	$662
Home/school learning packets	$2,058	$1,512	$10,800
Time for kids ($5/student)	$1,470	$1,080	$0
	$274,119	**$265,802**	**$201,853**
Percentage increase due to star resources	**30.68%**	**37.21%**	**14.43%**

Source: Adapted from "The STAR Schools Initiative at San Francisco Unified School District," PEL-039 (Harvard Business School Publishing, 2006), Exhibit 8, p. 26.

From 2002 to 2006, SFUSD's current expenditures decreased from approximately $487 million to $470 million, a compound annual growth rate of nearly –1 percent; but with enrollment declines, per-pupil spending was virtually flat at $8,309 in 2002 and $8,357 in 2006. Even though current expenses were projected to decrease further to $462 million in 2007, SFUSD still faced a shortfall due to declining enrollment and increased costs related to a new teachers' contract that the school board negotiated in 2006, which committed the district to more than $19 million in new annual spending beginning in 2007. After significant reductions in central office and noninstructional expenses, SFUSD still faced a shortfall of $5 million on its estimated $462 million operating budget, so district leaders explored options to further cut spending to cover the teacher salary increases. Because the STAR program accounted for $9.5 million each year, the team began to consider ways to reduce the program's supports in order to achieve the budget targets. Armed with survey data which showed that principals and teachers overwhelmingly cited the IRF and long-term substitute roles as the most effective parts of the intervention, district leaders considered reducing STAR resources, preserving these two positions as core to the strategy. When teachers and principals learned of the possible reductions, there was an outcry. As one teacher put it, "We accomplished the growth because of the extra money, because of the professional development, and the IRF position. If they take the resources away after we've progressed so much, it's almost like we're getting punished—these things helped us get where we are. If they take them away, it's like we're back at square one." A principal added, "Outside experts look at a program like STAR and think it's about reallocating and using resources differently. True, but it's also about more resources. STAR is designed well . . . but I just want to go on the record and say that part of our performance problem in the past was too few resources."

During the budget discussions, Ackerman left the district under pressure from her board, but an interim superintendent maintained STAR for 2006–2007, in part because twelve schools performed well enough to graduate from the initiative that year, thereby reducing the cost of the overall intervention. Over time, the district stopped funding parts of the strategy that it deemed less important and continued investments in IRFs, the nurses and parent liaisons, and the STAR Bonus. Every year a few schools performed well enough to graduate, while others were added to the program. As of the 2009–2010 school year, the strategy was still in place.

Montgomery County Public Schools' Red Zone/Green Zone Approach[13]

Serving 140,000 with a budget of $2 billion, Montgomery County borders Washington, DC, and is Maryland's largest and most affluent county. But in addition to the older, established neighborhoods and new upscale subdivisions, there are also deep pockets of poverty. The makeup of the student population in the county schools has changed dramatically over the last three decades, with the percentage of white students dropping from more than 80 percent to 40 percent and the Hispanic and African-American student population growing to represent approximately 45 percent of total enrollment. When Superintendent Jerry Weast arrived in Montgomery County Public Schools (MCPS) in 1999, the district had a strong reputation for quality. But along with the big demographic shifts, board members and community leaders were faced with the troubling reality that, along with some of the best schools in the country, Montgomery County had many schools that performed at levels similar to some of the lowest-performing urban schools in the country. The board hired Weast to create a new reality in which all students in the district had access to a great education.

Because of residential patterns, low-income and minority students were concentrated in particular areas of the county. Reading and math proficiency rates for schools in these areas were twenty to thirty-five points lower than schools in more affluent parts of the county. Describing the situation, Weast said, "The only thing we could predict was failure, and with a great deal of consistency. We could also predict who would fail because the evidence didn't show any . . . systemic approach to raising the level of education in our high poverty schools." As a first step, district leaders created two zones and labeled one Red and the other Green. Each zone accounted for roughly the same number of students but had significantly different demographics. Students in the Green Zone were predominantly white and came from middle-to-high-income families; those in the Red Zone were mostly African American, Hispanic, or recent immigrants and low income. In fact, with similar demographics, the Red Zone was larger than the public school districts in Atlanta, Boston, Denver, San Francisco, and Washington, DC (table 8.2).

Dividing MCPS into two zones did more than highlight the correlation between low-performing schools and high-minority populations; it formed the foundation of MCPS's strategy. Because predictable perfor-

TABLE 8.2
MCPS Red Zone/Green Zone demographics, 2009

	Red Zone	Green Zone
Enrollment	70,500	70,500
Minority	80%	43%
ESL	30%	10%
Free/Reduced Meals	51%	12%

Source: Childress, Stacey. "Six Lessons for Pursuing Excellence and Equity at Scale," Phi Delta Kappan, November 2009, vol. 91 no. 3, 13–18.

mance variability between student groups (and geographic regions) was the problem, the MCPS team believed that differentiation was the solution. The district set out to reduce variability in performance by allocating different levels of resources to schools in the Red and Green zones.

In order to garner support for this method of resource allocation, district leaders proposed a new way of thinking about equity: equity does not mean equal resources; it means equal opportunity. Unequal treatment was required to provide equal opportunity: more money, more talent, and more time were essential if the Red Zone students could be expected to rapidly meet the same standards as Green Zone students. In the past, MCPS had allocated resources equally across all schools based on enrollment numbers regardless of need or performance. In a series of community meetings in the fall of 1999, Weast explained the theory of unequal resource allocation, making the case that the Red Zone needed more time, better-trained teachers, and smaller class sizes to level the playing field. A number of parents in wealthier parts of the county did not like the idea of moving resources from the more advantaged schools their children attended to the low-performing schools. They were concerned that their children would be short-changed in the process and that performance across the district would go down. In part, the district's message hinged on doing "the right thing" for kids, but Weast also stressed the concept of a school district brand: good schools mean good neighborhoods, and good schools are good for property values. Improving schools in less affluent neighborhoods would be good for the whole county. Building sufficient (though not universal) support from Green Zone parents allowed the district to invest disproportionately in Red Zone schools.

District leaders believed their efforts would be diluted in trying to attack every grade at once, so they decided to focus first on early elementary literacy coupled with access to high school Advanced Placement (AP) and honors courses. The two were strongly linked—an internal research report found a high correlation between third-grade literacy proficiency and high school honors course enrollment. The correlation was equally strong across all four major racial and ethnic groups in MCPS. Based on this data, the team decided that one effective way to change achievement patterns predicted by race and income was to implement reform at both ends of the K–12 continuum, with emphasis on the neediest schools. Mapping backward from high school, the district set benchmarks for achievement starting in kindergarten that would prepare children for higher-level coursework through the next twelve grades. Weast explained the motivation for the approach: "We knew that if we did this right, we could push the capacity for higher achievement, grade by grade, and shut down the argument that children would not be ready."

The first wave of reforms was launched in sixty elementary schools in the Red Zone, which served 75 percent of the district's English language learner (ELL) population, 80 percent of all elementary students receiving free and reduced-price meals, 78 percent of the district's Hispanic students, and 70 percent of the African American elementary school students.

The district created full-day kindergartens and reduced class sizes in kindergarten through second grade. Called the Early Success Performance Plan, structural and curricular reforms at the focus schools were all aligned with the goal of improving third-grade literacy. Kindergarten class sizes were reduced to a student-teacher ratio of 15:1. MCPS invested in new kindergarten curricula and assessments and established a benchmark for kindergarten reading that was much more rigorous than what had previously been expected of kindergarteners. Other investments expanded instructional time without lengthening the school day through class size reductions and new requirements for time spent on certain content areas. The student-to-teacher ratio for first and second grades was reduced to 17:1, and reading instruction for all students was increased to ninety minutes, with students reading below grade level receiving an additional forty-five to sixty minutes of daily literacy instruction. Investments in teacher knowledge and skill were critical to the conversion, and the district eventually spent $50 million annually on targeted professional development to support the strategy.

The annual spending per student in 2000 was around $11,000. Eventually, the Green Zone "subsidized" the Red Zone by $2,000 per student annually. There were no actual transfer payments between zones—Green Zone spending did not decrease to pay for Red Zone increases—but the resource imbalance was real. Growth in Green Zone spending slowed significantly to permit new investments in the Red Zone. Between 2000 and 2008, overall per-student spending grew from $11,000 to $14,000. But Red Zone spending increased to $15,000 per student, while Green Zone spending only reached $13,000. Inflation during this period grew at 2.83 percent, with the Green Zone growing more slowly at 2.11 percent and the Red Zone growing markedly faster at 3.95 percent.

As long as revenue increased every year, the leadership team could invest disproportionately in the Red Zone without reducing resources in the Green Zone. In the spring of 2009, MCPS faced a $100 million revenue shortfall against projected expenses for the following academic year. As senior executives and board members were considering major cuts to core pieces of the strategy to balance the budget without alienating important stakeholders, the leaders of the district's three employees' unions brought a proposal to their members to defer $89 million in negotiated compensation in order to preserve investments in the strategy. As members of the superintendent's cabinet, the union presidents had helped craft the strategy and saw themselves as partners in the district's results. Many of the investments were in people (that is, union members), and deep cuts would have resulted in layoffs. The measure passed overwhelmingly and MCPS was able to maintain funding and staffing levels in both zones for the 2010 academic year. In November 2009, union leaders were again at the table with board members and district leaders searching for an additional $100 million in cuts, with all parties committed to preserving the investments in the Red Zone. Together, the multistakeholder teams working on the budget are attempting to ake Drucker's most painful step as effectively as possible.

New York City Department of Education: Funding the Autonomy/Accountability Exchange

Serving more than one million students in approximately 1,500 schools with an operating budget of $17 billion, the New York City school system was the largest in the United States in 2008. After thirty-two years of joint governance between thirty-two locally elected boards and a seven-member board appointed citywide by the mayor and five borough presidents, the system came under Mayor Giuliani's full control in 2000.[14] Michael Bloomberg inherited the schools when he became mayor in January 2002, and the following July he appointed Joel Klein as the system's new chancellor. Following a series of community engagement meetings during his first year, Klein unveiled the Children First reform agenda, named to show his commitment to putting the interests of "children first, not politics or bureaucracy."

The early years of Children First focused mainly on regaining control of what Klein described as a "chaotic and dysfunctional organizational structure." Klein noted that his administration's "first task was to lock the system down, establish some control, and bring coherence to the system." Klein grouped the thirty-two community districts into ten regional offices designed to support schools' operational and instructional needs. Using the regional offices to enforce standards and implement reforms, the DOE instituted a common math and literacy curriculum for grades K–8, ended social promotion, created 150 small schools to replace large failing high schools, and added math and literacy coaches as well as a parent coordinator position to every school.

Two years after establishing the regional offices, Klein's Children First message began shifting from regional control to school-level empowerment. The refined Children First strategy included three pillars of reform:

leadership, empowerment, and accountability. Klein remarked, "Our reform strategy is premised on the core belief that strong school leaders who are empowered to build and support teams and make instructional and managerial decisions and who are prepared to be held accountable for student performance will result in high-functioning schools."

As did Ackerman in San Francisco, Klein believed that if competent principals who were closest to the problems were empowered, then they would make better decisions about resources and academic programs than the central office could on their behalf. In order for empowerment to be effective, Klein also believed that principals needed to be held accountable for student performance.

> If we empower principals and hold them accountable for school results, we'll do two things—shift the locus of power from central office to the schools, and shift the organizational culture to a focus on results. However, I know that autonomy in and of itself is not going to guarantee success. But it will lead to innovation. And I suspect that if we're tight on accountability and instill an intense focus on student outcomes, we can also build into the equation some variability in terms of problem solving at the school level and learn from it.

Implementation of the autonomy for accountability exchange required a major overhaul of the resource allocation process along with investments in mechanisms to support the accountability and learning functions Klein described. Among the resource shifts that accompanied the strategy, two were especially emblematic of Klein's efforts to align resources with the autonomy/accountability exchange: Fair Student Funding (FSF) and a multifaceted accountability system.

In 2007, the New York City Department of Education (NYCDOE) implemented a new formula for allocating resources to schools. Similar to San Francisco's WSF, the FSF was designed to differentiate per-student spending by attaching dollars to students based on a number of learning characteristics. The change served two purposes. First, if principals were to be accountable for their students' learning, then it was critical that they receive resources based on their students' learning needs. Differential resources flowed to schools based on actual enrollment so that principals could create their academic plans and budgets in ways that were more responsive to their specific students' needs. Second, under the old allocation system, schools in more affluent neighborhoods spent more per student than schools in less affluent neighborhoods. By weighting the resources based on student characteristics, the district aimed to achieve more equitable school budgets.

Of the total $16.9 billion in 2008 spending, school budgets accounted for $8.7 billion. Approximately two-thirds of this was allocated through the FSF, with the balance allocated in lump sums according to categorical formulas such as federal Title I and state special education funds. Because of other changes aimed at increasing principal autonomy (for example, decoupling teacher seniority from hiring), principals controlled approximately 85 percent of the spending in their schools, the highest percentage of any large district committed to principal autonomy.[15] The 693 schools that were considered underfunded before the FSF received an additional $110 million under the new system. The NYCDOE decided to limit losses in schools that were considered overfunded before the FSF in order to protect them from significant decreases. These "hold harmless" concessions for 661 schools cost the district $237 million, more than twice the cost of increasing funding for disadvantaged schools. Because of these decisions, the resource imbalance between schools was not fully rectified in the first two years of the FSF.[16]

As the NYCDOE redesigned the allocation process to support principal autonomy, it also made systemwide investments in new accountability mechanisms from the top. Implemented in 2007, the accountability system included several components that required significant investments: progress reports, learning environment surveys, quality reviews, inquiry teams, and performance bonuses. The progress reports were published every year and awarded each school a letter grade A through F based on student achievement data and evaluations from parents, teachers, and students of its learning environment. Each school received an annual quality review, a visit from an outside reviewer who used a common rubric to assess the school's ability to use student data to improve instruction. Each school was also required to have an inquiry team, a group of teachers who worked together to diagnose and respond to the learning needs of students who were outside their "sphere of success." Depending on a school's performance on its progress report, the principal and teachers could receive performance bonuses. All of these costs, totaling $54.7 million in 2008, were carried by the central office rather than being devolved to school budgets.

In addition, the NYCDOE spent $80 million on outside contractors over three years to build the technical infrastructure to support the accountability mechanisms. The Achievement Reporting and Information System (ARIS) had a broader scope than accountability alone, but most observers, including the New York City Independent Budget Office, considered the capital and operating expenses related to the IT system part of the new accountability spending. Most of the funding to build ARIS came from private sources, such as the Fund for Public Schools, and did not require reallocation away from other activities.

FSF and accountability are clear examples of thinking about resource allocation from the bottom-up and top-down as an integral part of a strategy to improve performance. Both initiatives required significant political capital and reallocation that could only be mobilized at the top. From 2002 to 2008, the NYCDOE operating budget grew from $11 billion to $16 billion, funded mostly through increased allocations from state revenues and the city budget. Faced with a revenue shortfall for the 2010 annual budget, key elements of the accountability/autonomy exchange came under intense budget pressure. Even after a round of central office cuts and new revenue from the 2009 federal stimulus package, the shortfall for 2010 was estimated at approximately $400 million. After trimming school budgets by an average of 3 percent, the district still faced a shortfall of almost $200 million.

Klein implemented a freeze on hiring teachers from outside the district, which meant that principals were required to fill open positions with teachers who were in the "excess pool" because they had been unable to land positions in schools. As part of the autonomy/accountability exchange, Klein had allowed principals to hire candidates from inside or outside the district and without regard to seniority. To make this work, Klein had been willing to pay tenured teachers principals would not hire their full salaries even though they were not working in classrooms. This decision has reportedly cost the district as much as $200 million annually, which Klein was willing to cover centrally to meet his commitments to principals.[17] But in the face of a nearly $200 million gap after meaningful cuts had been made elsewhere, paying more than one thousand teachers for not working while hiring others from outside the system was no longer tenable at that scale.

Principals, however, appeared to be resisting Klein's requirement to hire from the pool. In mid-September 2009, two weeks into the new school year, schools still had 1,100 teacher vacancies, even though there were 1,500 teachers in the excess pool, suggesting that principals would rather leave a spot unfilled than hire a teacher they did not want. In a letter to principals on September 16, Klein set a deadline of October 30 for principals to fill the openings from the excess pool or lose funding for the positions. Klein asserted that these measures were necessary to "control costs." "Nobody dislikes this situation more than I do," Klein wrote to principals. "Limiting your hiring freedom goes against what I stand for, but because of the economic reality we must control costs and protect our schools from deeper budget cuts."[18] Klein faced and was willing to take Drucker's most painful step. In November 2009, the NYCDOE began reducing school budgets to account for the loss of open teaching slots principals had refused to fill from the excess pool.

A FRAMEWORK FOR ACHIEVING COHERENCE BETWEEN STRATEGY AND RESOURCE ALLOCATION

The cases of San Francisco, Montgomery County, and New York City share many common elements. One obvious similarity is that the superintendents had a clear strategy for improvement in place *before* they faced budget challenges. It is true that budgets grew in MCPS and NYC during the period examined in the cases, but per-pupil spending in NYC grew slower than the rate of inflation, and spending in San Francisco actually contracted in nominal and real terms. Spending per pupil in MCPS grew a bit faster in the early years than in the later years. Revenue reductions hit San Francisco by 2005 and MCPS and NYC in 2008, requiring the superintendents to protect key initiatives by cutting spending on activities that were less central to their strategies (see table 8.6). Even before the revenue reductions, each leader prioritized resource allocation as a critical component of implementing their strategy through the WSF, Red Zone/Green Zone, and FSF mechanisms. These changes were not driven by financial pressures but, rather, by a strategic insight about how to use existing resources more effectively to drive results for students.

When budget challenges did emerge, the leaders had a clear rationale for making cuts that could be explained in terms of the existing strategy. The cuts were not easy or popular, but they were defensible based on the theories of action at work in each city. Developing a strategy and allocating resources coherently might sound like common sense, but the examples highlighted in this chapter are not common practice. Of the twenty districts we studied in the Public Education Leadership Project , we saw evidence of this approach in only a few, including those in this chapter. In this final section, I describe a framework I developed with PELP colleagues to help others understand how leaders such as Ackerman, Weast, and Klein develop and implement effective strategies. The chapter closes with three recommendations for putting the ideas into practice.

The PELP Coherence Framework operates from the inside-out, prioritizing the teaching and learning that happens in the instructional core as the most important work in a school or district (see figure 8.2).

Leaders should develop a theory of action about how to maximize student learning and implement the theory through a strategy that is based on clear cause-and-effect relationships. In San Francisco and New York City, the superintendents believed that if principals had control over resources that flowed to them based on their students' needs, then they would make better decisions than would the central office given the proper incentives and supports. In Montgomery County, Weast's theory was a little different. He believed that if the central office distributed more resources to the

FIGURE 8.2
PELP coherence framework

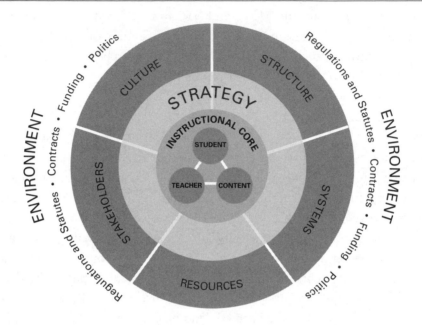

Source: Stacey Childress, Richard Elmore, and Allen Grossman, "Note on the PELP Coherence Framework," PEL-010, Harvard Business School Publishing, 2005.

struggling schools that needed them most and mandated K–12 standards and curriculum, then principals would adapt their schools' delivery of the curriculum to meet the standards even though their control over spending did not increase significantly. The basic premise of the framework is that district teams should organize various elements of the district to support the effective implementation of the strategy. The vignettes in this chapter focus specifically on the leaders' resource decisions, but they were working simultaneously in the other areas of the framework as well, redesigning systems and structures, changing the culture, and managing stakeholders. The key is that their actions were guided by an overarching strategy that was based in a cause-and-effect logic. This is sound advice for other district leaders. Three additional recommendations based on evidence from the cases focus specifically on resource decisions:

1. *Your strategy must be backed by a resource plan. If it is not, you don't have a strategy.* The three leaders from the cases saw resource allocation as a key part of their strategy rather than as a secondary set of choices. Each leader identified resource disparities as one of the root causes of the problem he or she was trying to solve. The animating assumption behind the WSF, FSF, and Green/Red Zone investments was that some students need *more* in order to reach high standards— more time, more support, more attention—all things that cost more money. As described earlier, each also had a clear sense of the causeand-effect relationships between their activities and the outcomes they desired. The concept model in San Francisco is a good illustration of this. These logic models help leaders integrate resource decisions into their strategic intent. When cuts were necessary, these models helped them decide what *not* to do. As Bower's research suggests, without a clear plan for allocating resources, an organization's actual strategy is determined by the uncoordinated decisions of many managers. Ackerman, Weast, and Klein integrated strategy and resource allocation in ways that allowed them to implement their intended strategies more effectively.

2. *Don't get trapped by the decentralization dogma.* Mechanisms such as the WSF and FSF were designed to help optimize performance at the school level by giving differentiated resources and decision-making authority to principals. But each superintendent also made top-down resource decisions to accelerate the strategy, consistent with the circumstances described earlier. When systemic barriers to improvement exist, no single school can make the size of investment required to remove them. Interventions such as mandatory full-day kindergarten in Montgomery County, the creation of the IRF role in San Francisco, and funding the salary of surplus teachers in New York were instrumental to ensuring that system-level capacity was greater than the

sum of the capacities of the individual schools. Similarly, each case
had an example of the power of central decision making when existing customers and investors were happy with the status quo: reducing
spending growth in the MCPS Green Zone, cutting spending on existing programs for low-income schools in San Francisco, dismantling
first the thirty-two and then the ten regions in New York. Each of these
decisions freed up resources for new strategic initiatives. And when
disinvestment was required, the will to abandon spending decisions
for the good of the system was marshaled centrally: deferring pay in
MCPS, the elimination of components of the STAR intervention, and
the change in the surplus teacher policy in New York. Creating a frame
for resource allocation that includes a thoughtful, dynamic blend of
bottom-up and top-down decisions is more likely to maximize performance at the school level as well as systemwide, especially when
revenues decline.

3. *If your strategy requires you to play Robin Hood, don't alienate those
   whose pockets you pick. You might eventually run out of other people's
   money.* As Ackerman, Weast, and Klein sought to optimize system-
   level performance, their resource choices were aimed at adding capacity to struggling schools without reducing capacity at stable or
   high-performing schools. STAR reallocated funds from other pools of
   money for low-income or low-performing schools rather than lowering the WSF for students who attended better-performing schools.
   Spending levels in Montgomery County's Green Zone never decreased.
   In fact, they grew every year to keep up with increases in teacher compensation, but grew slower than inflation rates. The Red Zone grew
   much faster. In New York City, even with the explicit equity goals of
   the FSF, Klein was careful to implement "hold harmless" provisions
   so that well-resourced schools would not experience disproportionate
   cuts to pay for increases in underresourced schools. One interpreta-
   tion of these actions could be that these leaders engaged in the layering
   behavior described at the beginning of the chapter and were unwilling
   to take Drucker's most painful step. Rather than cut old spending to

pay for new initiatives, they simply added more costs. Another way to interpret it, however, is that their decisions were aligned with ethical approaches to narrowing achievement gaps. Skeptics sometimes worry that districts will lower performance at the top so that closing gaps will be easier. My observations of districts around the country have produced no evidence of intentional behavior of this sort. Districts strive to raise performance for students at the top while accelerating performance even faster for students at the bottom, and Ackerman, Weast, and Klein attempted to make system-level resource decisions that were consistent with this aspiration. And politically, the optics of cutting costs in affluent, high-tax-bracket neighborhoods in order to increase costs in less-affluent, low-tax-bracket neighborhoods could derail the overall goals and strategy in these districts. The ongoing fragility of the Green Zone/Red Zone compact in Montgomery County is a testament to this challenge. When real revenue reductions occur, it is likely that cuts to activities that serve more affluent families will follow. If leaders alienate these stakeholders with their approaches to resource allocation when budgets are flush, they will find it even more difficult to preserve key strategic investments during financial crises.

Given the rarity of the strategic approaches to resource allocation described in these pages, it is clear that district leaders need more guidance and tools to help them make better decisions and manage the consequences, particularly when they are under enormous fiscal pressure. This chapter only scratches the surface of these important issues. Ideally, it will be part of a growing body of knowledge about how to allocate scarce resources strategically to maximize student performance.

9

First-Person Tale
of Cost-Cutting Success

Nathan Levenson

Despite declining resources, Arlington, Massachusetts, superintendent Nathan Levenson lead a team of committed administrators and a courageous school board from July 2005 through August 2008 to award-winning growth in academic achievement. The shrinking budget wasn't an obstacle to improvement; rather, it was an instrument of their success. More children learning, however, wasn't enough to calm the political firestorms that accompanied the tough and untraditional financial decisions that were necessary to raise student achievement.

AS I SAT IN THE high school library during the winter of 2005 being grilled by the seventeen-member Superintendent Search Committee, I was struck by how many questions centered on budgets and budgeting. No one asked me about reading instruction, what skills students should master in the twenty-first century, or how to close the achievement gap. But a school board member did ask, "Would you let people know what's in the budget?"

I was a bit disappointed. I had left the business world after twenty years to become a superintendent. I wanted to discuss my theories for accelerating student learning, but the committee only wanted to talk about money. As I moved through subsequent rounds of interviewing, I learned that reading couldn't be improved because "we had to cut reading teachers a few years back," that twenty-first-century skills couldn't be enhanced "because we had no money," and that we didn't know how big the achievement gap was "because we couldn't afford to fund the data analyst." This poverty mentality surprised me because the district spent the state average per pupil and had typical salary scales for a middle-class district. Little did anyone know that finding enough money to fulfill our grandest educational dreams would be easy, that raising student achievement wouldn't be hard, but that navigating budget politics would be fatal.

My MBA from Harvard Business School and experience as the "budget guru" on my hometown school board carried the day. Arlington hired a nontraditional superintendent. The public announcement said I was the man to navigate a tough financial situation and bring new ideas to the district. Privately, people whispered, "This is the end of 'old Arlington rule.'" The town had experienced a demographic shift from predominately middle-class, bluecollar, Irish Catholics who lived in town for generations to now include a mix of young, progressive, urban professionals. Unknown to me, I was the standard-bearer for the "New Arlington."

FIRST, SHOW ME THE MONEY

With contract signatures still damp, I launched a fifty-person listening tour with school committee members, central office staff, curriculum leaders, and principals. Very clear patterns emerged from the conversations.

The school board members were smart, caring, thoughtful, and somewhat lost. There was a desire, but no plan, for moving the district forward. Past fights over small funding disagreements still loomed large, and a desperate want for more resources nagged at them. Collectively they concluded that the district couldn't improve until we found more money.

The administrators had ideas but little hope. They knew exactly how to raise student achievement: provide more and better professional development, align the curriculum between grades, provide intensive intervention for struggling readers, mentor new teachers, and hire content-strong special education staff. Rather than being excited to share their ideas, many found our conversations depressing. Without more money, nothing would change, they told me. Like asking a man stranded on a desert island, "What would you want to eat if you were rescued?" it was merely hypothetical and a bit cruel. I pointed out that what they wanted didn't cost much, maybe $1 million, about 2 percent of our $50 million budget. Every administrator responded with tales of being denied a few thousand dollars for some top priority.

My last stop on the tour was the business office. At this point I thought I knew what to expect—"We have no money." Instead, I learned that we might end the year with a deficit (which is terrible) or we might end the year with a sizable surplus (which isn't much better), so I should prepare for both scenarios and be ready to spend-down any surplus on the last day of the year. I was mystified. With less than six weeks left in the school year, it should have been simple to forecast our ending balance. Yet, for a hundred reasons, no forecast was possible: we didn't have accurate budgets for many line items; purchase orders often get entered late; grants, which offset the operating budget, are handled by a different department and aren't accrued in real time; and so on. This made no sense to me, but I knew I wasn't going to get an answer until the last day of the fiscal year.

The listening tour revealed three truths: the school board didn't have a plan, vision, or strategy, but they did control the budget; the administrators knew what was needed, but no one asked them; and no one, including the superintendent, CFO, and school board, really knew where we spent our money.

THE CORNERSTONE: KNOWING THE PAST AND THE FUTURE

An old Russian proverb teaches, "If you don't know where you are going, any path will take you there." The Arlington Public Schools needed a strategy for raising student achievement. Since the school board had final say on the budget, I focused on them first. I created a best practice boot camp that included holding retreats, attending lectures, and using school board meetings to discuss journal articles. Many of our meetings looked like college seminars, with thought-provoking discussions and the Socratic method.

Within three months, there was broad agreement that standards-based education, a common curriculum, districtwide formative assessments, an unrelenting focus on reading, and sustained, focused professional development would help the students of Arlington. This was a comprehensive, interconnected plan, not a bunch of unrelated programs. The intellectual agreement was strong and deep. I was feeling good.

I was also naive. I had unknowingly fired the first shot in a bruising battle of attrition. The point of creating the strategy was to prioritize our time, energy, and resources. Our limited funds would be focused on the strategy, and administrators would be accountable for implementing the plan. While many lauded this, most failed to understand that, given limited resources, we could not continue to spend money on what *wasn't* critical to the strategy.

As we planned for the future, we also looked back in great detail at prior-year spending. We categorized, researched, clarified, and codified. Because we used purchase orders for all expenses, had a decent in-house payroll system, and tracked grants well, getting the information wasn't hard. Getting people to think strategically, rather than bureaucratically, was harder. For example, unspent textbook funds were used to pay a larger than expected heating bill. I wanted this recorded as "heat," but they put it in "textbooks." And a teacher who had been transferred to the reading department was recorded as "special education" because she still had her office in the special education wing.

The other challenge was creating a meaningful level of detail. Some line items contained only $200, another had $1 million marked "other," and a few combined a half-dozen unrelated programs. Because the business office seldom spoke to frontline staff or building principals, they had to guess where to charge many expenses. It took five months and ten revisions to create a clear, simple-to-understand listing of all prior expenses by activity and program.

SHIFTING FUNDS: WINNERS AND LOSERS

With the strategy in hand, we knew what we needed: more reading teachers, paid mentors, elementary math coaches, a better student information system, a data analyst, and stipends for teachers to develop a common curriculum and districtwide formative assessments. No new money was coming; in fact, over the next few years, inflation-adjusted per-pupil spending was forecasted to decline. There was only one option to implement our plan: we must shift spending from existing efforts.

We had plenty of money. We just weren't spending it on what mattered most to children. I was fortunate to be an outsider, both to Arlington and to education, for I could see where past practice had enshrined costly decisions that did not help kids or support the strategy. But my outsider status was also my curse. I could not see the landmines buried in times past.

The budget review had shone a light on past spending. The results were a bit shocking. We had a few tabloid-type embarrassments, such as $400 spent in overtime every Sunday for a custodian to close a single loose window or a teacher getting paid $1,000 per hour because her program had been cut back but not her work schedule. While wasteful and harmful to morale, this type of squandering didn't add up to a lot.

Good intentions also skewed our resource allocations. Treating everyone "equally" seems fair and is politically safe. No favorites means no enemies. In the Arlington elementary schools, for example, equal meant one reading teacher, one secretary, one nurse, one librarian, and one special education tester per school. Since some schools had twice as many students as others "same" did not seem fair to me. Arlington also had a cultural norm for the "equality of all subjects." This meant that every subject and every department should have roughly equal levels of administration. For example, math and home economics were equal, even though one was a core subject with thirty times as many teachers.

To implement our new strategy, we had to shift funds. That's code for saying, "Cut some existing staff and programs, so that we can add elsewhere." We had lots of possibilities. The first place I looked was the administrative staff. We had far too many noncore-subject department heads. The next target was federal grants. Each grant had an informal "owner," typically either the person who originally applied for the grant or the poor soul charged with filing the paperwork each year. The grant owners treated the funds as their own. While Arlington was meticulous in following the letter of the law, nearly all these funds were fritted away on ineffective programs, secretaries for the grant owners, and nice-to-have irrelevancies. Finally, the poster child of old decisions carried forward was our crossing guards, a small army of lovely women helping kids cross the street on the way to school. Seems great, but more parents were driving or walking their children to school. A study conducted by the police department and two pro bono traffic experts concluded that a third of the crossing guards crossed no children or that no children walked without a parent. Moreover, all the guards worked well beyond the time when children were walking to or from school.

By matching administrative staffing to the size and importance of the department, by redirecting certain grants, and by eliminating crossing guards from the unused routes, we could fund 100 percent of our strategy. I was on the top of the world . . . for a day.

ALL HELL BROKE LOOSE

The administrators who would be going back into the classroom rallied their teachers and told parents this was the first step in eliminating their programs completely. Grant owners, who lost control of their budgets, spread the rumor that I was going to spend the money illegally. The crossing guards screamed, "Children will die!" Week after week, school board meetings were packed with protesters. I was a crook and a baby killer, not a visionary or a financially savvy leader who found a way to make progress despite tough financial times.

As the school board debated the budget, the one thing both supporters and detractors could agree on was that if I had communicated better, there wouldn't be all the outcries. I disagree. I had spent five months laying the groundwork with the school board, the administrators, and the public. More than a dozen televised public meetings were held to explain the need to shift funds. I insisted on and received a half-dozen votes from the school board to bless, months in advance, the areas targeted for cuts and gains. I had shared the plan and how we would fund it in large groups, small groups, and with every individual impacted. The reality is, there is no way to soften the pain of "You are losing your job" or "You are losing your power."

I reminded the school board that this was exactly why they hired someone like me, and if they wanted *our* vision to become reality, they had to support the cuts needed to fund the new efforts. After a little horse trading (the crossing guards stayed, but their hours were cut to match the walking patterns) and much delay, I got all the money we needed. I also got a lot more than I bargained for. The budget debate also laid bare a fundamental divide within the community. Were math, engineering, and reading more important than woodshop, cooking, and free afterschool sports? Should years of service, rather than need, drive which positions are funded? The town was deeply, emotionally split on these questions. The majority favored the changes, but a vocal and sizable minority did not.

The crossing guard decision was my dumbest. It seemed so obvious. Six of the seven school board members ranked rationalizing the crossing guards as their top priority. The police chief and traffic experts created the plan. Hundreds of hours of field observations confirmed we had crossing guards at locations where no children walked without a parent or walked at all. The elementary principals supported the change. Crossing guard absenteeism was so high we couldn't even staff all the locations. We met regularly with the head of the crossing guards to keep them informed and included them on the planning committee.

Yet these sweet (except when hurling insults at me) little old ladies were all multigeneration Arlington residents. They protested the reduction in hours at school board meetings, town meetings, and public gatherings for two years. They unionized. Worst of all, they become a rallying cry for Old Arlington to retake a number of seats on the school board. In the end, I saved a few bucks but lost two school board members—a very bad trade.

I had won the budget battle but feared I might lose the war. Most of my political capital was gone. I made the calculation that raising student achievement significantly would restore peace and refill my spent capital.

After a frenetic summer of planning and training, we had everything we ever wanted come September. Five reading programs had been combined into a single new effort based on the National Reading Panel, with twice the reading staff all trained and fully equipped. We had expanded mentoring, added math and reading coaches, finished developing standards, created common assessments, and targeted our professional development. Scheduling was also revamped in order to put more time behind the strategically important subjects and efforts.

The shackles of poverty thinking had been broken. Most of the administrators now believed anything was possible. We even launched a leadership academy for teachers wanting to become administrators, added fifty stipend teacher leadership positions, and for the first time in ages had ample training and supplies to back the new efforts. There was an energy and determination in the district.

Unfortunately, special education costs were rising quickly, and tax revenue wouldn't cover the raises in the teachers' contract. Another year of budget cutting was coming.

WE, NOT I

After about a year, a subtle shift had taken place in the district. As curriculum became common across the schools, reading centrally managed, and professional development focused on supporting the strategy, many decisions affecting the entire district had to be made by my cabinet. Like most midsized school districts, the principals, curriculum leaders, and my direct reports constituted the superintendent's cabinet. Also like most superintendent's cabinets they were reluctant to speak their mind, listened more than participated, and criticized privately decisions they "supported" during meetings. They were called "the Leadership Team," but it wasn't really a team. It was a group of smart, caring, people who viewed their jobs as protecting their turf. Some harbored ill feelings toward their peers over past battles for money, time, and power. We started meeting with an executive coach to learn how to work as a team and make decisions for the good of the whole rather than in our narrow self-interests. There were tears, airing of old injustices, shouting, an occasional storming from the room, and a few resignations, but finally, after eighteen months, we had a breakthrough. The team, my cabinet, started thinking about the districtwide master plan, not the parochial interests of their own buildings. This dramatically improved the effectiveness of our budgeting, which allowed less funds to achieve more.

Running a school district is a team sport, despite the long tradition of silos, walls, and isolation. Even with the best programs and perfect tools, progress isn't possible until leaders work together. Spending some money on bringing your senior staff together is a great investment. Spending a bit more to facilitate teamwork and coach leaders is a wise use of funds. In the private sector this is common practice. In my former life as a business owner, I had an executive coach for years. Unfortunately, many school boards and administrators view this as wasteful or insulting. It is neither. I am certain that the academic gains we achieved couldn't have happened without investing in team building.

Developing the budget as a team also saved the district millions of dollars and allowed our most effective programs to continue despite a shrinking budget. I needed teamwork to build future budgets for two reasons. First, I had run out of ideas, and, second, I didn't have the political capital to sell any more hard choices on my own. Over the next two years we projected a funding shortfall of about 5 percent of the annual budget, and we wanted another 2 percent for expanding successful initiatives. Yes, I wanted to expand programs during years of budget cuts. The children of Arlington deserved nothing less.

In my cabinet of seventeen administrators, only two had much prior experience with budgeting. In the past, budgets were done to them. They complained, clawed back a bit for their departments or schools, publicly supported the superintendent, and privately groused. I needed them to take the lead, make the decisions, find the savings, and sell the plan. To turn budget development into a team exercise took training, time, and data.

The training covered basic finance, such as where our money comes from, what's driving the deficit, and how to understand detailed budget data. Even more time went to refining our strategy and reading articles about best practices for raising student achievement. No one is going to support laying off staff in their building or department for a plan they don't fully embrace, both intellectually and in their gut. More than fifty hours a year of group meetings were needed for budget training and decision making. You can't rush buy-in. Because our budget discussions constituted a debate of our priorities and of what's working or not, this time enhanced instructional leadership in the district. It wasn't a financial distraction but, rather, a constant focus on teaching and learning.

Without detailed student achievement data and accurate program costs, these would have been fifty useless hours. Without data, each department head loves every program and each principal knows that their staff is overworked. Data changed all that. For example, we shared the results of two secondary intervention programs, one in math and one in English. Personally, I loved the English program, championed it, and lavished resources on it. The math program was, at best, middling, or so I thought. The longitudinal data was striking. Many students skipped the English program altogether. Those who went, reported they liked the program but that their grades weren't improving. The math program had solid attendance, was oversubscribed, and students were making eighteen to twenty-four months' progress in a single year. It also cost 75 percent less in total and 90 percent less per student compared to the ineffective English program. With this data in hand, rather than the typical turf battle, we easily shifted funds from English to math and then revamped the English program, which has become more effective and cost effective.

Collectively, setting class size and staffing tested the team's commitment to serving the greater good. Since teachers make up 65 percent of a typical budget, it was critical to manage this cost. By sharing detailed information about each teacher's course load and student load, great things happened.

Elementary principals didn't push for yet smaller class size when they were made aware of the larger classes in middle school. Elementary principals even collectively voted on the distribution of teachers at each grade and school, trying to be fair to everyone and taking into account very specific needs like the mix of students in a particular cohort. These were thoughtful decisions that allocated resources far better than any central office process. By scheduling collectively, the elementary principals also found ways to share specialists, something that had eluded the district for years.

At the secondary level we discovered a number of departments that were over- or understaffed. The unofficial practice was to maintain status quo staffing in each department in each building. Over time, however, student course choices changed. For example, science, art, and Latin became more popular and fewer students were enrolling in home economics and Spanish. We discovered one school had many teachers paid full time for part-time work, and another had too many Spanish teachers but not enough Latin teachers. Only by having teacher-by-teacher class size data could we staff based on need. The information also made it easier for department heads to support necessary reductions, because they understood why the decisions were being made.

Perhaps the most powerful outcome of collective budgeting was reversing the incentive system. Because the administrators had meaningful say in how money would be spent, they wanted to find ways of freeing up funds. In the past, when superintendents asked for cost savings ideas, they heard, "You want to take things away from me, no thanks." In fact, nearly every cabinet member confessed to the executive coach that they had considered it their responsibility to protect their department or school from cuts. All that changed. During one year of budget cutting, principals offered up a laundry list of ineffective programs, underutilized staff, and options for running programs at a lower cost. They volunteered this information to save a districtwide reading effort they knew to be effective. In years past, the reading program was decimated to save better established, but less important, efforts.

During my second and third annual budgets, tax revenue failed to keep up with rising mandated costs and growing enrollment, making the annual rite of collective budgeting more difficult. At one point in my second budget we hit a deadlock. The team didn't want to decide how to balance the budget because the cuts would be too unpopular. They asked me to make the final decision, but I refused to let them off the hook. Instead, I gave them each a list of possible cuts, higher fees, and new revenue. They had to close the deficit by choosing options that covered our shortfall. They balked and said it was impossible, but this was exactly what they were asking me to do. They struggled to balance the budget and eventually rethought some long-held beliefs. Maybe we should charge, coupled with scholarships, for instrumental music programs, maybe we can raise lunch prices, and maybe we can live with slightly bigger fifth-grade classes. These represented major changes in thinking, decisions they wouldn't have supported if I had made them on my own. One principal said that the parents would never accept this, but that if they had to wrestle with this problem like we did, they might come to the same conclusion.

I took this suggestion to heart. Working with the school board, we emailed and posted online a survey that asked parents and taxpayers to balance the budget, given the same choices the leadership team had. More than a third of the parents responded, fifty times the typical turnout at any public forum. Many parents talked to administrators, hoping that other, less painful choices existed. The administrators responded sincerely that these were the best options. When forced with tradeoffs, rather than just given the opportunity to criticize our decisions, the parents voted in overwhelming numbers to raise certain fees, but not others, and to trim some programs, but not others. It was thoughtful and it finalized our budget with little commotion.

UNINTENDED CONSEQUENCES

In my worldview, the budget should fund the strategy and feed only effective programs. We therefore had to collect data to know which programs were successful. This created a lot of headaches for me and the leadership team, because it also meant we knew which schools, programs, and teachers weren't successful. Armed with this information, we praised those doing well and supported, coached, and prodded the less successful. To me, and many on my cabinet, it seemed immoral to stand by and let ineffective teachers, programs, or schools persist when we knew we had the tools and money to do better.

Could you offer tenure to a teacher when you knew nearly all of her students made only six months' progress each year in reading? Could you keep a dropout prevention program in which few students graduated despite the "wonderful" teacher? What do I do with a hard-working principal who opted for an alternative literacy program but had the worst reading results in the district? In the end, principals raised the bar for achieving tenure, ineffective programs were cut, and a few tough superintendent-principal conversations took place. Each action raised student achievement and ensured that our funds created learning. Each action also hurt morale and further drained my political capital. I wondered if the reason so few school districts measure success in detail is because not knowing is easier.

In another unintended consequence, I found myself expending a lot of energy defending small expenses. When people are being laid off, every decision comes under the microscope. The three most hotly debated budget decisions I made had a few things in common. They didn't cost much, benefited the district greatly, supported our strategy, saved the district lots of money, were commonplace in the private sector, but they just weren't tolerable in a public school setting.

The big offenders were $15,000 for team building and executive coaching for my cabinet, $10,000 to run a leadership academy for teachers aspiring to become administrators, and $65,000 for a cost containment specialist. By all measures, these were successful efforts. The executive coach greased the implementation of standards-based education and professional development reform. The academy had a waiting list, and half the participants eventually became leaders in the district. And the purchasing expert saved four times their salary the first year and fifteen times the next year. Yet these were all flashpoint issues. Shouldn't our administrators naturally work well together? If teachers want to learn leadership, shouldn't they get a master's degree?

And why are we overpaying for purchased items in the first place? The truth was the administrators worked in silos and protected their turf, the higher education programs didn't meet our needs, and, although we usually paid reasonable prices, we seldom got the best price on major purchases.

I held firm during my third budget. These small, unorthodox expenditures were the low-cost, high-impact ideas needed for us to do more with less. For many in the community, however, a tough economic time was the wrong time to try something new. I postponed the final budget vote to drum up support; I lobbied and I won. The strategy prevailed, but I was again weakened by winning.

With the benefit of hindsight, I should have found a better way to explain the benefits and should have better appreciated how atypical some ideas appear in the K–12 setting, even though they are commonplace in the nonprofit and private sector. Most superintendents know this from coming up through the ranks, but they don't know how much it hampers moving a district forward when they don't measure what's working or invest in leadership development and proactively managing cost control.

PARTNERS TO SHARE THE LOAD

During my second year, I realized there was a limit to how much I could shift and cut. I had enough money to meet the academic needs of our students, but I knew we were underserving their social and emotional needs. Historically, the district was very thin in this area.

I created a task force to research the local options available to students and families seeking counseling. We held focus groups with local mental health providers and clinics. We learned that many mental health providers who serve children don't have much business during the day and that older children don't want to go to a counselor after school. (Telling your coach you can't play this afternoon because you have a mental health appointment isn't cool.) Within two years we had partnered with five different organizations, providing over a $1 million of services a year to our students at no cost to the district. We provided top-notch drug and alcohol addiction counseling, summer support programs, school counselors in every building, anger management training, family counseling, and supervised diversion from criminal prosecution for first-time nonviolent offenders.

After screening the agencies, we welcomed them into our buildings. We provided space, invited them to our weekly student support meetings, and included appointments on student schedules. They became part of the fabric of the schools. Aside from a few start-up costs and paying for a small amount of supervision, the services were free to the district. Private insurance paid for therapists (with fees waived for students who couldn't pay), some of whom were graduate student interns supervised by one of our partner organizations. One counseling agency raised its own funds, and one intensive program served enough tuition-paying out-of-town students to fully cover the cost of serving Arlington students.

Buoyed by the success of our mental health partnerships, we expanded the concept, but with a new twist—we would do good for the students and increase revenue as well. Parents clamored for more middle school afterschool activities at the same time that we were considering cutting the few afterschool stipends due to budget woes. Partnering with a local interfaith group, we solicited bids for someone to run a fee-based afterschool program with scholarships available to children who couldn't pay. We also added summer programs, expanded day care for our staff, increased elementary afterschool offerings, and added preschool programs through collaboration with third parties.

These alliances not only provided services we could never afford, but we charged rent for most of them to be housed in our schools. This covered 1 percent of the entire budget (more than our Title 1, Title 2, and Title 3 funding combined). Best of all, we could provide need-based scholarships and still run the programs at below-market fees.

The concept grew to include the academic side as well. To support our goal of making the high school experience more global, we joined with foreign exchange programs that recruited tuition-paying students to attend

Arlington High for a year. This quickly attracted about twenty students from around the world and generated $200,000 per year of new revenue to the district.

NO SOLUTION WITHOUT A SPECIAL EDUCATION SOLUTION

From the day I first arrived in Arlington, I knew that our students with special needs achieved at unacceptably low levels, despite providing ever-increasing resources. For three years I spent nearly a quarter of my time spearheading a comprehensive special education reform effort in conjunction with the broader changes under way. By replacing common practices with best practices, the results were impressive.

The number of special education students scoring proficient or advanced on MCAS (the state accountability test) increased by 26 percent in English and 22 percent in math over three years in the schools participating in the reform program. The increases at the high school level were even more significant (see figure 9.1). Achievement declined in the control group. The number of formal parent complaints to the Department of Education dropped from twenty-five to zero, and parent satisfaction, as measured by an independent survey company, increased substantially. Special education costs grew by less than 2 percent per year, well below the rate of salary increases. Prior to my arrival, costs were growing by 10 percent a year (see figure 9.2).

My first step in rethinking special education was to create a team of special educators who liked to think outside the box. I supported them with financial expertise from the business office, a data analyst from general education, and a skilled transportation director. They were asked to review the effectiveness of current programs and determine in fine detail what was driving our ever-increasing costs.

What we learned turned conventional wisdom on its head. While parents and staff believed more money would increase student achievement, we found that increasing student achievement would actually lower costs.

FIGURE 9.1

The achievement gap between students with special needs and their general education peers

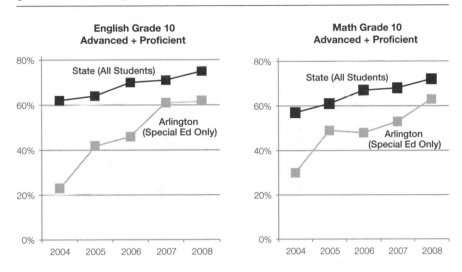

The achievement gap between students with special needs and their general education peers narrowed dramatically, while real spending decreased.

Source: "Seeking Effective Policies and Practices for Students with Special Needs" (Cambridge: Rennie Center for Education Research & Policy, 2009).

This was true for two reasons. First, nothing is more expensive than a child not learning. If you help student reach grade level quickly, you will save years of future remediation costs. Second, we were spending substantial sums of money on ineffective programs. We didn't need more money; we needed programs that worked better.

An IEP (individual education plan) is a legally binding document that outlines the services a student with special needs must receive. Technically, IEPs are reviewed every year and students are reassessed every three years. In reality, once a child starts receiving special education services, they continue through twelfth grade. This means the decision to provide special education services to a third grader is a ten-year financial commitment.

FIGURE 9.2

Growth in special education spending

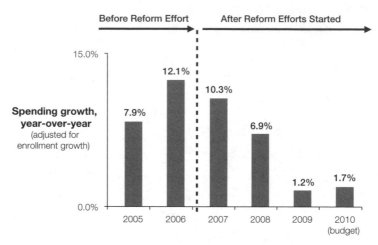

*Special education costs increased
by less than inflation while student achievement soared.*

Source: Arlington Public School year-end reports and approved school budgets compiled by author.

Special education is the most expensive form of remediation, requiring substantial testing, meetings, paperwork, and lawyers. In many districts, including Arlington when I arrived, it is also the easiest route to obtaining remedial services. Children couldn't receive intensive reading support, speech, or counseling without an IEP. At the secondary level, math and English remediation was reserved for special education students only. This encouraged staff and parents to fight for a child to be classified as special needs.

Despite its great expense, special education remediation wasn't very effective. The supplemental instruction came from a special education teacher who may not be a trained in math or reading, and the lessons were disconnected from the instruction in the classroom. In many cases, a teacher assistant with no formal training provided the bulk of a student's instruction. Worse yet, reading help often came during math time, creating a new area of weakness.

IT'S READING, STUPID!

In Arlington, like most districts, the number-one reason students enter special education is for difficulty with reading. Nationwide, up to 40 percent of all students on IEPs have reading problems, and 80 percent of students with the most common learning disability simply haven't learned to read.[1] Fortunately, the National Reading Panel, a group of experts brought together by Congress, has laid out a clear, effective plan for addressing reading difficulties in elementary students. Under their plan, most children can read at grade level by third grade or sooner. If we taught more children to read, we would change their lives for the better and spend less on special education.

This seemed like a miracle to me. There was a program that worked! All my administrators believed the program would work in Arlington, and many had begged for something similar in years past. Yet when I told my leadership team that we would commit to the National Reading Panel's recommendations, rather than applause my announcement was met with anxiety and reluctance.

"Nate, you don't understand," every comment began. "We have five different remedial reading programs already (Title 1, special education, ELL, voluntary desegregation, and general education), and classroom teachers use over fifty different approaches." "This requires regular district wide assessments, and we don't do that." "All teachers and schools would have to use the same program. That's a mandate, and that's an ugly word." And the most anxiety-provoking concern was never stated out loud: "Some of our administrators, reading specialists, and teachers won't accept a new program. It would be insulting to their past efforts."

Well, they were right, I didn't understand. As I told my wife at one point, "If we don't implement a new large-scale reading program based on proven best practices, then I didn't want to be a superintendent any more. But if we do, I might not get to stay a superintendent." I placed all my chips on this effort.

At the start of my second year, I ended five ineffective reading programs and placed all reading staff under one leader. The money that we shifted from grants and the administrative reorganization funded additional high-quality reading teachers and intensive professional development. All teachers—classroom, remedial, and special education—used the same program and pacing. Principals were evaluated based on reading results in their building, and we mandated thirty minutes of phonics each day as part of ninety minutes of the daily required English language arts. And while teachers had a great deal of input into designing and adjusting the districtwide plan, they couldn't individually change the plan.

In the end it worked better than I could have hoped for, but not as well as I needed. The number of students K–2 not reading at grade level dropped by 52 percent. Two thirds of K–2 students who started the year behind in reading made more than one year's progress. Referral rates to special education dropped. Within three years reading ceased to be a special education service for nearly all children.

New teachers welcomed the structure provided by the reading program. Some principals delayed retirement or became reinvigorated. As a district, we learned how to implement large-scale change, empower teachers, and encourage instructional leadership by the principals. Parents were thrilled, especially parents of students with special needs. Their kids could read! Nearby districts came to study what we did, with envy.

Despite the results, about half of the veteran teachers and most of the staff running the old programs resented the new effort. As the positive results were shared publically, things got worse. Instead of basking in the glow of our success, they believed the data denigrated their prior years of teaching. Their feelings were hurt, and I was the cause. The situation was best summarized by a former teacher and union official speaking at a town meeting. I remember her saying something like, "Mr. Levenson, my grandson couldn't read well and now he can because of your reading program.

Thank you. Now that I have given you your due, you don't appreciate the great, dedicated teachers we have." She went on to criticize many of the changes that made the reading program possible and made it clear that she wished I had never come to Arlington.

KNOWING WHAT YOU TEACH

The success in elementary reading encouraged us to look at math and English at the secondary level. In a typical week I would spend a few hours visiting classes. One day in a special education resource room in a secondary school I watched a bright, caring, passionate veteran teacher stand at the board and try to explain math to one student, English to another, biology to a third, and U.S. history to a fourth. Several thoughts hit me at once: we would never allow this teacher to teach any of these subjects to general education students because she wasn't certified in any of these fields; every student sitting in front of her had already been taught that day by a certified teacher and still they struggled; after not learning from an expert in the field, we were sending them to a generalist; and not a single general education math, science, or English teacher would agree to teach outside their field, yet we expected special education teachers to teach all subjects. None of this made sense to me, yet I knew this was the norm in most districts across the country.

We implemented a commonsense plan that didn't add one penny to the budget. Math and English remediation became open to all students (general education and special education alike) and was taught by general education teachers with expertise in the subject matter. The classes were 50 or 100 percent longer and staff was now handpicked (similar to how we handpick teachers for Advanced Placement classes). These programs were cost neutral in the short run because they only required shifting resources from special education to general education. In the long run they will decrease costs by reducing the need for future services. High school test scores for students with special needs rose so dramatically that Arlington was profiled by the Rennie Center for Education Research and Policy as one of the fastest improving districts in the state.[2]

This strategy did create some pushback. Special education teachers felt devalued when their numbers decreased as we shifted to general education content–trained staff. In one school, both general education and special education staff were so fierce in their opposition that the changes weren't implemented at all, and they organized a parent revolt by suggesting that students wouldn't learn and that laws would be broken. The results speak for themselves. In the eight schools that embraced the changes, proficiency rates for students in special education rose by 26 percent in English and 22 percent in math. At the school that rejected change, achievement dropped in English and was flat in math.

LOGIC IN THE MIDST OF EMOTION

While my preference was to help children learn without the cost and bother of special education, many children would still rightfully qualify for an IEP. By incorporating a Five Why analysis to our most expensive programs, we learned how to improve the lives of students with disabilities and still lower costs. The Five Why approach is simple and powerful. As the name suggests, you ask the question *Why?* five times to understand the root cause of a problem. We applied the process to our three fastest-growing costs in special education: out-of-district placements, teaching assistants, and related services like speech and language and occupational therapy.

For example, question one: Why do we have so many special education students being educated out-of-district at the district's expense? Answer: We don't have programs to meet their needs in-district. Question two: Why don't we have programs to meet their needs in-district? Answer: Their needs are so substantial it would be more expensive to have in-house programs. Question three: How expensive would it be to have in-house programs? Answer: We don't know. Question four: Why don't we know? Answer: We aren't sure what services we must provide or how much staff we need for each program. Question five: Why don't we know what services to provide or how much staff to hire? Answer: We don't have programs like these in-house, so we haven't seen them.

In short, we sent students to very costly out-of-district placements simply because we always had. After some field research, we learned that we could run our own top-quality programs with identical staffing levels and services as the out-of-district schools for 40 percent less per student. The savings came from less transportation (much shorter rides), lower facility costs (we owned the buildings), and no marketing costs. Many parents preferred that their children attend school in the community, so these new programs were popular. Over the next few years, Arlington opened eight programs and saved more than $5 million cumulatively.

The same approach helped us rethink the use of paraprofessionals (teaching assistants) for including students with special needs in the general education classroom. Paraprofessionals were a big expense and growing fast. Conventional wisdom said that "the more paraprofessionals, the better," and the budget reflected this thinking.

As we looked for more cost-effective ways to meet the needs of struggling students, it was surprising to learn that paraprofessionals were, unintentionally, sometimes detrimental to many students. They hovered beside their assigned child and created a social barrier, stifling peer interaction and defeating one of the primary benefits of inclusion. What's more, often having a paraprofessional *decreased* the instruction a student received from the classroom teacher who felt a student with a teaching assistant already has 100 percent of an adult's time, unlike classmates without a paraprofessional. So the students with the greatest needs got the least attention from the teacher certified in the subject matter. In the worst case, the paraprofessional actually did the work for the student under the guise of helping. Paraprofessionals also can foster a sense of dependency, which is an anchor to students after graduation. While some students do absolutely need paraprofessionals for health and safety reasons, they are not a panacea.

It turned out that paraprofessionals were easy to add, but more targeted, more cost effective help was almost impossible to include in the budget. We had created a system that made the path of least resistance both expensive and ineffective. In one case, a teacher advocated strongly for a full-time paraprofessional for a student prone to outbursts in class. This would cost $30,000 a year ($300,000 over the education of the student). The decision was historically left to a team of special educators and teachers at the building level. They could hire a paraprofessional without central office approval. But what the student really needed was two weeks of a behaviorist's time, though there was never money in the budget for this "frill." In hiring a behaviorist, we learned that the outbursts were infrequent. She observed the student and identified the triggering factors. She created a behavior plan for the student, codified the warning signs, and coached the teacher. Within a few weeks, a paraprofessional was no longer needed.

The last major special education effort we tackled was bringing more planning and consistency to determining which students received speech and language therapy, occupational therapy, and counseling. In doing so, we utilized benchmarking, the process of comparing how others do the same things we do. In Arlington the results were surprising. It turned out that despite desperate pleas for more therapists and testers, we exceeded the like-community benchmarks by 25 and 15 percent, respectively. Yes, staff was working long days, but we had more staff than most.

What was wrong? We weren't good at scheduling. One therapist scheduled 25 percent of her time to escort students to and from class, while others had the students come to them. Therapists also lacked the authority to ask classroom teachers to accommodate more efficient schedules. We also realized that staff was assigned to buildings, not by student caseload. If School A really needed 1.25 therapists and School B needed 0.75 therapists, each got 1. Obviously, the therapist in School A felt overloaded and asked for more staffing.

We moved scheduling to a highly skilled administrator. Because she was a peer of the principals, she could say, "We need Mary and John at the same time. Let's find a way to work this out." She could also balance caseloads more fairly. The net effect was that we increased effective capacity by 25 percent; so when we added new in-house programs, we didn't have to hire more staff.

Rethinking special education allowed Arlington to raise achievement, please more parents, and control costs. By controlling the growth in special education spending, our other efforts could be fully funded.

LESSONS AND IMPLICATIONS

Looking back, I'm proud of our results, but battered and bruised from the process. A relatively small, but mean-spirited group of protesters regularly packed school board meetings; sent anti-Semitic notes, e-mails, and voice-mails; made threats against me and my family; and whispered ugly, fabricated innuendos to discredit me, the staff, and the community members who supported the reforms. I'm often asked, "Would you do it again?" or "What would you do differently next time?" The more important question, however, is, "What would make it less difficult to make the same decisions next time?" Four changes would ease the way for superintendents to do more with less.

Increase External Pressure So Data, Not History, Drive Budget Decisions. Greater urgency and more external pressure for raising student achievement would make it easier to put the needs of children before those of the adults in the schools. For most superintendants and school boards, it is in their self-interest to minimize changes to existing staffing and programs. Currently, the negative repercussions from shifting resources are worse than the repercussions from not raising student achievement. There has to be more pain from maintaining the status quo than from implementing change. This is not the case in most districts.

School districts must make shifting funds based on strategy and need normal, not radical. School boards must demand that programs are measured for effectiveness and that only successful ones continued. Using beginning- and end-of-year assessments, it is not difficult to know which programs are meeting their stated objectives. Detailed class size and teacher case load data must be collated and drive staffing decisions. Finally, when a report indicates that a third of the crossing guards cross no children, it should be taken for granted that this can't continue.

Make School Boards More Like the Senate.   Before school boards can make budgeting and staffing more data driven and fluid, the structure of school boards must change. Every year is an election year, and every hard decision is kindling for a challenger to unseat the incumbents. Since shifting funds creates a loss for someone, moving funds to support student need and the vision is politically harmful. The more progress you make, the more inclined friends of the harmed parties are to run for the board to reinstate the past. In Arlington three seats on the school board were won by candidates running on the platform to stop the reforms and turn back the clock. Their campaigns were fueled by the attempted cuts to the crossing guards, the reduction in administrators (some of whom lived in town), and the imposition of a common reading curriculum, which upset some of the veteran staff (who also lived in town).

A possible solution is to make school boards more like the U.S. Senate. The Senate, unlike the more politically reactive House of Representatives, is considered more deliberate because its members run for office less frequently. If school board members were elected to six-year terms, with elections every three years, a superintendent and the board would have the time and consistent support to create a strategy, make the tough decisions, and weather the storm.

If elections were every three years, then vocal minorities would have less clout, the risk to sitting board members would be reduced, and a strategy could be put in place long enough to be measured on its results. A stable school board would also empower a superintendent to make bolder decisions without the fear that after the next election their decision will be overturned.

A Broader Skill Set.   Even if superintendents have a clear strategy for raising student achievement and strong school board support, they also need a breadth of expertise. The traditional path to a superintendency—from classroom teacher, to assistant principal, to principal, to central office, to superintendent—often does little to build competency in financial management, team building, systemic planning, and selling unpopular decisions. Former military officers and teachers turned school business managers often have the right stuff. Both have risen through politically complex environments, have experience in budgeting, and are comfortable with data-driven decision making.

To be fair, many nontraditional superintendents also lack key skills, notably the political and cultural awareness needed to survive realigning the budget and to shepherd large-scale change through a foreign culture. Had I spent twenty years as an educator, I would have known to avoid the crossing guard issue, despite the obvious waste. I would have foreseen the hurt feelings of some veteran staff who objected to a common curriculum. But my training and life experience put more emphasis on achieving results and tolerated a bit more discomfort along the way.

Whether a district is headed by a traditional or nontraditional superintendent, the senior leadership team needs vision, political acumen, and financial expertise.

Start from Scratch.   If structural changes to school governance aren't possible, then starting from scratch is an alternative. Nearly all of the pushback from using the budget to drive academic improvement stems from cutting legacy decisions, not from objections to what is being added. My decisions to increase reading support, add in-house autism programs, or teach more engineering weren't controversial. Cutting home economics or ending an ineffective remediation program to pay for the new programs was. A reconstituted school, a charter school, or a rebuilt-from-scratch district like New Orleans doesn't have old decisions and staffing patterns to undo. In these situations, 100 percent of the funds can be directed to the strategy.

THE AFTERMATH

I was hired to be an agent of change, and few question that the Arlington Public Schools changed under my leadership. On the plus side, academic achievement increased substantially, program offerings expanded, leadership capacity blossomed, and financial controls came into being. The district won a number of awards and commendations, and other districts came to study our reading program, methods of budgeting, and special education reforms. On the flip side, the changes divided the town and angered some veteran staff. Shortly after my contract was renewed for another three years, and just as the next firestorm began to spark, I resigned. I had had enough.

It is interesting to look back and see what stuck and what faded away in the twenty four months since I left Arlington. The reading program, some of the special education reforms, the partnerships with social service agencies, the teamwork within the administrative cabinet, the common curriculum, and the common assessments are all alive and well. The town, however, is more divided than ever. While Old Arlington's anger was directed at me, my leaving only redirected it to the new superintendent and the school board. The underlying friction continues to split the community.

It seems that I inherited a status quo and, unfortunately, created a new one. Few, if any, of the initiatives have been canceled, but most new efforts are on hold. The leadership and school board are gun shy. They fear becoming the target of a vocal and, at times, cruel minority. I think the lesson they draw from my tenure is that significant progress is possible despite tight budgets, but the political and personal price is too high. A *Boston Magazine* article written more than a year after I left the district concluded, "In the end, it turned out that Levenson had made the mistake of thinking that when Arlington residents said they were ready for change, they actually meant it."[3]

10

Overcoming the Political Barriers to Change

Martin R. West

AN ERA OF UNPRECEDENTED belt-tightening appears to be looming for American public education. The pressures facing school districts in the wake of the 2008–2009 financial crisis, already strong despite the flow of temporary federal stimulus funds, are poised to intensify as that funding recedes. There are signs that taxpayers have begun to balk at the ever-growing bill for public education. State pension funds have been decimated by the economic downturn, even as unfunded obligations for retiree health care mount at an alarming pace. Over the long run, the needs of a steadily aging national population will place competing demands on federal, state, and local budgets.

What remains to be determined is what these changes will mean for the quality of education offered to American students—and, by extension, for the nation's economic, political, and social well-being. Just as private-sector businesses are known to use economic downturns to streamline operations and boost productivity, the ongoing recession has undoubtedly led district and state officials to take a fresh look at spending priorities and practices in K–12 education. Media reports now highlight examples of school districts rethinking teacher compensation and evaluation systems, lifting restrictions on class size, making greater use of online instruction, and closing long-underutilized schools. The preceding chapters make the case for reform, innovation, and experimentation in each of these areas and in many more.

Yet the evidence compiled in this volume also reveals the vast distance between changing the conversation about school reform and changing actual policy. The most common steps districts have taken thus far range from superficial changes that offer only marginal cost reductions (like adjusting thermostats), to temporary measures that cannot be sustained over time (like delaying textbook purchases or scheduled pay increases), to actions that clearly threaten to undermine student learning (like engaging in seniority-based layoffs, shortening the school year, or adopting a four-day week). Understanding why this is the case is essential to devising appropriate solutions.

In this chapter I contend that the barriers to cost-cutting reform in American education are fundamentally political. In particular, the electoral incentives facing the more than 13,500 school boards charged with the day-to-day management of school districts do not incline them to challenge established routines in pursuit of greater productivity, even when budgets are tight. By definition, enhancing productivity requires either that resources be reallocated from less efficient to more efficient uses or that inefficient practices be altered. Either approach imposes concentrated costs on discrete constituencies who will readily mobilize against change, and the structure of local education politics works to their advantage.

School board elections are low-turnout affairs in which information about candidates and their positions is notoriously difficult for voters to obtain, enabling organized interests to exert outsized influence. Teacher unions, in particular, can be relied on to oppose vigorously changes they perceive as threatening their members' interests. But they are hardly alone: proponents and beneficiaries of programs of all kinds emerge regularly to defend the status quo against proposed reforms. The general public, which stands to benefit from improved productivity through reduced tax burdens, increased property values, and access to better schools, is far more difficult to mobilize for political action.

The familiar bias against change that results when the costs of reform are concentrated and the benefits diffuse is reinforced by the broader political environment in which school districts operate. A heavy reliance on categorical spending by the federal government and the states restricts the ability of districts to reallocate funds to their most important priorities, while additional rules and regulations limit experimentation with new models of staffing or instructional delivery. Existing federal and state accountability policies reward educators for boosting test scores but pay scant attention to how much has been spent to accomplish that goal. Survey evidence predictably reveals that the general public is far better informed about student outcomes than they are about education spending.

To be sure, poor fiscal management on the part of school districts has many causes. A dearth of information attributable to antiquated data systems and limited analytic capacity does hinder the ability of district leaders to manage their budgets. We do not yet know how best to design alternatives to existing policies on matters such as teacher compensation and evaluation; it is more likely that no one optimal design exists. The inertia endemic to large public bureaucracies, combined with cultural norms formed over decades of adhering to existing practices and protocols, work against large-scale change. These factors, however, reflect underlying political realities; they are symptoms, not the root cause. Addressing them without altering the political incentives facing district leaders is unlikely to have more than a marginal impact on their decisions.

To the extent that this diagnosis is correct, it should inform the development of policies that will help districts overcome the barriers to cost-cutting reform. Above all, it highlights the need for measures that can change school board politics and free district leaders to seek efficiencies in the interests of both students and the general public. I conclude the chapter by identifying steps that could accomplish this goal.

THE NEED FOR CHANGE

It may seem short-sighted to forecast anything but continued spending growth in American public education. As James Guthrie and Arthur Peng document in chapter 1, public school budgets historically have been well protected during times of economic contraction and the beneficiaries of additional resources when the economy expands. As a consequence, real per-pupil spending on public education has increased more than three-fold since 1970. It is reasonable enough to conclude that, as the American economy returns to growth, so too will education spending.

Yet several factors suggest that the fiscal challenges now facing school districts will persist into the future. Consider first evidence from surveys measuring Americans' support for education spending and their confidence in the public schools. For the years 2007–2009, an annual poll administered under the auspices of *Education Next* and Harvard University's Program on Education Policy and Governance (PEPG) asked Americans a battery of questions about these topics.[1] The surveys conducted in February–March 2008 (when the Dow Jones Industrial Average had fallen just 10 percent from its peak) and in February–March 2009 (when the Dow bottomed out while the survey was in the field) provide an ideal opportunity to gauge the impact of the economic downturn on public attitudes.

The results confirm that support for spending on public school declined precipitously with the state of the economy. The share of Americans who say that spending on public schools should increase fell by 15 percentage points between 2008 and 2009, from 61 percent to 46 percent; the percentage calling for education spending to "greatly increase" fell by half, from 18 percent to 9 percent. A separate question showed that the share of Americans supporting increased teacher salaries fell from 69 percent to 56 percent. Not surprisingly, confidence that more spending would improve student learning also dropped from 60 percent to just over half. The levels of support registered by questions on school spending and teacher salaries should be interpreted cautiously: Americans routinely express support for more spending on a variety of specific government programs while also calling for tax cuts. Yet the sizable drop in the level of support for additional spending over the course of a single year is noteworthy.

The 2009 *Education Next*–PEPG survey also revealed that the grades the public assigned to the nation's public schools dropped to the lowest levels on record—not only in the three-year history of that survey but also over the four decades for which comparable data is available from the *Phi Delta Kappan*/Gallup survey.[2] Only 18 percent of respondents gave the nation's public schools an A or a B grade in 2009, while 25 percent assigned a D or F. Americans have long assigned their local public schools higher grades than those assigned to the nation's schools as a whole. In 2008, for example, 40 percent of Americans assigned their local public schools an A or B grade while only 20 percent did so for the nation's schools as a whole. Even so, the same survey revealed that the public evaluates its local post office and local police force much more favorably than their local schools: the shares assigning the post office and police an A or B were 64 percent and 70 percent, respectively.

Of course, public support for education spending may well recover with the economy, and entrepreneurial political leaders could exploit Americans' flagging assessments of their public schools to make a case for still more investment. Other signs, however, point in the direction of continued strain on school district budgets. A 2010 study of state pension funds for teachers and other government employees conducted by the PEW Center on the States documented a $452 billion gap between the $2.8 trillion in total long-term liabilities and current funding levels.[3] Other analysts contend that this estimate, which takes at face value the optimistic expected rates of return used by most public-sector actuaries, dramatically understates the true shortfall.[4] Retiree health care and other nonpension benefits, which continue to be funded almost entirely on a pay-as-you-go basis, represent another half-trillion dollars or more in unfunded commitments.[5]

The nation's ongoing demographic transition to an older population will present additional challenges. The U.S. Census Bureau projects that the number of Americans sixty-five years and older will increase by 120 percent by 2050, while the number of five- to seventeen-year-olds will increase by just 75 percent.[6] As soon as 2025, senior citizens are likely to outnumber the nation's school-age population for the first time in our nation's history. There is evidence that elderly voters are somewhat less likely to support spending on public schools, especially when they retire to an area to which they do not have strong personal ties.[7] Much more important, however, are the growing demands that this politically active demographic group will place on government budgets.

While projections of future circumstances are necessarily uncertain, it therefore seems more than likely that school districts are entering a time of prolonged fiscal stringency. Moreover, the productivity of the nation's public school system should be a concern for policy makers irrespective of what the future holds. Even as real per-pupil spending has increased rapidly over the past four decades, high school graduation rates and test scores have remained essentially flat, suggesting a substantial decline in system productivity.[8] As Stanford economist Caroline Hoxby points out, this decline threatens the most important historical source of American economic growth, "its comparative advantage in producing goods and services that make intensive use of educated labor."[9] Maintaining this advantage hinges on the nation's ability to produce educated workers relatively cheaply.

It is also worth noting that, although the preceding discussion suggests that fiscal challenges will come only in the future, many school district leaders have long felt as if they are already here. A 2000 survey conducted by the American Association of School Superintendents found that "inadequate financing" was the issue most commonly identified by the nation's superintendents as the chief factor inhibiting their effectiveness (a response given by 44 percent of superintendents).[10] Comparable surveys administered in 1982 and 1992 found much the same pattern.[11] In other words, school districts' historically privileged fiscal position has not meant that their leaders have not perceived a need to become more efficient. Why, then, have they not been able to do so? What are the barriers to change?

SUPERFICIAL BARRIERS TO CHANGE

Discussions of the obstacles to sound financial management and cost-cutting reform in public education often emphasize surface-level considerations that, although important, cannot on their own explain the failure of most school districts to take the steps necessary to become more efficient.

Policies designed to address these barriers in isolation are unlikely to be effective in promoting change.

Information Deficits

Perhaps the most commonly lamented barrier to reform is simply a lack of the type of information necessary to make sound decisions concerning resource allocation. Anecdotal evidence of the information deficits plaguing school districts large and small is easy to find. Dennis Chaconas lost his job as superintendent of the Oakland, California, public schools in 2003 when a newly installed computer system revealed a previously hidden $40 million operating deficit from the prior fiscal year and projected similar deficits going forward.[12] When Harvard Business School graduate Nathan Levenson arrived in 2005 as superintendent of the Arlington, Massachusetts, Public Schools, he was taken aback, as he writes in chapter 9, by the fact that "no one, including the superintendent, CFO, or school board really knew where we spent our money."

The absence of sound information on which to base budgetary decisions should not be confused with the absence of raw data. School districts today are awash in data on not only financial matters but also, due largely to No Child Left Behind and state accountability laws, student performance on standardized tests. However, because school districts rarely consider information technology to be a core function, the information systems that contain these data are frequently assembled on the cheap and are hopelessly out of date. Related data are often housed in distinct systems without a common architecture, making it difficult for policy makers to make timely connections. As Harvard researcher and former budget director for the Los Angeles Unified School District board Jon Fullerton explains, district "budgeting systems do not connect automatically with accounting systems, and both may be isolated from the human-resources systems that track who is hired, when, and for how much."[13] Linking these systems to data on student achievement, as is necessary to evaluate the cost-effectiveness of specific programs in improving student learning, represents an additional hurdle.

Staff capacity is another constraint on the quality of the financial information available in school districts. Superintendents are typically hired
based on their reputation for instructional leadership rather than for being
skilled fiscal managers. Salary comparisons indicate that competent business managers and chief financial officers can earn substantially more in
private-sector organizations than they can in school districts of the same
scale, again reflecting the perception that financial matters are peripheral to
the district's core instructional activities.[14] Rather than recruit outside talent, many school districts instead promote business managers from within,
an approach that ensures local knowledge but limits exposure to ideas and
practices in other industries. And while many school districts employ a
number of highly competent researchers with solid analytic skills, their
time and energy are often taken up by compliance and reporting requirements rather than the types of exercises that could inform policy making.

These constraints highlight the need for the types of analyses illustrated
in this volume by Marguerite Roza, Michael Casserly, and the Boston
Consulting Group's (BCG) education practice. Roza demonstrates how a
series of simple per-unit cost calculations based on readily available data
can inform policy makers forced to choose between, for example, teacher
layoffs and increases in class size. Casserly's ongoing work with the Council on Great City Schools' Performance Management and Benchmarking
Project, by providing comparative data on operations spending across fifty
large urban school districts, has the potential to help urban school districts
identify areas of inefficiency and to target cost-saving efforts accordingly.
BCG's work goes a step further by drawing on the consultancy's vast experience with private-sector firms. These and similar analyses should inform
school districts' resource allocation decisions at all times and are particularly useful in times of fiscal stringency.

Yet BCG's experience in Delaware also highlights the degree to which
political realities can limit the value of this type of work. As described in
chapter 7, although their cost study was commissioned by the governor
and nominally included all public spending in Delaware on preK–12 education, its mandate did not extend to matters directly related to student

achievement. As a result, key cost drivers such as class size were deemed "too close to instruction to be explored." High-cost but controversial matters such as employee benefits were discussed but, in light of their political sensitivity, recommended "for further study." Implementation of even their more straightforward recommendations has been slow and uneven. Ultimately, the analysts were forced to conclude that "strong leadership is a necessary condition for success, given the emotional response that often comes with cost efficiency and reduction initiatives."

Before concluding that district inefficiencies stem primarily from a lack of information, we need to ask why, if new forms of information have the potential to increase efficiency, they do not already exist. The constraints districts face in terms of data infrastructure and staff capacity are of their own making, a consequence of decades of investment and management reflecting other priorities. Providing district leaders with new information without changing their incentives to put that information to use is unlikely to result in changed behavior.

Lack of Policy Know-How

A second common explanation for school districts' failure to alter inefficient practices is that they simply do not know how to do so. This diagnosis resembles critiques of reform efforts that rely on external accountability to press schools to improve their performance without providing them the tools and expertise needed to do so. Harvard's Richard Elmore, for example, contends that "low-performing schools, and the people who work in them, don't know what to do. If they did, they would be doing it already."[15] Inefficient and cash-strapped school districts may find themselves in much the same situation.

This explanation also captures an important reality. Our knowledge of how to design alternatives to existing policies is quite limited, even in key areas such as teacher compensation. A strong case can be made that the salary schedules now in use throughout American public education, which ignore differences in the scarcity and value of teachers' skills, the difficulty of their assignments and the caliber of their work, are poorly designed to recruit and retain the most essential and effective teachers. Districts seeking to improve their efficiency of spending on personnel, which typically represents the bulk of overall budgets, could therefore be expected to focus their attention on this area.

Yet the most widely discussed alternatives to traditional teacher compensation systems present challenges of their own. Basing a portion of teacher pay on students' progress on standardized tests is currently viable for no more than 40 percent of most districts' teachers (those who teach math or reading in self-contained classrooms in grades four to eight), yet we have little evidence on the validity of subjective evaluation mechanisms that would need to be used for the rest. We do not have solid evidence on the extent to which merit pay schemes based on standardized tests would undermine the quality of education by promoting an unhealthy focus on test preparation. Nor do we know the appropriate balance between incentives for individuals, teachers grouped by grade or subject area, or entire schools. It is widely speculated that rewarding individual teachers based on their performance could undermine the collegiality and cooperation that is essential for educational success, but others worry that group-based incentives are too weak an intervention and would allow teachers to "free-ride" on the efforts of others. Even economist Eric Hanushek, perhaps the leading academic researcher making the case for the use of performance-based compensation systems to improve teacher quality, admits that "we have little experience with how to structure incentives."[16]

A lack of experience, however, cannot explain a lack of experimentation. In fact, it is the resistance to experimentation with alternatives to the single salary schedule that is primarily to blame for the absence of rigorous evidence as to which alternatives are worth pursuing. It may be that the obstacles to implementing performance-based compensation systems in large public bureaucracies like school districts are too severe and that the currently dominant systems represent the least-bad alternative. But given the consensus concerning the importance of teacher quality for students' academic success, the fact that a majority of district budgets is typically devoted to teacher salaries, and the clear shortcomings of the status quo, one would expect to see more school districts engaged in an active consideration of alternatives than has been the case.

Nor can a lack of rigorous evidence explain school districts' attachment to failed programs and policies, even in times of fiscal distress. In 2009, as the public schools were experiencing the first significant fallout from the economic downturn, Marguerite Roza and Raegen Miller published a report documenting that districts nationwide spend more than $8.6 billion annually on paying high salaries to teachers with master's degrees.[17] This amounts to 2.1 percent of total spending on public education (or roughly $174 annually per pupil), and it is being spent despite the fact that a large body of research finds that teachers with a master's degree in education (the credential held by 90 percent of teachers with graduate training) are no more effective than other teachers in raising student achievement. Yet the political obstacles to eliminating this long-established perquisite have been sufficient to prevent almost any discussion of the issue among districts and states seeking to cut costs.

Bureaucratic and Cultural Inertia

School districts' seeming reluctance to experiment with potential cost-cutting reforms may simply reflect the inertia that often characterizes large public bureaucracies. This inertia manifests itself in—and is in turn reinforced by—the widely used practice of incremental budgeting as a basis for policy making. In other words, school districts typically determine their current-year budget allocations by taking the past year's budget and adding or subtracting increments to each major program area. The default, any deviations from which must be explicitly justified, is for each program area to receive the same percentage increase or decrease as the district's overall budget. A pervasive norm that the pain of budget cutbacks should be shared equally makes this default especially potent in times of fiscal distress.

Incremental budgeting is an alternative to more comprehensive approaches widely used in other industries. Zero-based budgeting, for example, requires the managers of each program area within an organization to document annually the costs of the specific services they are required to deliver. Activity-based costing similarly compares the costs of service delivery to external benchmarks and uses the results to identify opportunities for saving. Both of these approaches can be enhanced by evidence concerning the cost-effectiveness of specific programs in achieving their goals. Each aims to ensure that an organization's spending is efficient and consistent with its strategic priorities.

Incremental budgeting in public education can be defended on the grounds that it is simpler than more comprehensive approaches and that it makes sense in light of the tight constraints on resource allocation within school districts. The practice tacitly acknowledges the fact that much of a school district's budget each year is already spoken for, either because of regulations attached to categorical state and federal funding streams or because it has effectively been committed to teacher and staff salaries. Moreover, avoiding wholesale changes to spending allocations may reduce the likelihood of unintended consequences stemming from sudden policy shifts.[18]

Yet incremental budgeting clearly biases the policy making process in favor of the status quo, making structural changes less likely in times of plenty and potentially undermining system performance when school budgets are in decline. When new funding becomes available, district leaders often take the opportunity to invest in new programs reflecting their current priorities without reallocating funds away from existing programs. As in any organization, however, not every new program will be effective. This makes it essential to reevaluate past investments on an ongoing basis to ensure that programs remain aligned with district priorities and are accomplishing their goals. In contrast, across-the-board spending reductions impact each of a district's programs without regard to their importance or effectiveness.

Budgeting practices are not adopted in a vacuum, however, but are devised to reflect political needs. And it is from this vantage point that incremental budgeting offers school district leaders a number of advantages. Each line item in a school district budget serves a distinct constituency. As Fullerton points out, "School boards and superintendents are understandably hesitant to mobilize too many stakeholders against them at once by saying 'Let's rethink our whole approach.' In normal years, the incremental approach enables district leaders to limit the stresses around budgeting by focusing on a few specific changes. As a result, the incremental approach is likely to lead a long and healthy life in school district budgeting."[19] His observation again confirms the central role of politics in shaping how school districts approach fiscal decisions.

POLITICS AND SCHOOL PRODUCTIVITY

The pervasive influence of politics on school district budgeting and policy making, although often overlooked, is easy to understand. All but a handful of the nation's school districts are governed by boards chosen through popular elections. These officials exercise their mandate within bounds set by state and federal policy makers facing electoral pressures of their own. Governance by elected school boards promotes transparency, provides a venue for stakeholder input on district policy making, and, in principle, allows for a measure of democratic accountability to local citizens. Unfortunately, it also makes it difficult for districts to respond sensibly to fiscal pressures. Existing state and federal policies, meanwhile, provide few incentives for district leaders to pursue cost-cutting reforms and often limit their ability to respond flexibly to budget cutbacks.

Interest Group Politics Within School Districts

Local school governance is largely an exercise in interest group politics. While regular elections allow ordinary citizens to hold school board members accountable for district performance, very few take advantage of this opportunity. Voter turnout in school board elections is notoriously low, often lingering in the single digits even when measured as a percentage of registered voters. These abysmal turnout rates in part reflect the fact that school board elections are typically held on different days than the contests for national or statewide office that tend to attract voters to the polls. In 1986, California revised its election code to allow school districts to move their elections from the off-cycle (odd) years to on-cycle (even) years. In research exploiting this policy change, Christopher Berry and Jacob Gersen show that turnout among eligible voters between 1996 and 2004 averaged 40 percent in districts holding their elections on-cycle, as compared to just 18 percent across districts that continued to hold their elections in odd years.[20]

Even when voters show up at the polls, many lack even the most basic knowledge necessary to make informed decisions. A 2001 study by Public Agenda found that 62 percent of adults could not name a single member of their local school board, and 63 percent could not name their superintendent. The authors were forced to conclude that "most people, for whatever reason, are simply not active in or mindful of school affairs on a routine basis."[21] One reason may be the shockingly small amounts of money even successful candidates spend on their campaigns. A national survey conducted by Frederick Hess and David Leal in 2001 found that more than 76 percent of school board members had spent fewer than $1,000 on their last election; fewer than 1 percent spent as much as $25,000.[22] Such low levels of campaign spending make it difficult for voters to acquire information on candidates and their positions.

In a low-turnout, information-poor environment, any group that is able to mobilize even a relatively small number of voters to support a particular candidate or slate can exercise outsized influence. It is no surprise, then, that fully 62 percent of superintendents and 69 percent of board members nationwide express agreement with the statement that school board meetings are "dominated by people with special interests and agendas."[23] A superintendent considering strategies to reduce costs must therefore be attentive to the various constituencies in the district that could be organized in response to a given change.

No group is better positioned to influence election outcomes on a regular basis than the unions representing teachers and other district employees, which benefit from a steady flow of resources from membership dues and agency fees and have ready access to a large number of potential voters and campaign workers. School board elections offer these employees the unusual opportunity to influence the makeup of the management team with which they will be bargaining over district policy. Predictably, Hess and Leal found that school board members described teacher unions as "very active" in local school board elections in 31 percent of school districts nationwide and either "very" or "somewhat" active in 57 percent—a significantly higher share than groups representing parents, religious interests, or the business community.[24]

Political scientist Terry Moe has carried out the most systematic research on union influence in school board elections.[25] In a study of 245 California school districts between 1998 and 2001, Moe found that candidates endorsed by the local teacher union were fifty-six percentage points more likely to win a board seat than were unendorsed candidates. By way of comparison, incumbent candidates were only 47 percent more likely than challengers to gain a seat. A related study of individual voter records from nineteen school board and school bond elections held between 1997 and 2000 in Los Angeles and Orange counties revealed that teachers who lived in the same district in which they worked were two to seven times more likely to vote than were other citizens. The median turnout gap between teachers and other citizens living in the same district was 36.5 percentage points, a huge increase over median turnout rates of 9 percent in school board elections and 23 percent in school bond elections. While Moe's evidence on turnout comes only from California, the *Education Next*–PEPG survey provides suggestive evidence that similar patterns hold more generally. Fifty-five percent of public school teachers nationwide reported in 2008 that they had voted in the most recent school board election in their district, as compared with just 33 percent of nonteachers.

The influence of teachers and teacher unions in local school politics has important consequences for educational productivity and for efforts to improve it in response to fiscal pressures. In the majority of school districts nationwide which engage in formal contract negotiations with unionized employees, the collective bargaining process provides teacher unions with a unique venue through which to shape district policy. Topics typically covered in teacher collective bargaining agreements range from the bread-and-butter issues of salaries and benefits to procedures for teacher evaluation, allowances for preparation time, limitations on student contact time

and class size, and a host of other work rules that structure everyday practice in the district's schools. Indeed, the 199 contracts on file at the Bureau
of Labor Statistics in January 2005 spanned, on average, 105 pages.[26] Their
sheer scope ensures that virtually any attempt to change an established
policy or practice will conflict with the contract in some way and therefore
require union approval. Accordingly, even researchers who downplay the
role of teacher unions as a proactive force shaping district policy generally
acknowledge that they have the ability to veto major policy changes.[27]

When the funds available to a school district are increasing, superintendents and school boards have the option of using salary and benefit increases
to win concessions from unions on contract provisions they believe interfere
with district performance. New York City schools chancellor Joel Klein was
widely praised between 2002 and 2006 for negotiating a series of contract
changes including shorter summers, a six-period work day, streamlined
grievance procedures, and a reinstatement of a policy under which teachers
patrolled school lunchrooms. Yet he was only able to convince United Federation of Teachers president Randi Weingarten to go along with these changes
by agreeing to increase teacher salaries by more than 40 percent, something
he was in a position to do because the performance of the city's economy
and the settlement of a long-running school finance lawsuit had generated
an infusion of new funds.[28] In a subsequent negotiation, Klein won union
approval for a modest merit pay program for schools serving low-income
students only by agreeing to modify pension policies such that a twenty-
five-year veteran could retire at age fifty-five, rather than sixty-two, with 50
percent of her salary guaranteed for life.[29] An early evaluation showed that
the merit pay program failed to improve performance at eligible schools,
perhaps because the potential bonuses were relatively small (3–7 percent of
annual salaries) and were allocated to school-level compensation commit-
tees rather than directly to individual teachers.[30] Yet the enhanced pension
benefit, estimated to be worth $250,000 to each veteran teacher, will remain
in the contract even if the program is jettisoned.[31]

Yet when available funds are steady or in decline, the options facing district leaders are more limited—and far less attractive. In February 2010,

Central Falls, Rhode Island, superintendent Fran Gallo attempted to implement a turnaround plan in her district's long-struggling high school that would have lengthened the school day and required teachers to receive more extensive professional development. However, negotiations with the local teacher union broke down when Gallo was unable to commit to offering teachers enough additional pay for their increased hours. In response, Gallo persuaded the district's board to impose an alternative plan calling for all ninety-three faculty and staff members to be fired at the end of the school year, with no more than 50 percent to be rehired later. The board's decision received national media attention and supportive comments from President Barack Obama and Secretary of Education Arne Duncan. But it also touched off a firestorm of protest and critical attention in the state and beyond. A week later Gallo reopened negotiations with the union in the hopes of reaching a compromise that would avert the mass firings.[32]

Although its outcome remains unresolved, the Central Falls episode also highlights the pressure on district leaders to maintain tranquil relations with their teachers. Superintendents in large urban districts consistently report being urged by civic officials, business leaders, and philanthropists to avoid conflict and to partner with the local union. And as Arne Duncan's own experience suggests, the safest path to professional success as a superintendent is to cultivate a reputation for being a consensual leader who keeps all parties at the bargaining table. Parents and the voting public frown on labor conflict and teachers' strikes for good reasons, not least among them the disruptions for families and their children's schooling that are caused by even temporary school closings. Yet the resulting pressure on superintendents to acquiesce to union demands makes it difficult for them to pursue reform, especially when they are unable to offer salary or benefit increases in exchange for desired concessions.[33]

While teacher unions have unmatched resources and a presence in school districts nationwide, they are hardly the only group that is active in local school politics. Virtually every program that districts enact creates a constituency of one form or another that can be mobilized to avoid cutbacks, even if the threatened program is ineffective or has outlived its purpose. This dynamic is nicely illustrated in chapter 9, where Arlington Public Schools superintendent Nathan Levenson describes his seemingly commonsense attempt to eliminate crossing guards at little-used intersections and to reduce the hours of all crossing guards to correspond to the times of day when children actually walked to schools. This cost-cutting measure, which had been endorsed by local police, traffic experts, and the district's elementary school principals, was intended to free resources for additional reading teachers, a better student information system, a data analyst, and stipends for teachers to develop a common curriculum and benchmark assessments, among other strategic investments. Yet protestors accusing Levenson of risking students' lives soon became a regular fixture at school board meetings, and in the end he was only able to push through the reduction in hours. More important, the crossing guards issue became the centerpiece of a vitriolic election campaign that cost Levenson two supportive board members.

The threat of political backlash understandably influences how even reform-minded district leaders approach budget cutbacks. Superintendent Jose Torres of School District U-46 in Elgin, Illinois, recently described being forced by budget cuts to decide between eliminating transportation for preschool or for afterschool extracurricular programming. While he considered the former pivotal to his goal of narrowing the district's achievement gaps and the latter largely extraneous, he noted that political pressures weighed in the opposite direction. Parents of students in the afterschool programs already benefited from the district's provision of transportation, expected it to continue in the future, and were poised to oppose service reductions. In contrast, parents of the young children who would enroll in early childhood education had not yet experienced the service and would be unlikely to make noise. Torres explained that his decision would inevitably come down to whether the expected long-run academic benefits of boosting preschool enrollment were sufficient to outweigh the political costs that would be incurred in making that investment—a refreshingly candid admission but hardly a recipe for sound fiscal policy making.[34]

State and Federal Policy Constraints

In addition to the internal political constraints on school boards and their appointed superintendents, the state and federal policies that shape district policy making also tend to work against cost-cutting reform. First, the accountability programs developed under the federal No Child Left Behind Act and its state-level predecessors focus exclusively on improving student test scores and closing achievement gaps without considering whether school districts achieve these goals in a cost-effective manner. District leaders who succeed in shaving costs while holding performance constant can therefore expect little public recognition or reward, even as spendthrift leaders who eke out test score gains are lavished with praise. When budgets decline, outcome-based accountability systems are helpful in pressing districts to seek out those cost-cutting measures that are least likely to impact student achievement adversely. Yet by ignoring inputs they create asymmetric incentives under which productivity gains are only formally recognized if they are accomplished through noticeable improvements in student achievement.

Accountability programs' inattention to inputs, combined with the extraordinary complexity of school finance systems, makes accurate information on school spending difficult for the public to obtain. The 2009 *Education Next*–PEPG survey showed that Americans are able to provide reasonably accurate assessments of the national graduation rate and the relative standing of American students on international assessments of math and science. When asked to assign letter grades to specific schools in their community, their assessments tend to correspond well to publicly available information on the proficiency rates of the school's students on state tests.[35] These findings diverge sharply from those of surveys asking respondents to estimate average teacher salaries in their state and how much was spent to educate each student in their local school district. On average, respondents to the 2007 survey underestimated average teacher salaries in their state by more than $14,000, or nearly one-third of the actual average salaries of $47,000. The average per-pupil spending estimate was $4,231 dollars, and the median response was just $2,000, whereas the actual average spending per pupil in their districts exceeded $10,000.[36] These contrasting levels of public aware-ness about student outcomes and spending inputs both reflect and work to reinforce a one-dimensional rewards system in which student outcomes are valued but productivity is ignored.

Second, much of the federal and state funding that now accounts for the bulk of total spending on K–12 education comes in the form of categori-cal grants that restrict the use of funds to specific purposes. Federal Title I-A funding for compensatory education, for example, must be spent only on low-income students or in schools that have a sufficient concentration of poverty to qualify for schoolwide programs. State funding systems also commonly allocate dollars to specific purposes such as textbook purchases, facilities improvement, vocational education, or nutrition programs. These restrictions, which are often accompanied by strict maintenance of effort re-quirements, are meant to ensure that districts use external funds in a manner consistent with their purpose and not as a substitute for local spending. State legislators may also recognize that districts will face strong pressures in the collective bargaining process to use any unrestricted state funds to increase teacher pay. A consequence, however, is that districts facing budget cutbacks are limited in their ability to repurpose funds to protect their top priorities.

Finally, a host of state laws and regulations stifles the ability of school districts to develop alternative approaches to staffing, instructional deliv-ery, and the procurement of instructional materials in response to revenue declines. In California and Florida, for example, incentives and mandates to reduce class size have forced school districts to devote inordinate re-sources to hiring additional teachers and constructing new facilities that might have been used to make teacher salaries more competitive or for other purposes altogether. State regulations on teacher certification and statutory provisions concerning evaluation, tenure, and dismissal constrain districts' options for recruiting new talent into the classroom and manag-ing their teacher workforces.[37] As John Chubb and Terry Moe have recently demonstrated, outdated state regulations have slowed the spread of online instruction and open source curricular materials in K–12 classrooms, even as they have spread like wildfire among homeschoolers and in the growing ranks of virtual charter schools.[38] Meanwhile, burdensome textbook procurement and approval policies increase administrative costs for districts and, by limiting the market to providers large enough to navigate the approval process, have prevented the kind of competition that could drive down costs.[39] In short, even reform-minded district leaders inclined to challenge the status quo often find that their hands are tied.

ENABLING REFORM

Overcoming the barriers to cost-cutting reform in American school districts will require improved analytic capacity and a newfound willingness to reconsider failed policies and to experiment with novel approaches to organizing and delivering instruction. Above all, it will require unprecedented political will on the part of school boards and superintendents who too often have been captive to beneficiaries of the status quo. The federal government, states, foundations, and the public at large all have roles to play in creating an environment in which change is possible.

Federal Policies

Much ink has been spilled proposing revisions to the accountability provisions of the federal Elementary and Secondary Education Act (ESEA), now long overdue for congressional reauthorization. Commonsense changes with broad support include incorporating measures of student achievement growth into school ratings, better differentiating between schools at varying levels of performance, and abandoning the utopian goal that all students achieve proficiency in core academic subjects by 2014. Modifications along these lines are essential in order to improve the quality of information about school performance provided by the law and to enhance the credibility of federal education policy. Yet none of these widely discussed changes would address the basic inattention to productivity that characterizes current educational accountability systems at all levels.

A reasonable first step to address this shortcoming would be for Congress to require the disclosure of average per-pupil spending at the level of the state, district, and school alongside the test-based metrics that now dominate school report cards. State education agencies should then be encouraged to develop and disseminate "return on investment" performance measures that attempt to adjust for cost differences across districts and schools. Although such adjustments would necessarily be imperfect, even relatively crude measures would enhance the transparency of information about school spending and call attention to the need for reform in such places as New Jersey's so-called Abbott Districts and in states like Rhode Island that devote incredible resources to public education yet achieve dismal results. By requiring that school spending reports reflect actual teacher salaries rather than the districtwide averages, the new federal requirement could also highlight disparities in spending within districts caused by the migration of experienced teachers to schools serving more advantaged students and create pressure for equity-oriented reform.

In addition, Congress should continue to expand the use of competitive grants such as Race to the Top, the Investing in Innovation Fund (i3), and the Teacher Incentive Fund as a substitute for the formula-driven categorical spending programs that have historically dominated federal education spending. It is too early to ascertain the overall success of the ongoing Race to the Top competition, by far the largest and most ambitious federal effort along these lines. Even so, there is little doubt that the program has provided leverage for state legislatures to consider more far-reaching reforms than would have been the case had the same funds been distributed through traditional mechanisms. At the same time, ongoing competitive grant programs should deemphasize support from local stakeholders as a selection criterion, as this practice only strengthens the hand of organized interests resistant to change. Instead, the Department of Education should condition eligibility for future competitions on the implementation of funded proposals and be aggressive about withdrawing funding from states failing to carry out promised reforms. Nor should grant competitions require applicant states to demonstrate that they have and will maintain past education funding levels, as this creates disincentives for efficiency-enhancing reform. Finally, programs such as i3 that are intended to foster and scale-up successful innovations should pay careful attention to issues of cost-effectiveness and sustainability when evaluating proposals.

State Policies

State governments must first of all resist the temptation respond to budget difficulties by weakening policies promoting accountability and subjecting school districts to authentic competition. Accountability systems that accurately measure school performance and include meaningful rewards and sanctions can strengthen the hand of district leaders eager to press for change. States should therefore continue to invest in the development of data systems that provide more detailed information on the performance of individual students and their academic progress over time. States should also foster competition among schools and districts through mechanisms such as charter schooling, school vouchers, and funding systems that link state and local funding to actual per-pupil enrollment. Such mechanisms, if designed such that dollars actually follow students to schools of their choice, can promote innovation and create a situation in which maintaining the status quo threatens budgets and jobs, giving management, local union leaders, and other stakeholders a common purpose in improving efficiency.

State legislatures should minimize the use of categorical grant programs and work to lift legal restrictions on the ability of districts to manage their funds and personnel flexibly. In particular, limits on class size and on the use of virtual instruction as an alternative to traditional classroom instruction should be eliminated. At the same time, states should craft new laws and regulations that constrain the outcomes of local collective bargaining negotiations to reflect performance and productivity concerns (for example, by requiring that teacher evaluations, tenure decisions, and compensation be based substantially on student achievement and limiting the use of experience and education credentials as a basis for compensation). Such mandates must be carefully designed in light of the limited capacity of many districts to measure teacher performance reliably and their collective inexperience with policies of this kind. Yet affirmative mandates that allow districts a measure of flexibility to respond to local circumstances have the potential to stimulate innovation even when new funds are not available to compensate groups opposed to change.

Finally, state legislatures should consider changing the mechanics of school board elections in two ways: by requiring that they be held at the same time as contests for statewide and national offices and by extending the time school board members hold their seats before facing reelection. Although hard evidence on the consequences of these changes is lacking, scheduling school board elections contemporaneously with other major elections would likely increase turnout among the general public and therefore limit the influence of special interests. Extending the terms of school board members could reduce superintendent turnover (and the policy incoherence it causes) and make it easier for superintendents to pursue politically challenging reforms. Both of these strategies are more widely applicable than placing control of school districts in the hands of local mayors, a policy that has yielded encouraging results in some locales but the merits of which likely depend on the mayor in question.

Foundations, Local Officials, and the General Public

Foundations can encourage cost-cutting reform by investing in district analytic capacity and by prioritizing issues of cost-effectiveness and sustainability when awarding grants. The cost of upgrading a district's data management systems is typically quite modest as a share of per-student spending, especially when evaluated over the system's expected lifetime and against the likely benefits of improved information to guide district policy. Nonetheless, the absence of a specific constituency that stands to benefit can make it difficult for superintendents to free up the necessary resources. In New York City, private funding allowed Joel Klein to construct the district's vaunted Achievement Reporting and Information System (ARIS) without reallocating funds away from other activities, providing a model for grantmaking in other districts. Foundations have also played a key role in supporting the recent emergence of a thriving sector of charter management organizations, human capital providers, and other entrepreneurial organizations working with and alongside school districts to improve student outcomes. As they continue this activity, foundations should pay attention not only to the results such organizations are producing but also to their cost and therefore the extent to which they provide an opportunity to improve system productivity.

Local officials concerned with the productivity of their area's schools may wish to follow in the footsteps of former New York City councilwoman Eva Moskowitz and hold hearings on the district's collective bargaining agreements, inviting public scrutiny and media coverage. Moskowitz's hearings were especially valuable in providing reporters a context for writing about the implementation of the contracts covering both teachers and noninstructional employees and their impact on district operations. Officials and civic leaders must also ensure that influential members of the local media are aware of contract provisions and have information on the nature, conduct, and outcomes of grievance and arbitration proceedings that determine how contracts are implemented.

Finally, parents, the business community, and the general public cannot continue to tolerate tepid district leadership. As simple as it sounds, local communities need to demand that school boards and superintendents work aggressively to eliminate efficiencies, to manage based on performance, and to stand up to organized interests opposed to change. The barriers to cost-cutting reforms are fundamentally political, and mobilizing those who pay the price for unproductive schools can make the crucial difference.

11

Conclusion

Eric Osberg

AMERICAN PUBLIC EDUCATION is facing a fiscal crisis, one that is unlikely to get significantly better absent important, structural changes in schools. As Frederick Hess notes in the introduction to this volume, the short-term problem is acute—significant state budget shortfalls are expected through 2013. At the same time, this is not just a short-term problem. James Guthrie and Arthur Peng put it quite simply in their chapter: "A hundred-year era of perpetual per-pupil fiscal growth will soon slow or stop. The causes of this situation are far more fundamental than the current recession. Schools should start buckling their seat belts now."

Despite such dire warnings, which have been sounded from coast to coast from many observers and analysts of our public schools, it is fair to say that too few school districts are willing or able to take the necessary steps to ensure their long-term fiscal solvency, to ensure that they are able to meet their missions and obligations to provide a high-quality education to all their students, even with reduced or tightened budgets.

Schools are facing pressure from two sides: the fiscal and academic fronts. Even as budgets tighten, the expectations for student achievement from states, the federal government, and even much of the public have not waned—nor should they. How can forward-thinking district leaders begin to "buckle their seat belts" and prepare their schools for a world in which they must do more with less? How can policy makers foster an environment for schools and districts in which it is possible to undertake the significant structural reforms they must consider? We believe those seeking answers can find them here, for the contributors to this volume bring varied backgrounds and viewpoints and offer a correspondingly wide range of intriguing ideas and solutions.

INCREMENTAL AND TRANSFORMATIVE APPROACHES

On the one hand, several authors offer compelling evidence and examples of how it is possible to improve on the existing model of schooling—to make it more efficient, more focused, and more responsive to economic realities. As Michael Casserly discusses in chapter 4, the efforts of the Great City Schools to optimize their operational and administrative functions are commendable and necessary. They have identified millions in savings that can be redirected into classrooms or saved from their bottom lines. Likewise, a team from Boston Consulting Group shows in chapters 7 and Stacey Childress shows in chapter 8 that committed district leaders can restructure how they staff their central offices or how they fund their schools in order to more effectively and efficiently fulfill their core missions to serve their students well.

On the other hand, several contributors demonstrate that—regardless of whether we have squeezed every drop of productivity from our current construct of schooling—we could dramatically improve the cost-efficiency of schooling if we radically rethink some of its basic assumptions. Fine-tuning today's model of district-based schooling may be sufficient to stave off fiscal calamity in the near term, but to produce better results more efficiently over the long haul, education must begin to mimic other industries that have found innovative ways to reconfigure and deploy their staffs and to use technology to achieve productivity gains. Today's schooling is a people-intensive industry, a fact that has not changed in hundreds of years. In fact, with the steady decline in student-teacher ratios in the past half-century, it has actually become *more* labor intensive. While other industries have boosted productivity per worker in innumerable ways over the last few decades, often with technology, education has moved in the opposite direction.

Both the incremental and the transformative approaches to making schools and districts more efficient have considerable merit, and, indeed, both are essential to meeting the large and long-term financial challenges facing schools. Yesterday, today, and twenty years from now, it will be imperative that schools and their systems be run by smart, creative, and dogged administrators who continually seek to do a little more with a few pennies less. A district that finds ways to maximize the number of buses in daily operation, for example, may find that tomorrow brings new challenges in food service or procurement. It must also guard against the possibility that its ground-breaking work in busing operations will grow obsolete as new schools, the aging of the buses, changes in the market for bus drivers, or other circumstances require it to think anew about that function. The efficient, effective fiscal stewardship of an organization is a continual process in which there is no single finish line—only a constant struggle for continuous improvement.

Better use of measurement tools and careful analytics is a straightforward but essential step, as both Casserly and Marguerite Roza demonstrate. The creation and use of key performance indicators in America's largest urban districts provides evidence that what gets measured gets attention; in the first few years using this tool, these districts improved the efficiency of their custodians, the age of their bus fleets, the costs of their food supplies, their use of electricity, and more.

In chapter 3 Marguerite Roza also shows that districts willing to undertake detailed analyses of all aspects of their programs—from English to art to track to cheerleading—are likely to be surprised by the areas of potential savings that become apparent. Using her methodology of calculating the per-student costs of classes, programs, sports, and other school activities, expensive outliers can be diagnosed and corrected—for example, by combining expensive elective courses or by outsourcing niche offerings (like photography) to a local community college or even an online provider. By targeting limited resources on the highest priorities, the result can be a more efficient use of personnel—the greatest cost to schools—and more effective schools.

And yet this continual struggle to fine-tune the current model of running schools should not leave us content that such improvements will be *sufficient*, even while they remain necessary. To stay ahead of the coming fiscal tidal wave that Hess foreshadows, fundamentally new models of schooling are needed.

LABOR COSTS

James Guthrie and Athur Peng's trenchant analysis makes clear why this is so: for decades, we have poured increasing funds and personnel into education with little or no long-term improvement in performance. This problem could have been seen coming decades ago—and indeed it was, at least by some astute observers. Education scholar Michael Kirst wrote in 1982, for example, that "in the past, lasting changes have tended to take the form of reform by addition. We have added functions, categorical programs, and additional layers of school personnel. But a single example will show that the period of reform by addition is over: If the pace at which we increased instructional personnel over the past twenty years were to continue, the national average pupil/teacher ratio (not counting aides) would be 12 to 1 by the year 2000."[1]

While we have not yet reached 12:1, the ratio has fallen to less than 16:1 and shows little sign of slowing—indeed, it may reach 14:1 within the decade (see chapter 1, figure 1.4 in this volume). While recent layoffs in many districts may extend this horizon, the long-term trend remains. Roza has argued that "one way to think about declining productivity in education is to attribute it to Baumol's disease . . . a tendency for costs in service industries to rise even as outputs stay the same." She asks, "Is Baumol's disease inevitable in education?" and firmly concludes that it is not.

> Service industries have re-thought the ways they hire and reward employees, so that employees are more personally connected with desired outcomes. Supply chain enhancements have yielded productivity gains by better connecting stages of production.

In contrast, the core processes involved in public education have remained virtually unchanged during the past 50 years: buildings consisting of classrooms are designed around uniformly paid career teachers, who are assigned to guide a group of same-aged children through an antiquated curricula delivered in nine-month segments . . .

. . . Clearly charter and private schools may provide some insights into alternative approaches. But there also could be relevant lessons gleaned from learning systems that occur in other oft-overlooked settings.

Home schooling and distance learning offer very different ways of producing student learning. Education systems in other countries also do things very differently. Even in our country, students learn piano, take swimming lessons, participate in driver's education, learn from franchised tutoring programs (e.g., Sylvan), or tackle what look like school topics in non-school settings (e.g., foreign language programs, science camps, or Kumon math programs).

In each of these learning models, while the delivery system is dramatically different than that of the typical school, one can't help but notice that students do learn.[2]

To improve productivity in schooling, district leaders must be willing (and politically able) to grapple with the cost of their teaching forces. As Steven Wilson points out in chapter 5, "Any serious appraisal of the question must begin with teachers, for spending on teachers represents a school district's single largest expense—in 2006, 45 percent of total expenditures in public education." And there are numerous ways to grapple with this cost. Districts across the country have already increased class sizes, and surely this is a smart strategy, for American public schools do not seem to have benefited from the dramatic reduction in class sizes over the prior three decades: student-teacher ratios have plummeted with no apparent corresponding improvement in educational outcomes. And so, in Wilson's anonymous northwestern district, an increase in class size, from a 15:1 student-teacher ratio to one of 17:1, results in savings equal to 5 percent of the district budget—savings that may have little or no negative impact on student achievement. (Indeed, Wilson carefully dissects the research and finds "limited" evidence and perhaps no reliable proof that schools' clinging to smaller classes is of much benefit to students.)

Teacher compensation must also be addressed. Wilson suggests that cost-cutting districts could actually pay many or most teachers *more*, thereby boosting teacher quality, if they rethink salary structures, staffing levels, and how teachers are deployed. For example, the generosity of teacher pensions and health benefits, relative to employees in other sectors, leaves fewer dollars available for base salaries and is a fiscal problem with which policy makers and school leaders will eventually be forced to grapple. In the meantime, their failure to align teacher benefits with those of other comparable professions bloats districts' budgets at significant cost; such benefits comprise up to 2 percent of district budgets.

The contributors also show how the reliance on experience and credentials in teacher compensation leads to substantial inefficiencies, with pay largely divorced from questions of teacher efficacy or student learning. Roza's 2007 analysis of teacher contracts found such raises combine to comprise more than 12 percent of district budgets. These often trace their roots to teacher contracts, which hinder cost-saving efforts in other ways—for example, when districts must abide by their provisions to base layoffs on teacher seniority rather than merit. When districts let go only the least experienced and thus least expensive teachers—regardless of their effectiveness—a greater number of them must be fired. Roza calculates that a district needing to reduce its salary expenditures by 5 percent would need to lay off 50 percent more personnel under a seniority-based policy than under a seniority-neutral policy.[3] This makes little financial or educational sense. (Thankfully, in 2009 Arizona passed a law banning the use of seniority in layoffs, and the Obama administration's strong emphasis on judging teachers by their classroom results may lead to a changing mind-set about this issue in particular.)

Beyond the fundamentals of compensation itself, many other factors conspire to inflate the cost of teachers in district budgets: the inability to quickly and cost-efficiently remove ineffective instructors from the classroom; high rates of absenteeism; spending on professional development that is arguably wasteful and ineffective; and the widespread use of teacher aides. Wilson estimates that a concerted effort to extract savings from these areas could yield another 5 percent in savings. Tackling such costs would be far more difficult for most districts than optimizing their busing operations, but it is a challenge that should not be avoided.

OPPORTUNITIES FOR INNOVATION AND LEADERSHIP

In the longer term, those states, districts, entrepreneurs, and school leaders willing to supplement (and in part replace) teachers with technology can expect the greatest potential savings. Wilson's proposed learning labs, which could save eight teacher FTEs per school, might yield savings of 5 percent. John Chubb suggests that hybrid schools, part virtual and part traditional, might do even a bit better than this, yielding savings of 8 percent relative to district schools. In chapter 6, he calculates that models of schooling which are fully online could be 10 percent cheaper than traditional brick-and-mortar schools (after offsetting the tremendous savings in teacher costs with the investments in technology and other costs specific to the online model).

Of course, technology is not a panacea. While it may be transformative for many districts, which either adopt forms of virtual learning or must compete for students with other schools or providers that do, its educational effectiveness is not yet fully proven. Still, districts need the creativity and entrepreneurial spirit to harness its potential in order to serve students well while cutting costs. Many of us—among the public, students, school leaders, and teachers—are accustomed to thinking of "schooling" as a relatively small group of students sequestered in a single room in front of a single teacher (perhaps with an aide). It need not always be so for all students all the time. Schools must do more to emulate those service sectors that have harnessed technology to boost their productivity and effectiveness.

A fundamental barrier to cost-efficiency in education is the pervasive mind-set that all reform must be, in Kirst's words, "by addition." The continual reduction in class sizes by adding teachers is one manifestation of this problem, albeit the most ubiquitous, but is not just limited to the teaching pool. Witness, for example, the perpetual "adequacy" campaigns and lawsuits around the country, some successful, arguing that the schools in this city or that state cannot be expected to successfully educate their pupils without greater infusions of dollars. And even some districts frequently cited as models of fiscal reform—for example, the emphasis in Montgomery County, Maryland, on directing funding to high-poverty schools and New York City's Fair Student Funding (or weighted student funding)—were made possible by increasing budgets that enabled the districts to shift funds while essentially holding harmless the budgets of many schools that otherwise stood to lose funding.

Childress describes the phenomenon of reform by addition well:

> District leaders have plenty of ideas for improving performance, but when they launch these new initiatives, they often leave the old ones in place. This practice is financially possible as long as revenue grows faster than inflation and negotiated increases in compensation. The net effect is layer upon layer of activities, many of which have little going for them but the fact that they exist. Shutting them down would require releasing or reassigning employees and changing the services received by some students whose parents are strong advocates for the existing arrangements. Rather than jeopardize support for their initiatives by antagonizing powerful stakeholders, superintendents invest in their new ideas without disrupting existing programs.

In short, changing this mentality in education is a leadership challenge. Unfortunately, again in Childress's words, "district leaders have not developed a habit of weighing the relative impact of various activities so that they can starve ineffective ones in order to feed promising ones." With district leadership typically dominated by former teachers or education administrators—transplants from the private sector are the exception rather than the norm—this financial, analytic mind-set does not come naturally to many superintendents. And given the historical norm of ever-increasing funding for schools, there has been little incentive or urgency for superintendents or other education leaders to focus on developing these skills over others.

In chapter 9, former Arlington, Massachusetts, superintendent Nathan Levenson reminds us that districts whose leadership teams lack the capacity to undertake careful financial analyses; who cannot plan strategically; and most importantly, who cannot build support for "unpopular decisions," are more likely to fail in their quests to thoughtfully enact significant cost savings. The task of strategically cutting costs, or of maintaining costs but aligning them with the strategic goals, is a large undertaking. In chapter 7 representatives of the Boston Consulting Group provide a useful glimpse into what it can entail: analyzing cost-saving measures in other sectors, utilizing scale curves to understand administrative cost structures, or enacting a vast, strategic reorganization of roles and personnel.

Clearly, to undertake such initiatives—or even to manage the experts who might be charged with their implementation—requires a savvy superintendent who can manage change, manage people, and manage complex organizations. As the authors write, "Strong leadership is a necessary condition for success, given the emotional response that often comes with cost efficiency and reduction initiatives. Leaders and their direct reports must clearly and frequently communicate the case for change to the organization. They must stand firm by decisions in the face of multiple debates not supported by facts. Last, they must be able to guide and motivate the organization through difficult periods that have the potential for very sharp declines in morale."

Several contributing authors offer useful advice on how district leaders can effectively communicate fiscal reforms. Roza shows the power of framing the choice and its alternatives; budget cuts may be seen as less draconian and painful when it is known that even less popular cuts are under consideration. And yet too few districts follow this advice. As she reports,

In the spring of 2009, many districts . . . announced layoffs as though there were no other options. Teachers and parents, in many cases, vigorously opposed the layoffs. In many districts, including Seattle Public Schools, teachers picketed layoff decisions at the district's headquarters . . . A few districts, however, did indeed enact layoffs as one of several trade-offs. And other districts made different decisions. For example, teachers in the William Floyd District in Long Island traded portions of their salaries to avert layoffs of nineteen district employees.

And Levenson argues succinctly that leaders should "stop talking about cost-cutting. Talk instead about cost-effectiveness. Cost-cutting assumes we are taking something away from children. No wants to support it. Cost-effectiveness means getting the same or better results for less money. No one wants to not support that."[4]

We hope the leadership and management lessons offered here will be useful to those district and education leaders who must ensure their districts and schools are able to do more with less.

POLITICAL AND POLICY BARRIERS

Even for those leaders with the will and wherewithal to push for significant change, political barriers loom large. Garnering political and popular support for always-unpopular decisions to reduce outlays or reconfigure school operations can be a crippling hurdle for any of the measures addressed in this volume. Students, families, and employees become accustomed to the ways their schools operate, and it's simply human to resist painful change. Inertia is a powerful force. Equally powerful are education's interest groups, which are well organized and focused—often focused on securing greater funding, even conditioned to expect that change will not occur absent new resources—whereas those who might oppose such spending, taxpayers in particular, are dispersed, unorganized, and relatively uninformed. The results are predictable and well chronicled.

Martin West concedes in chapter 10 that these political challenges are considerable, but they may not be insurmountable. Perhaps the most important contribution state and federal policy makers can make toward rectifying public education's fiscal crisis is to provide district and local leaders the support and the cover they need to make painful changes.

Such cover could take many forms. For example, as West notes, reforms could address the fact that accurate and comparable spending data are rarely available, and almost never are they linked to student achievement data. State scorecards that graded districts not just on their academic performance but on their academic *efficiency*—on student learning per dollar spent—would be helpful to leaders seeking support for fiscal reforms in their districts. Unfortunately, West argues, today "district leaders who succeed in shaving costs while holding performance constant can . . . expect little public recognition or reward, even as spendthrift leaders who eke out test score gains are lavished with praise." If state and federal expectations of schools included an emphasis on fiscal success, not just academic achievement, district and school leaders could harness this external pressure and, in Levenson's words, help ensure that "data, not history, drive budget decisions."

States can also encourage districts or cities that wish to restructure their governance arrangements in order to empower their superintendents. Mayoral control, for example, can limit the often counterproductive politics of school boards, which can prevent district leaders from instituting uncomfortable changes or in seeing those changes through to completion. As Casserly writes, the "alignment of resources with strategic priorities . . . takes careful assessment and analysis, target setting, prioritizing, planning, confidence building and time, something that an impatient public isn't always inclined to grant. But the task is highly complex and will require patience as schools struggle to get this right."

Levenson grappled with such challenges in Arlington, leading him to conclude that school boards should perhaps be "more like the Senate," with elections every six years rather than every few years. Regardless of their particular forms, reforms are needed to increase the likelihood that the long-term priorities of students, families, and taxpayers will gain political traction sufficient to overwhelm the short-term demands of adult interest groups and others resistant to change.

State and federal policy can also encourage and support specific reforms that are most likely to be cost effective. For example, given that the best data available suggest that charter schools operate at 80 percent of the cost of district schools and provide comparable (and occasionally better) academic results, cost-conscious policy makers should free them from barriers to growth. First among these barriers are enrollment caps and limits on the number of charter schools, but equally problematic are local school boards or district leaders who inhibit the birth of new charter schools or the operation of existing ones in their backyards.

Virtual and online forms of schools and courses face similar opposition, and state and federal policies could do more to encourage their growth. It is time to modernize state laws limiting the enrollments of online schools or policies that were designed for traditional schools and thus unable to smoothly incorporate virtual or hybrid forms of learning.

Finally, as West notes, federal and state policy makers could greatly aid local district and school leaders striving to better manage their budgets by freeing them of many of the mandates imposed from above by federal and state laws and regulations. For example, he notes that the "heavy reliance on categorical spending by the federal government and the states restricts the ability of districts to reallocate funds to their most important priorities, while additional rules and regulations limits experimentation with new models of staffing or instructional delivery."

Today, even with decade after decade of new spending, there is little cause for satisfaction with the performance of our schools, the level of student achievement, or our progress in combating socioeconomic gaps in achievement. For the sake of our students, the time is now for schools to find paths toward greater productivity. Doing so will require schools to rethink what a teacher does and how he or she is paid, what a school looks like, and what programs it offers. Must a student learn only from those teachers located in his or her particular school building? Why can't we use technology to give Susie exposure to the award-winning physics teacher in the next county, or even three thousand miles away, rather than give her only the option of the two mediocre science teachers in her building (if she even gets to choice among them)? Why can't technology, like teacher aides, do more to assist teachers in their classrooms—administering lessons, practice problems, and other exercises—while at the same time making easier the task of compiling their results, analyzing student learning, and devising appropriate interventions for each child?

The challenges and barriers to fundamental, long-term reform of schooling are indeed formidable, so it is not unreasonable for superintendents to focus first on the changes that are simplest or least controversial. Indeed, all district leaders should immediately take some of the most fundamental, yet important steps described in this volume: they should seek to optimize their noninstructional operations, they should analyze all their costs at the unit level, and they should flatten and modernize their central office structures.

But it is equally true that cash-strapped districts cannot simply close a few school buildings, lower the cost of food services, or raise class sizes slightly and expect to put their fiscal challenges behind them. Changes such as those may indeed be needed—and plenty of districts have and will continue to implement them—but to address the coming crisis of state budget deficits and national debt, more dramatic change is needed. We hope district leaders will heed the arguments provided in this volume about the power and cost-efficiency of virtual learning models, whether in conjunction with or in lieu of traditional classrooms. It is also essential that, regardless of the number of teachers schools and districts employ, they structure their roles and compensation to maximize the return on this core investment in schooling rather than simply continue to pay them and deploy them in the ways of the past.

The types of reforms, political changes, leadership skills, and management disciplines the authors describe here are essential today, in times of fiscal crisis, and will continue to be invaluable when economies recover and revenues increase, for we can never alleviate the need to spend our educational dollars in ways that are the least wasteful and the most beneficial to students. Indeed, the dual pressures for improved academic results and greater financial efficiency are here to stay, and addressing them will require everyone with a stake in our education system to rethink fundamental assumptions and embrace significant change. Only with this mindset can schools both stretch their dollars and serve students best.

Notes

Introduction

1. Noelle Ellerson, "A Cliff Hanger: How America's Public Schools Continue to Feel the Impact of the Economic Downturn" (Arlington, VA: American Association of School Administrators, 2010).

2. "State Budget and Finance: Trends and Challenges," Nelson A. Rockefeller Institute of Government, Sept. 25, 2009, http://www.rockinst.org/pdf/government_finance/2009-09-25-Boyd_Pew_presentation.pdf.

3. Ashlee Vance, "Microsoft Plans to Cut 5,000 Jobs," *New York Times*, Jan. 22, 2009, http://www.nytimes.com/2009/01/22/technology/22iht-23soft.19595492.html.

4. Peter Burrows, "Cisco to Restructure up to 2,000 Employees out of Jobs: But Just Don't Call Them Layoffs," *Business Week,* Feb. 4, 2009, http://www.businessweek.com/the_thread/techbeat/archives/2009/02/cisco_to_restru.html.

5. *Looking Back, Looking Forward: How the Economic Downturn Continues to Impact School Districts* (Washington, DC: American Association of School Administrators, 2009), http://www.aasa.org/uploadedFiles/Resources/files/LookingBackLookingForward.pdf.

6. Chester E. Finn Jr., *Troublemaker: A Personal History of School Reform since Sputnik* (Princeton, NJ: Princeton University Press, 2008), 284.

7. W. Norton Grubb, *The Money Myth: School Resources, Outcomes, and Equity* (Russell Sage Foundation Publications, January 2009); Gary Burtless, *Does Money Matter? The Effect of School Resources on Student Achievement and Adult Success* (Washington, DC: Brookings Institution Press, 1996); Helen Ladd, *Handbook of Research in Education Finance and Policy* (Routledge, 2007); James Guthrie, Matthew G. Springer, Anthony Rolle, and Eric A. Houck, *Modern Education Finance & Policy* (Allyn & Bacon, 2006).

8. Carolyn Busch and Allan Odden, *Financing Schools for High Performance: Strategies for Improving the Use of Educational Resources* (San Francisco: Jossey-Bass, 1998).

Chapter 1

1. The absence of mention of education or schooling from the U.S. Constitution appears not to have been a frivolous omission or unconscious lapse of consideration. At the time of the Constitution's framing, most of the soon-to-be states' constitutions already had provisions by which the state would assume responsibility for education.

2. See *Campbell County, State of Wyoming, et al. v. State of Wyoming, et al.* 907 P.2d 1238, 1995 Wyo.; *Serrano v. Priest*, 5 Cal.3d 584 (1971); *Washington v. Seattle School District No. 1*, 458 U.S. 457 (1982); or *Tennessee Small School Systems v. McWherter*, 851 S.W.2d 139.

3. A seldom-recognized irony is that in the school year immediately following enactment of Proposition 13, an overwhelmingly popular initiative that withdrew $5 billion in tax revenues out of the state's public economy, public schools in California received more per pupil than in the previous year. California had a $7 billion state surplus (and protected by Governor Jerry Brown) that the legislature could draw to compensate for local property tax revenue losses.

4. Robert Novy-Marx and Joshua Rauh, "The Liabilities and Risks of State Sponsored Pension Plans," *Journal of Economic Perspectives* 23 (Fall 2009): 191–210.

5. Robert Clark, "Retiree Health Plans for Public School Teachers after GASB 43 and 45," paper presented at the National Center on Performance Incentives for a conference on Educator Pension Systems (Nashville, TN: Vanderbilt University, 2010).

6. When there are many local school districts in a state, and when they contribute a large share of school revenues, state per-pupil mean spending is higher.

Chapter 2

1. All quotes, unless noted, come from interviews conducted by the author in 2009.

2. http://www.ecs.org.

Chapter 3

1. Michele McNeil, "Governors, State Legislatures Seek Ways to Limit Damage," *Education Week*, January 5, 2009, http://www.edweek.org/ew/articles/2009/01/07/16session_ep.h28.html.; Michele McNeil, "Districts Scrounge for Low-Pain Budget Cuts," *Education Week*, January 15, 2009, http://www.edweek .org/ew/articles/2009/01/15/18scrounge.h28.html?tmp=619749410.

2. Since not all the money will go to K–12 education (some will go to higher education, etc.), we should anticipate some level of expenditure of less than that in K–12 education.

3. Or $1,016 per student per year if expended over two years.

4. Based on author's conversations with district officials in 1999. District name and those of officials held for confidentiality.

5. "NYC Public School Principals Divided over ARIS System, Gotbaum Survey Says," Office of the Public Advocate press release, August 20, 2009, http://pubadvocate.nyc .gov/new_news/8.20.09ARIS.html.

6. Marguerite Roza, "Breaking Down School Budgets," *Education Next* 9, no. 3 (Summer 2009).

7. For a relative comparison of costs, benefits can be excluded.

8. Based on author's calculations.

9. Michael DeArmond and Dan Goldhaber, *A Leap of Faith: Redesigning Teacher Compensation* (Seattle: Center for Reinventing Public Education, University of Washington, 2008).

10. Marguerite Roza, *The Tradeoff Between Teacher Wages and Layoffs to Meet Bud get Cuts* (Seattle: Center for Reinventing Public Education, University of Washington, 2009).

11. Winnie Hu, "The New Math: Teachers Share Recession's Pain," *New York Times*, May 22, 2009, http://www.nytimes.com/2009/05/24/education/24teachers.html.

12. Nancy Badertscher, "Budget Cuts Target Substitute Teachers," *Atlanta Journal Constitution*, November 2, 2009, http://www.allbusiness.com/education-training/ teaching-teachers/13369637-1.html.

13. Based on interviews by the author with district leaders, in a Colorado district, in 2003. District and officials' names held for confidentiality.

14. The name of the school has been changed to protect confidential conversations, 2008, with district leaders.

15. For a more complete description of the technique, see Marguerite Roza and Claudine Swartz, "School Spending Profiles: A Framework to Enlighten Resource Allocation Decisions," *Public Budgeting and Finance* 27, no. 1 (Spring 2007), 68–95.

16. Marguerite Roza and Raegen Miller, *Separation of Degrees: State-by-State Analysis of Teacher Compensation for Master's Degrees* (Seattle: Center on Reinventing Public Education, University of Washington, 2009).

17. Kate Walsh and Christopher O. Tracy, *Increasing the Odds: How Good Policies Can Yield Better Teachers* (Washington, DC: National Council on Teacher Quality, 2005).

18. National Council on Teacher Quality, *Teacher Quality Bulletin* 10, no. 10 (November 2009).

Chapter 5

1. U.S. Department of Education, National Center for Education Statistics, "Table 174: Summary of Expenditures for Public Elementary and Secondary Education, by Purpose; Selected Years, 1919–20 through 2005–06," *2008 Digest of Education Statistics,* comp. Thomas D. Snyder, Sally A. Dillow, and Charlene M. Hoffman, NCES 2009-020 (Washington, DC: Government Printing Office, 2009), 250; and "Table 180: Expenditures for Instruction in Public Elementary Schools, by Subfunction and State or Jurisdiction; 2004–05," ibid., 260.

2. "Table 32: Historical Summary of Public Elementary and Secondary School Statistics; Selected Years, 1869–70 through 2005–06," ibid., 60; and "Table 80: Staff Employed in Public Elementary and Secondary School Systems, by Functional Area; Selected Years, 1949–50 through Fall 2006," ibid., 117.

3. "Table 64: Public and Private Elementary and Secondary Teachers, Enrollment, and Pupil/Teacher Ratios; Selected Years, Fall 1955 through Fall 2017," ibid., 98.

4. U.S. Department of Education, National Center for Education Statistics, *NAEP 2008 Trends in Academic Progress,* comp. Bobby D. Rampey, Gloria S. Dion, and Patricia L. Donahue, NCES 2009–479 (Washington, DC: Government Printing Office, 2009).

5. "Chart B1.1: Annual expenditure on educational institutions per student in primary through tertiary education," *Education at a Glance 2009: OECD Indicators,* (Organization for Economic Cooperation and Development, 2009, 2002).

6. U.S. Department of Education, National Center for Education Statistics, *Highlights from PISA 2006: Performance of U.S. 15-Year-Old Students in Science and Mathematics Literacy in an International Context,* comp. Stéphane Baldi, Ying Jin, Melanie Skemer, Patricia J. Green, Deborah Herpet, and Holly Xie, NCES 2008-016 (Washington, DC: Government Printing Office, 2007), 6, 12.

7. "Table 64," *2008 Digest of Education Statistics,* 98.

8. Eric A. Hanushek and Steven G. Rivkin, "Understanding the Twentieth-Century Growth in U.S. School Spending," *Journal of Human Resources* 32, no. 1 (1996): 45.

9. "Class Size," National Education Association, http://www.nea.org/home/13120.htm; "Class Size Counts: The Research Shows Us Why," American Federation of Teachers, http://archive.aft.org/pubs-reports/downloads/teachers/Policy3.pdf. The AFT Web site text continues: "High academic standards and a challenging curriculum, safe and orderly classrooms, and qualified teachers are no less significant in the arsenal of solid research-proven reforms. And, in fact, when smaller class size is pursued in conjunction with these standards-based reforms, the combined impact on student achievement is far greater than either strategy alone."

10. Tom Loveless and Frederick M. Hess, eds., *Brookings Papers on Education Policy 2006–2007* (Washington, DC: Brookings Institution, 2007), 2.

11. Douglas N. Harris, "Class Size and School Size: Taking the Trade-Offs Seriously," in ibid., 153.

12. Ibid.

13. Gary Hopkins, "The Debate over Class Size, Part 2: The Critics Have Their Say," *Education World,* February 23, 1998.

14. Eric A. Hanushek, "Some Findings from an Independent Investigation of the Tennessee STAR Experiments and from Other Investigations of Class Size Effects," *Education Evaluation and Policy Analysis* 21, no. 2 (1999): 150, 155–156.

15. Diane Whitmore Schanzenbach, "What Have Researchers Learned from Project STAR," in Loveless and Hess, *Education Papers on Education Policy 2006/2007,* 213.

16. Alan B. Krueger and Diane M. Whitmore, "The Effect of Attending a Small Class in the Early Grades on College Attendance Plans," (Princeton, NJ: Princeton University, April 1999), 1.

17. Jay P. Greene, *Education Myths* (Oxford: Rowan & Littlefield, 2005), 53.

18. Caroline M. Hoxby, "The Effects of Class Size on Student Achievement: New Evidence from Population Variation," *Quarterly Journal of Economics* 115, no. 4 (2000): 1239–1285.

19. The results of the 1994 NAEP were released in 1995. See also California Senate Bill 1777, passed in 1996; George W. Bohrnstedt and Brian M. Stecher, eds., *What We Have Learned about Class Size Reduction in California* (Sacramento: California Department of Education, 2002), 25.

20. "Fingertip Facts," California Department of Education, http://www.cde.ca.gov/ ls/ cs/k3/facts.asp.

21. "2002–03 Statewide Summary Data," California Department of Education, http:// www.cde.ca.gov/ls/cs/k3/sum02.asp.

22. Bohrnstedt and Stecher, *What We Have Learned about Class Size Reduction in California,* 7.

23. Ibid., 5, 35, 37.

24. Ibid., 49.

25. Christopher Jepsen and Steven Rivkin, "Class Size Reduction and Student Achievement: The Potential Tradeoff between Teacher Quality and Class Size," *Journal of Human Resources* 44, no. 1 (2009): 245.

26. Joshua D. Angrist and Victor C. Lavy, "Using Maimonides' Rule to Estimate the Effect of Class Size on Scholastic Achievement," *Quarterly Journal of Economics* 114, no. 2 (2009): 533–576; Alan Krueger, "Experimental Estimates of Education Production Functions," *Quarterly Journal of Economics* 114, no. 2 (2009): 514; Steven C. Rivkin, Eric A. Hanushek, and John F. Kain, "Teachers, Schools, and Academic Achievement," *Econometrica* 73, no. 2 (2005): 447.

27. Jepsen and Rivkin, "Class Size Reduction and Student Achievement," 224.

28. Ibid., 247.

29. Bohrnstedt and Stecher, *What We Have Learned about Class Size Reduction in California,* 38.

30. Greene, *Education Myths*, 56.

31. Ibid., 56–57.

32. Ludger Wössmann and Martin West, "Class-Size Effects in School Systems around the World: Evidence from Between-Grade Variation in TIMSS," Harvard University, Program on Education Policy and Governance, Working Paper No. PEPG/02–02 (2002): 31–32.

33. "About KIPP," Knowledge Is Power, http://www.kipp.org/about-kipp/results.

34. "Common Questions about KIPP," Knowledge Is Power, http://www.kipp.org/ 01/resultsofkippsch.cfm.

35. "About KIPP," Knowledge Is Power, http://www.kipp.org/about-kipp/results, accessed October 24, 2009.

36. Quoted in Abigail Thernstrom and Stephan Thernstrom, *No Excuses: Closing the Racial Gap in Learning* (New York: Simon & Schuster, 2003), 57.

37. Elizabeth Word, John Johnston, and Helen Bain, *Student/Teacher Achievement Ratio (STAR), Tennessee's K–3 Class Size Study: Final Summary Report, 1985–1990* (Memphis: Tennessee Department of Education, 1990), 11.

38. For SABIS 2009 MCAS results for the NCLB low-income subgroup, see http://profiles.doe.mass.edu/mcas/subgroups2.aspx?linkid=25&orgcode=04410505&fycode=2009&orgtypecode=6&. For Springfield Public Schools low-income subgroup, see http://profiles.doe.mass.edu/mcas/performance_level.aspx?linkid=32&orgcode=02810000&orgtypecode=5&.

39. "The Top of the Class 2008: The Complete List of the 1,300 Top U.S. High Schools," *Newsweek,* May 17, 2008, http://www.newsweek.com/id/39380/?q=2008/ state/601/.

40. Steven F. Wilson, *Learning on the Job: When Business Takes on Public Schools* (Cambridge, MA: Harvard University Press, 2006), 122.

41. Rocketship Education, "Rocketship Education: Achieve," http://www.rsed.org/achieve.

42. Rocketship Education, "Rocketship Education 2009 Academic Results Highest Performing in San Jose and Santa Clara County, Tops Palo Alto Unified," press release, September 16, 2009, http://www.rsed.org/downloads/rsed_09_results_release_9.16.pdf.

43. Michael Barber and Mona Mourshed, *How the World's Best Performing School Systems Came out on Top* (McKinsey & Co., 2007), 11–12.

44. Ibid., 12.

45. Steven Brill, "The Rubber Room: The Battle over New York City's Worst Teachers," *New Yorker,* August 31, 2009.

46. The New Teacher Project, "Executive Summary," *Teacher Hiring, Transfer, and Assignment in Chicago Public Schools,* July 2007, http://www.tntp.org/files/TNTPExecSumm-Chicago.pdf.

47. V. Dion Haynes, "Rhee Seeks Tenure-Pay Swap for Teachers: Giving Up Seniority Would Boost Salary If Benchmarks Met," *Washington Post,* July 3, 2008.

48. Kieran M. Killeen, David H. Monk, and Margaret L. Plecki, "School District Spending on Professional Development: Insights Available from National Data (1992–1998)," *Journal of Education Finance* 28 (Summer 2002): 28.

49. For instance, consider an audit of professional development spending in Chicago in 2002. The districts spent nearly $200 million on professional development "without any 'overarching strategy' for improving instruction" and with no requirement for proof of improvement. Rosalind Rossi, "Schools Get Millions; Results 'Unclear,'" *Chicago Sun-Times,* November 15, 2002.

50. Sean Corcoran, William Evans, and Robert Schwab, "Changing Labor Market Opportunities for Women and the Quality of Teachers 1957–2000," NBER American Economic Review Papers and Proceedings, May 2004, 94 (2) Working Paper No. 9180 (2002).

51. "Assessing Scientific, Reading, and Mathematical Literacy : A Framework for PISA 2006," Programme for International Student Assessment (Paris, France: OCEd, 2006)..

52. Barber and Mourshed, *How the World's Best Performing School Systems Came out on Top*, 18.

53. Kwok Chan Lai, "The Qualifications of the Teaching Force in the Hong Kong Special Administrative Region, China," 35–37; Hidenori Fujita, "The Qualifications of the Teaching Force in Japan," , 47; Ee-Gyeong Kim, "The Quality and Qualifications of the Teaching Force In the Republic of Korea," 64–69; Steven K. S. Tan and Angela F. L.

Wong , "The Qualifications of the Teaching Force: Data from Singapore," 80-81; Richard M. Ingersoll, "The Preparation and Qualifications of the Teaching Force in the United States, 101–104, all in *A Comparative Study of Teacher Preparation and Qualifications in Six Nations,* ed. Richard M. Ingersoll (Philadelphia: Consortium for Policy Research in Education, 2007).

54. "NYC Teaching Fellows: Program Overview," NYC Teaching Fellows, http://www.nyctf.org/the_fellowship/prgm_overview.html.

55. "About the NYC Teaching Fellows," NYC Teaching Fellows, http://www.nycteachingfellows.org/mypersonalinfo/downloads/NYCTFpresskit.pdf.

56. U.S. Department of Education, Office of Innovation and Improvement, *Innovations in Education,* November 2004, http://www.ed.gov/admins/tchrqual/recruit/altroutes/report_pg13.html.

57. "NYC Teaching Fellows: Program Overview."

58. Marguerite Roza and Raegen Miller, *Separation of Degrees: State-by-State Analysis of Teacher Compensation for Master's Degrees* (Seattle: Center on Reinventing Public Education, 2009).

59. Steven G. Rivkin, Eric A. Hanushek, and John F. Kain, "Teachers, Schools, and Academic Achievement," *Econometrica* 73, no. 2 (2005): 449–450.

60. "Systemic Reform," Harrison School District No. 2, http://www.hsd2.org/departments/human-resources/eandr#systemicreform.

61. Frederick M. Hess and Martin R. West, *A Better Bargain: Overhauling Teacher Collective Bargaining for the 21st Century* (Cambridge, MA: Harvard University, Program on Education Policy and Governance, 2006), 2.

62. Barber and Mourshed, *How the World's Best Performing School Systems Came out on Top,* 20.

63. Michael Podgursky, "Fringe Benefits," *Education Next* 3(3): 71–76.

64. Hess and West, *A Better Bargain,* 24.

65. Robin Chait, *Current State Policies That Reform Teacher Pay* (Washington, DC: Center for American Progress, 2007), 19–20.

66. Caroline M. Hoxby and Andrew Leigh, "Pulled Away or Pushed Out? Explaining the Decline of Teacher Aptitude in the United States," *American Economic Review* 94, no. 2 (May 2004): 236–240.

67. Thomas Toch, "Five Myths about Paying Good Teachers More," *Detroit News,* October 13, 2009.

68. Ibid.

69. Hess and West, *A Better Bargain,* 24.

70. Ibid., 25, citing Leslie Moye, Ann Duffet, Jean Johnson, and Steve Farkas, *Stand by Me: What Teachers Really Think about Unions, Merit Pay and Other Professional Matters* (New York: Public Agenda, 2003): 24–25.

71. Joshua H. Barnett, Gary W. Ritter, Marcus A. Winters, and Jay P. Greene, *Evaluation of Year One of the Achievement Challenge Pilot Project in the Little Rock Public School District*, (Fayetteville: University of Arkansas Department of Education Reform, 2007), 9–11.

72. James W. Guthrie and Patrick J. Schuermann, "The Question of Performance Pay," *Education Week,* October 29, 2008.

73. Emily Ayscue Hassel and Bryan C. Hassel, *3X for All: Extending the Reach of Education's Best* (Chapel Hill, NC: Public Impact, 2009).

74. Podgursky, "Fringe Benefits," 74.

75. Robert M. Costrell and Michael Podgursky, "Teacher Retirement Benefits," *Education Next* 9(2): 59.

76. Hess and West, *A Better Bargain*, 26.

77. Podgursky, "Fringe Benefits," 72.

78. Raegen T. Miller, Richard J. Murnane, and John B. Willett, "Do Teacher Absences Impact Student Achievement? Longitudinal Evidence from One Urban School District," Working Paper No. 13356, National Bureau of Economic Research, August 2007, http://www.nber.org/papers/w13356.

79. U.S. Department of Education Office of Special Education and Rehabilitative Services, *A New Era: Revitalizing Special Education for Children and their Families* (Washington, DC: Government Printing Office, 2002), 25.

80. Ibid., 26.

Chapter 6

1. Gary T. Kubota, "Teachers Approve Contract," *Honolulu Star Bulletin*, September 23, 2009, http://www.starbulletin.com/news/20090923_Teachers_approve_contract.html.

2. "California: Now Issuing IOUs for Income Tax Refunds," *TurboTax Support*, July 15, 2009, http://blog.turbotax.intuit.com/2009-tax-law-changes/california-is-sending-ious-to-taxpayers/.

3. "Schools Across the District Finalize Budget Adjustments," press release, DC Public Schools, October 2, 2009, http://www.dcps.dc.gov/DCPS/About+DCPS/Press+Releases+and+Announcements/Press+Releases/Schools+Across+the+District+Finalize+Budget+Adjustments.

4. The factors that predict and fail to predict teacher success have been the subject of more research than any other influence on student achievement. Representative studies include Eric A. Hanushek, "Assessing the Effects of School Resources on Student Performance: An Update," *Educational Evaluation and Policy Analysis* 19, no. 2 (1997):141–164; Daniel D. Goldhaber and Dominic J. Brewer, "Does Teacher Certification Matter? High School Teacher Certification Status and Student Achievement," *Educational Evaluation and Policy Analysis* 22, no. 2 (2002):129–145; and Linda Darling-Hammond, "Teacher Quality and Student Achievement: A Review of State Policy Evidence," *Education Policy Analysis Archives* 8, no. 1(2000).

5. *Economic Stimulus Package (ARRA) Guidance to Governors from Secretary of Education Arne Duncan*, April 1, 2009. Accessed at www2.ed.gov/policy/gen/leg/recovery/index.htm/#apps.

6. Schools will attempt to cushion the potential blow to students with home assignments during days off; no educator wants the students to lose out. But everyone agrees the loss of in-school instructional time puts student achievement at risk.

7. Ian McGugan, "Too Many Cars, Too Few Customers," *Financial Post*, November 21, 2009,http://www.financialpost.com/story.html?id=2248928.

8. International comparisons of education spending vary somewhat depending on which measures are employed, but every analysis places the United States among the top spenders. See, for example, Michael Barber and Mona Mourshed, *How the World's Best Performing School Systems Came out on Top* (McKinsey & Co., 2007).

9. The latest figure reported by the federal government is for the 2005–2006 school year, when total public school expenditures totaled $529 billion. *Digest of Education Statistics 2008*, Institute of Education Sciences, National Center for Education Statistics, Table 174, U.S. Department of Education, http://nces.ed.gov/programs/digest/d08/tables/dt08_174.asp.

10. These well-known indicators are explicated and documented in Terry M. Moe and John E. Chubb, *Liberating Learning: Technology, Politics, and the Future of American Education* (San Francisco: Jossey Bass, 2009).

11. William Howell, Martin West, and Paul Peterson, "The Persuadable Public," *Education Next* 9, no. 4 (2009), http://educationnext.org/persuadable-public/.

12. The 70 percent figure is the sum of the federal accounting categories, "instruction" (51.9%) and "other school services" (18.3 %). *Digest of Education Statistics 2008*.

13. The most successful is arguably the Japanese (and Asian) model of giving teachers larger classes but more time to prepare, fewer classes to teach, and better compensation. See Harold W. Stevenson and James M. Stigler, *Learning Gap: Why Our Schools Are Failing and What We Can Learn from Japanese and Chinese Education* (New York: Simon & Schuster, 1992).

14. These schools numbered 219 in 2009. *National Charter Schools Directory,* Center for Education Reform, http://www.edreform.com/charter_directory/SpecialtyProfile .cfm?&spec_id=5.

15. "Learning on Demand: Online Education in the United States, 2009," Sloan Consortium (Newburyport, MA 2009).

16. "Learning on Demand: Online Education in the United States, 2009," Sloan Consortium (Newburyport, MA 2009).

17. The classic model is attributed to Madeline Hunter. See, for example, Madeline Hunter, *Mastery Teaching: Increasing Instructional Effectiveness in Elementary and Secondary Schools, Colleges and Universities* (Thousand Oaks, CA: Corwin Press, 1992).

18. Lesson differentiation through methods such as "pyramid planning" is how teachers are taught to address the diverse classroom, but the methods inevitably compromise what some students can learn.

19. The problem is perhaps best expressed in the School of One project launched by the New York City Public Schools in the summer of 2009 to offer students fully customized instruction. The project, serving one pilot middle school, explains that even the most successful teachers in the entire school system fail to help a third of their students reach state proficiency levels in reading and math.

20. Urban schools are as likely as suburban schools to have instituted policies to limit cell phone and iPod use during class time.

21. Studies of online learning, covering many programs still in their infancy, find student achievement gains at least as strong as those in traditional settings. See Rosina Smith, Tom Clark, and Robert L. Blomeyer, *A Synthesis of New Research on K–12 Online Learning* (Naperville, IL: North Central Regional Education Laboratory, 2005); Cathy Cavanaugh, Kathy Jo Gillan, Jeff Kromrey, Melina Hess, and Robert Blomeyer, "The Effects of Distance Education on K–12 Student Outcomes: A Meta-Analysis," (Naperville, IL: Learning Points Associates, North Central Regional Education Lab, 2004).

22. *Digest of Education Statistics 2008.*

23. Moe and Chubb, *Liberating Learning,* chap. 5.

24. *Digest of Education Statistics 2008.*

25. Details on technology spending in brick and mortar schools are discussed in Moe and Chubb, *Liberating Learning,* ch. 4.

26. Because teachers at all grade levels are given planning time away from students, the number of teachers needed to cover a student day exceeds the number of periods in a day: one teacher covers only five- or six-sevenths of a student day; the rest of the day must be covered by other teachers.

27. In elementary schools, the single period of online instruction requires half a teacher (one teacher supervising two classes), a savings of .5 teachers from the total otherwise necessary of 7. A savings of .5 teachers from the total of seven is a 7 percent personnel savings. In middle schools the savings is double that, or 14 percent, because online instruction occupies two periods. In high schools, three online classes (rather than two) are supervised by one teacher, and online instruction occupies three periods per day. So the teacher savings equal two-thirds of a teacher for three periods, or two whole teachers for every seven previously needed, a savings of 29 percent.

28. The savings are calculated as follows. In the scenario in which online learning occupies one period in elementary, two periods in middle, and three periods in high school, the savings in traditional teachers equals $800 per student. Since the cost of software for a single online class is $5,000 versus the $13,000 price tag of a traditional class, the online class is 5/13 the price of the traditional class per student. Applying a 5/13 software deduction to the $800 savings per student in our hybrid model yields a $500 per-student all-in savings per student from hybrid instruction.

Chapter 7

1. The Steering Committee and the Boston Consulting Group, *Vision 2015*, 5, http://www.vision2015delaware.org/resources/Vision2015report1-26.pdf.

2. *Vision 2015*, 13.

3. *Vision 2015*, 21.

4. LEAD Committee, *Report on Education Funding in Delaware: Executive Order 98*, 3, www.doe.k12.de.us/reports_data/lead.shtml.

5. The LEAD Committee's final *Report on Education Funding in Delaware* and accompanying documents also include minor recommendations for cost efficiency within the state's Department of Education.

6. Ohio Legislative Service Commission, *The Effects of the Exemption of School Construction Projects from Ohio's Prevailing Wage Law*, SB 102 Report, 2002.

7. Rosalind Rossi, "Budget Crisis Threatens School Jobs," *Chicago Sun Times*, January 23, 2006.

8. David Mendell, "City Schools to Cut 70 Office Jobs, Save at Least $14 Million," *Chicago Tribune*, May 31, 2006.

Chapter 8

1. Peter Drucker, "Managing for Business Effectiveness," *Harvard Business Review*, May–June 1963, 53–60.

2. This deceleration in growth rates and subsequent decline in revenues hit California districts earlier than those in the rest of the country due to the way the state's school funding mechanisms operate.

3. For a list of case studies developed by PELP faculty members, see http://www.hbs .edu/pelp/casestudies.html.

4. William Ouichi, *Making Schools Work* (New York: Simon & Schuster, 2003) and *The Secret of TSL: The Revolutionary Discovery That Raises School Performance* (New York: Simon & Schuster, 2009).

5. Joseph L. Bower, *Managing the Resource Allocation Process,* revised edition, (Boston: Harvard Business Press, 1986).

6. Among others, such notables as Robert Burgleman, C. K. Prahalad, and Clayton Christensen replicated Bower's findings.

7. Joseph L. Bower and Clark G. Gilbert, eds., *From Resource Allocation to Strategy* (New York: Oxford University Press, 2005).

8. Donald Sull, "When the Bottom-Up Resource Allocation Process Fails," in *From Resource Allocation to Strategy,* ed. Joseph L. Bower and Clark G. Gilbert (New York: Oxford University Press, 2005).

9. Thomas Eisenmann and Joseph L. Bower, "The Entrepreneurial M-Form: Strategic Integration in Global Media Firms," *Organizational Science* 11, no. 3 (2000): 348–355.

10. Clayton M. Christensen and Joseph L. Bower, "Customer Power, Strategic Investment, and the Failure of Leading Firms," *Strategic Management Journal* 17, no. 3 (1996): 197–218.

11. Donald Sull, "No Exit: The Failure of Bottom-up Strategic Processes and the Role of Top-down Disinvestment," in Bower and Gilbert, *From Resource Allocation to Strategy.*

12. The descriptions of the STAR strategy and resource allocation in this section are adapted from Stacey Childress, "The STAR Schools Initiative at San Francisco Unified School District," PEL-039 (Boston, MA: Harvard Business School Publishing, 2006). All direct quotes from Arlene Ackerman and other SFUSD staff members are from this case.

13. This section draws heavily on two pieces: Stacey Childress, Denis Doyle, and David Thomas, *Leading for Equity: The Pursuit of Excellence in Montgomery County Public Schools* (Cambridge, MA: Harvard Education Press, 2009); and Stacey Childress, "Six Lessons for Pursuing Excellence and Equity at Scale," *Phi Delta Kappan* 91, no. 3 (2009). All direct quotes from Jerry Weast are from *Leading for Equity.*

14. The section draws on Stacey Childress, "Focusing on Performance at the New York City Department of Education," PEL-054, Boston, MA: Harvard Business School

Publishing, 2008 (rev. ed.). All direct quotes from Joel Klein originally appeared in this publication unless otherwise noted.

15. Ouchi, *The Secret of TSL*.

16. Ana Champeny, "New Funding Formula Seeks to Alter School Budget Disparities," New York City Independent Budget Office Fiscal Brief, October 2007, http://www.ibo.nyc.ny.us/iboreports/FairStudentFunding2.pdf.

17. Jennifer Medina, "Amid Hiring Freeze, Principals Leave Jobs Empty," *New York Times*, August 28, 2009.

18. Joel Klein, letter to principals, September 16, 2009, attained from district by author.

Chapter 9

1. *Seeking Effective Policies and Practices for Students with Special Needs* (Cambridge, MA: Rennie Center for Educational Research and Policy, 2009), 2.

2. Ibid., 4.

3. Francis Storrs, "Dispatch: Sex and the School District," *Boston Magazine*, October 2009.

Chapter 10

1. Complete survey results are available in William G. Howell, Martin R. West, and Paul E. Peterson, "What Americans Think about Their Schools," *Education Next* 7, no. 4 (2007): 12–26; William G. Howell, Martin R. West, and Paul E. Peterson, "The 2008 *Education Next*–PEPG Survey of Public Opinion," *Education Next* 8, no. 4 (2008): 12–26; William G. Howell, Martin R. West, and Paul E. Peterson, "The Persuadable Public," *Education Next* 9, no. 4 (2009): 20–29. Except where noted, all references in this chapter to results from the *Education Next*–PEPG surveys are drawn from these articles.

2. Historical results from the annual *Phi Delta Kappan*/Gallup polls are available at http://www.pdkintl.org/kappan/poll.htm.

3. Pew Center on the States, *The Trillion Dollar Gap: Underfunded State Retirement Systems and the Roads to Reform* (Washington, DC: The Pew Charitable Trusts, 2010).

4. See, for example, Josh Barro and Stuart Buck, "Underfunded Teacher Pension Plans: It's Worse Than You Think," *Manhattan Institute Civic Report* 61 (April 2010); Andrew G. Biggs, "An Options Pricing Method for Calculating the Market Price of Public Sector Pension Liabilities," *AEI Working Paper* 164 (February 2010).

5. Pew Center on the States, *The Trillion Dollar Gap*.

6. U.S. Census Bureau Population Division, 2008 National Population Projections, "Projections of the Population by Selected Age Groups and Sex for the United States: 2010 to 2050," http://www.census.gov/population/www/projections/2008projections .html.

7. Michael B. Berkman and Eric Plutzer, *Ten Thousand Democracies: Politics and Public Opinion in America's School Districts* (Washington, DC: Georgetown University Press, 2005): 128–144.

8. Eric A. Hanushek, "The Failure of Input-Based Schooling Policies," *Economic Journal*, 113, no. 485 (2003): F64–F98.

9. Caroline M. Hoxby, ed., *The Economics of School Choice* (Chicago: University of Chicago Press, 2003), 293.

10. Thomas E. Glass, Lars Bjork, and Cryss C. Brunner, *The Study of the American School Superintendency, 2000: A Look at the Superintendent of Education in the New Millennium* (Arlington, VA: American Association of School Administrators, 2000): 70, table 5.27.

11. Ibid., 68–69.

12. Jon Fullerton, "Mounting Debt," *Education Next* 4, no. 1 (2004): 11–19.

13. Ibid., 18.

14. Ibid., 16, figure 4.

15. Richard Elmore, "Unwarranted Intrusion," *Education Next* 2, no. 1 (2002): 33–34.

16. Eric Hanushek, "An Effective Teacher in Every Classroom: A Lofty Goal, but Can It Be Done?" *Education Next* 10, no. 3 (2010): 48.

17. Marguerite Roza and Raegan Miller, *Separation of Degrees: State-by-State Analysis of Teacher Compensation for Master's Degrees* (Washington, DC: Center for American Progress, 2009).

18. For an influential defense of incremental policy making in public agencies, see Charles E. Lindbloom, "The Science of 'Muddling Through,'" *Public Administration Review* 19, no. 2 (1959): 79–88.

19. Fullerton, "Mounting Debt," 13.

20. Christopher R. Berry and Jacob E. Gersen, "The Timing of Elections," *University of Chicago Law Review* (forthcoming 2010).

21. Steve Farkas, Patrick Foley, and Ann Duffett, *Just Waiting to Be Asked: A Fresh Look at Attitudes on Public Engagement* (New York: Public Agenda, 2001), 15.

22. Frederick M. Hess and David L. Leal, "School House Politics: Expenditures, Interests, and Competition in School Board Elections," in *Besieged: School Boards and the*

Future of Education Politics, ed. William G. Howell (Washington, DC: Brookings Institution Press, 2005), 236, figure 10.1.

23. Farkas, Foley, and Duffett, *Just Waiting to Be Asked*, 10.

24. Hess and Leal, "School House Politics," 241, table 10.4.

25. Terry M. Moe, "Political Control and the Power of the Agent," *Journal of Law, Economics, and Organization* 22, no. 1 (2006): 1–29.

26. Frederick M. Hess and Martin R. West, *A Better Bargain: Overhauling Teacher Collective Bargaining for the 21st Century* (Cambridge, MA: Harvard University Program on Education Policy and Governance, 2006).

27. See, for example, Jeffrey R. Henig, Richard C. Hula, Marion Orr, and Desiree S. Pedescleaux, *The Color of School Reform: Race, Politics, and the Challenge of Urban Education* (Princeton, NJ: Princeton University Press, 2001).

28. Peter Meyer, "New York City's Education Battles," *Education Next* 8, no. 2 (2008): 11–20.

29. Elisa Gootman, "Teachers Agree to Bonus Pay Tied to Test Scores," *New York Times*, October 18, 2007.

30. Serena Goodman and Lesley Turner, "Group Incentives for Teachers: The Impact of NYC School-Wide Bonus Program on Educational Outcomes," *Columbia University Department of Economics Discussion Paper* 0910-05 (August 2009).

31. Meyer, "New York City's Education Battles."

32. Linda Borg and Paul Davis, "Central Falls Superintendent Acts to Fire City's High School Teachers," *Providence Journal*, February 11, 2010; Kate Zezima, "A Vote to Fire All Teachers at a Failing High School," *New York Times*, February 23, 2010; and Jennifer D. Jordan, "Schools Chief, Teachers Agree to Resume Talks," *Providence Journal*, March 4, 2010.

33. Frederick M. Hess and Martin R. West, "Strike Phobia: School Boards Need to Drive a Harder Bargain," *Education Next* 6, no. 3 (2006): 39–48.

34. Jose Torres comments at "Penny Saved: How Schools and Districts Can Tighten Their Belts While Serving Students Better," a conference sponsored by the Thomas B. Fordham Institute and the American Enterprise Institute, Washington, DC, January 11, 2010.

35. Matthew M. Chingos, Michael Henderson, and Martin R. West, "Citizen Perceptions of Government Service Quality: Evidence from Public Schools," Unpublished manuscript, Harvard Graduate School of Education (June 2010).

36. William G. Howell and Martin R. West, "Is the Price Right? Probing Americans' Knowledge of School Spending," *Education Next* 8, no. 3 (2008): 37–41.

37. Emily Cohen, Kate Walsh, and RiShawn Biddle, *Invisible Ink in Collective Bargaining: Why Key Topics Are Not Addressed* (Washington, DC: National Center on Teacher Quality, 2008).

38. John E. Chubb and Terry M. Moe, *Liberating Learning: Technology, Politics, and the Future of American Education* (San Francisco: Jossey-Bass, 2009).

39. Frederick M. Hess, *Education Unbound: The Promise and Practice of Greenfield Schooling* (Alexandria, VA: ASCD, 2010).

Chapter 11

1. Michael W. Kirst, "How to Improve Schools Without Spending More Money," *Phi Delta Kappan* 64, no. 1 (1982): 6–8.

2. Marguerite Roza, "Must Public Education Suffer from Baumol's Disease?" *Denver Post*, August 1, 2008.

3. Marguerite Roza, *Seniority-Based Layoffs Will Exacerbate Job Loss in Public Education* (Seattle: Center on Reinventing Public Education, University of Washington, 2009), http://www.crpe.org/cs/crpe/download/csr_files/rr_crpe_layoff_feb09.pdf.

4. Nate Levenson, "A Win-Win Approach to Reducing Special Education Costs," *District Management Journal* 1 (Spring 2009): 20–43.

About the Editors

Frederick M. Hess is a resident scholar and the director of education policy studies at AEI, executive editor of *Education Next*, and author of the *Education Week* blog "Rick Hess Straight Up." His many books include *Education Unbound* (ASCD, 2010), *Common Sense School Reform* (Palgrave Macmillan, 2004), *Revolution at the Margins* (Brookings Institution Press, 2002), and *Spinning Wheels* (Brookings Institution Press, 1998). His work appears in scholarly and more popular outlets, such as *Teachers College Record, Harvard Education Review, Social Science Quarterly, Urban Affairs Review, Chronicle of Higher Education, U.S. News and World Report, Washington Post*, and *National Review*. He serves on the review board for the Broad Prize in Urban Education and on the boards of directors for the National Association of Charter School Authorizers and the American Board for the Certification of Teaching Excellence. A former high school social studies teacher, Hess teaches or has taught at the University of Virginia, the University of Pennsylvania, Georgetown University, Rice University, and Harvard University.

Eric Osberg is the vice president and treasurer of the Thomas B. Fordham Institute. He is also a research fellow at the Hoover Institution. He is primarily responsible for financial and managerial issues at Fordham, and also works on policy projects related to school finance. From 1997 to 2000, Osberg worked for Capital One Financial in Vienna, Virginia, where he helped develop the company's telecommunications line of business, America One.

About the Contributors

Michael Casserly serves as executive director of the Council of the Great City Schools, the nation's primary coalition of large urban public school systems. Before assuming this position in January 1992, he served as the organization's director of legislation and research for fifteen years. He is currently spearheading efforts to boost academic performance in the nation's big city schools; strengthen management and operations; challenge inequitable state financing systems; and improve the public's image of urban education. Casserly has also written numerous studies, reports, and op-ed pieces on urban schools, including CCSO's "Beating the Odds," report series—the nation's first look at urban school performance on state tests. He is considered by many to be one of Washington's best education advocates and lobbyists and an expert on urban education, governance, finance, and federal legislation and policy. His legislative work has been the subject of a college textbook on how Capitol Hill really works. *Washington Almanac* listed Casserly one of Washington, DC,'s four hundred most powerful individuals, and *USA Today* called him a "crusader" for city schoolchildren. Casserly is a U.S. Army veteran.

Stacey Childress is deputy director of innovation at the Bill and Melinda Gates Foundation. Previously, Childress was a senior lecturer in the general management unit at Harvard Business School and a cofounder of the Public Education Leadership Project at Harvard University. She studied entrepreneurial activity in public education in the United States, including the behavior and strategies of leadership teams in urban public school districts, charter schools, and nonprofit and for-profit enterprises with missions to improve the public system. She is also interested more generally in a range of social enterprise topics, including international social entrepreneurship. Childress has authored more than two dozen case studies about large urban districts and entrepreneurial education ventures and is the coauthor with Richard Elmore and Allen Grossman of the *Harvard Business Review* article "How to Manage Urban Districts." She is also a coeditor, with Susan Moore Johnson, Allen Grossman, and Richard F. Elmore of the book *Managing School Districts for High Performance: Cases in Public Education Leadership* (Harvard Education Press, 2007). Before working in academia, Childress was a cofounder of an enterprise software company and spent ten years in a Fortune 500 company in sales and general management. Early in her career, she taught in a Texas public high school.

John E. Chubb is the chief executive officer of Leeds Global Partners, LLC. Until recently, Chubb was chief development officer and senior executive vice president of EdisonLearning, which he helped found in 1992. EdisonLearning is the nation's leading education reform company, working typically with disadvantaged communities to create innovative charter schools, to turn around underperforming public schools, and to bring online educational solutions to schools and families. Prior to assuming his current role in 2008, he served as EdisonLearning's chief education officer. Before joining Edison, he was a senior fellow at the Brookings Institution and a professor of political science at Stanford University. He currently is a distinguished visiting fellow at the Hoover Institution at Stanford University and a member of Hoover's task force on K–12 education. Chubb is the author or editor of numerous books, including *Liberating Learning: Technology, Politics, and the Future of American Education*, with Terry M. Moe (Jossey-Bass, 2009); *Learning From No Child Left Behind,* (Hoover, 2009); *Within Our Reach: How America Can Educate Every Child* (Roman and Littlefield, 2005); *Closing the Achievement Gap*, with Tom Loveless (Brookings Institution Press, 2001); and *Politics, Markets, and America's Schools*, with Terry M. Moe (Brookings Institution Press, 1990). His articles have appeared in the *New York Times, Wall Street Journal, Education Next, The Public Interest,* and *American Political Science Review,* among other publications. He Chubb has served as an adviser to the White House under the Reagan first Bush adminstrations, numerous state governments, and public and private schools and school systems.

Jill Corcoran joined the Chicago office of the Boston Consulting Group in 2001. She is currently the director of social impact. While at BCG, Corcoran has worked with clients across industries on strategy development, organization design, large-scale transformation, and organization start-up. In the last four years, she has focused on public education and nonprofit clients. Examples of her work in public education include assisting with start-up of the National Math and Science Initiative; supporting Chicago Public Schools on a high school transformation effort; helping develop the strategy and launch the plan for Advance Illinois, a statewide education advocacy organization; and designing a support organization for Chicago's Renaissance 2010 schools. Prior to joining BCG, Corcoran worked in education policy and program evaluation for Mathematica Policy Research. She holds an MBA from Chicago Booth, where she received the George Hay Brown Marketing Prize; an MPP from the University of Chicago's Harris School of Public Policy Studies; and a BA in sociology, summa cum laude, from Harvard University.

Reginald Gilyard joined the Boston Consulting Group in 1996 and is a core leader in the firm's education practice. He currently serves as partner and managing director, and he has worked with private- and public-sector clients. His experience in the education sector has included developing a strategic plan to improve teacher effectiveness in the Prince George's County, Maryland, school system and leading efforts to support New Orleans Recovery School District in opening thirty-four post-Katrina public schools. He also led the development of various strategic plans for the Los

Angeles Unified School District, Seattle Public Schools, and the Cleveland Metropolitan Schools District. Prior to joining BCG, Gilyard was a project manager in the U.S. Air Force, where he led USAF officers and civilian defense contract professionals in the development, production, and fielding of logistics and intelligence systems.

James W. Guthrie is a senior fellow at the George W. Bush Institute and a professor of Public Policy and Education at Southern Methodist University. Previously, he was the Patricia and Rodes Hart Professor of Educational Leadership and Policy and director of the Peabody Center for Education Policy at Peabody College of Vanderbilt University, where he conducted research on education policy and finance. He is founder and chairman of the board of Management Analysis & Planning, Inc. (MAP), a private-sector management consulting firm specializing in public finance and litigation support. He was previously a professor at the University of California, Berkeley, for twenty-seven years. Guthrie has been a consultant to the governments of Armenia, Australia, Chile, Guyana, Hong Kong, Pakistan, Romania, and South Africa and has extensive experience consulting for the World Bank, UNESCO, and the Organization of American States. He is the author or coauthor of fourteen books and more than two hundred professional and scholarly articles. He is past president of the American Education Finance Association and served as editor-in-chief of the *Encyclopedia of American Education* (2002) and as editor Vanderbilt University's ten-volume Peabody Education Leadership Series.

June Kronholz is a Washington, DC–based writer. She previously worked for the *Wall Street Journal* as a foreign correspondent in London, Africa, South Asia, the Philippines; and Hong Kong; as the *Journal*'s bureau chief in Boston and deputy bureau chief in Washington; and as a *Journal* reporter in Washington, DC, where she covered education for a decade.

Nathan Levenson has spent much of his career in the private sector as a strategic planning management consultant, as an owner of a midsized manufacturer of highly engineered machinery, and as a turnaround consultant helping struggling firms. A passion for public education led to a career switch that included six years as a school board member, working as assistant superintendent for curriculum and instruction in Harvard, Massachusetts, and, most recently, as superintendent of the Arlington, Massachusetts, Public Schools. Levenson was hired as an agent of change in Arlington during a turbulent time in a divided community. He oversaw all academic and operational aspects of a district with nine schools and $50-plus million budget. He helped create and champion an intensive reading program that reduced the number of students reading below grade level by 52 percent and revamped special education services that lead to a 24 percent improvement in academic achievement in English and math. By redesigning the district's budgeting, custodial, financial accounting, and leadership structure, the district created $1.5 million in savings. A multipronged reform to deliver special education services more cost effectively also helped curb more than $3 million in spending. During Levenson's leadership, the Arlington Public Schools built partnerships with local nonprofits to provide, at little or no cost, nearly $1 million of social services per year.

Lane McBride is a principal in the Boston Consulting Group's Washington, DC, office. With BCG since 2003, Lane has managed education projects at the state and local level, encompassing a variety of topics including transformation strategy, performance management, teacher effectiveness, and cost efficiency. Through these efforts, he has extensive experience working with education stakeholders, including students, teachers, administrators, unions, foundations, charter schools, other nonprofits, and the private sector. Lane's experience outside of education includes work in consumer goods and retail, with a particular focus on qualitative and quantitative consumer research.

Arthur Peng is a research associate at the Peabody Center for Education Policy at Vanderbilt University. Peng is a graduate assistant for the National Center on Performance Incentives and is currently a PhD candidate in the

Department of Leadership, Policy and Organizations at Vanderbilt University's Peabody College. His research interests include educational policy, with a particular focus on the impact of measurement issues on the estimates of value-added school, teacher, and program effects. The primary focus of his recent work has been on evaluations of performance-pay programs in Texas, New York, Colorado, and North Carolina; an examination of achievement tradeoffs and NCLB; and an analysis of volatility in school-level test scores and its implications for monitoring school performance over time.

Jamal Powell is a principal in the Atlanta office of the Boston Consulting Group. He is a core member of the company's social impact practice network and consumer practice area. He has extensive experience working with clients across the education landscape, including state education authorities, public school districts, charter school authorizers, and education advocacy organizations. His work within the education sector has included working with District of Columbia Public Charter School Board to revise their performance management framework as well as leading strategy development and implementation planning efforts to transform Dallas Independent School District (Dallas Achieves), including central office cost reduction and development of performance management and accountability systems. Powell has also developed a comprehensive teacher effectiveness strategy for the School District of Palm Beach County, Florida, and assisted in the transformation of the New Orleans public schools' post–Hurricane Katrina. Before BCG, he spent three years in investment banking with Morgan Stanley, where he worked in the real estate division. During his time at Morgan Stanley, he spent one year based in Tokyo and traveling throughout the region. Powell also participates as a member of the Managing for Excellence Committee for the Community Foundation for Greater Atlanta.

Marguerite Roza serves as a research associate professor with the Center on Reinventing Public Education at the University of Washington. Roza's research focuses on education spending and productivity. Her recent research has produced fiscal projections of the effect of the recession on education. Additionally, her work has documented the real dollar implications of education policies once realized inside schools across schools within districts. Her calculations of dollar implications and cost-equivalent tradeoffs have prompted changes in education finance policy at all levels in the education system. Roza's work has been published Education Sector, the Brookings Institution, *Education Next*, and the *Peabody Journal of Education*. Prior to joining the University of Washington faculty, she served as a lieutenant in the U.S. Navy teaching thermodynamics at the Naval Nuclear Power School.

Martin R. West is an assistant professor of education at the Harvard Graduate School of Education. He also serves as an executive editor of *Education Next*, a journal of opinion and research on education policy; is deputy director of the Program on Education Policy and Governance at Harvard University; and is an affiliate of the CESifo Research Network. Before joining the Harvard faculty, West taught at Brown University and was a research fellow at the Brookings Institution.

Steven F. Wilson is founder and president of Ascend Learning, a charter school management organization in New York City, and a senior fellow at Education Sector in Washington, DC. He is a former executive vice president for product development at Edison Schools and senior fellow at the Center for Business and Government of the John F. Kennedy School of Government, Harvard University. His most recent book, *Learning on the Job: When Business Takes on Public Schools* (2006), which examines the first decade of private management of public schools, was awarded the Virginia and Warren Stone Prize. Wilson founded and served as CEO of Advantage Schools, an urban charter school management company. Prior to founding Advantage, he was special assistant for strategic planning for Massachusetts governor William Weld, whom he advised on education policy during the passage and implementation of the state's 1993 comprehensive education reform act. He also oversaw the Weld administration's privatization programs and drafted the governor's plan to reorganize state government. Wilson is the former executive director of the Pioneer Institute for Public Policy Research. His first book, *Reinventing the Schools: A Radical Plan for Boston* (1992), led to the establishment of Massachusetts charter school law, which Wilson drafted.

Index

Abbott Districts (N.J.), 284
absenteeism. *See* teacher absenteeism
academic outcomes
    educational spending and, 12–13
    outcome-based accountability systems, 281
    public awareness of spending and,
        266–267, 277, 281
    See also student achievement
accountability, 13
    autonomy/accountability exchange,
        224–228, 229, 231–232
    federal and state policies, 265, 269, 285
    mechanisms for, 226–227
    outcome-based systems, 281
    for progress, 122, 283
accounts payable, 109
achievement. *See* student achievement
Achievement Challenge Pilot Project,
    147–148
Achievement First, 132, 140–141
Achievement Reporting and Innovation
    System (ARIS), 74, 227, 286
Ackerman, Arlene, 214–215, 217, 219, 225,
    229, 231, 232, 233
activity-based costing, 274
ACT test, 128
"adequacy" campaigns, 295–296
administration
    compensation of, 159
    cost-cutting in, 16, 239–240
    See also central office support
Advanced Placement (AP) courses, 75, 76–78,
    222

advisors
    for online instruction, 169
    student behavior advisors, 215, 258
AERA (American Educational Research As-
    sociation), 127
African American students
    achievement-related challenges, 201, 214
    low proficiency rates, 220–221
    in special education, 150
AFT (American Federation of Teachers), 127
alternative education, 64
American Association of School Superinten-
    dents, 268
American Educational Research Association
    (AERA), 127
American Federation of Teachers (AFT), 127
American Institutes for Research, 76
American Recovery and Reinvestment Act
    (ARRA) of 2009, 33, 35, 37, 73, 156
annual quality review, 226–227
AP (Advanced Placement) courses, 75, 76–78,
    222
ARIS (Achievement Reporting and Innova-
    tion System), 74, 227, 286
Arlington (Mass.) Public Schools
    cost-cutting example, 235–262, 269
    political barriers to change, 269, 280
ARRA (American Recovery and Reinvestment
    Act) of 2009, 33, 35, 37, 73, 156
Ascend Learning (charter school manage-
    ment), 15
assistant principals, 52
asynchronous instruction, 165, 167–168

Atkins, Norman, 142
audit of spending data, 182–187
    analogous efforts, 185
    comparison of best practices, 184–185
    comparison of estimates of outsourcing,
        185
    funding formula incentives, 185–186
    inter-district comparisons, 183
    interstate comparisons, 183
    public policy objectives and, 186
    use of professional judgment in, 186–187
    use of scale curves, 183–184
automation
    cost savings through, 53–54
    of Key Performance Indicators, 119
autonomy/accountability exchange, 224–228,
        229, 231–232
auxiliary services
    counseling, task force on options in,
        248–249
    custodial (*See* custodial services)
    food service (*See* food service)
    power indicators in, 103, 115
    printing operations, 62
    security, 79, 108
    service costing, 72, 75–81
    study of information services, 101–102
    transportation (*See* transportation)

baby boomers, 43–44
Ballmer, Steven, 3
ballotpedia.org, 66
Baumol's disease, 292–293
BCG. *See* Boston Consulting Group
behavior management
    options in counseling services, 248–249
    in pre-referral programs, 151
    in special education, 258
    student behavior advisors, 215, 258
Bellevue Public Schools case study, 125–153
benchmarks
    developed from data collection and analy-
        sis, 14–15
    in finding "economies of scale," 184
    in service costing, 79
    for student achievement, 222

benefit cutting
    health care benefits, 1
    pension plan benefits, 1, 42–43, 56–57
    as strategic move, 47, 56–59
Berdnik, Christopher, 56, 58–59, 62, 67
best practices
    analyses of, 119–120
    "boot camp" on, 237–238
    comparisons of, 184–185
    delayering and, 202
    documentation of, 100
    in purchasing, 119, 184–185
    in special education, 250
Bill & Melinda Gates Foundation, 15
Bistany, Ralph, 134–135
block scheduling, 52
Bloomberg, Michael, 224
boards of cooperative educational services
        (BOCES), 64–65
Boston Consulting Group (BCG), 15, 290
    budget analyses by, 270, 297
    large-scale cost cutting, 179, 187, 192, 195,
        202, 204, 208
    limitations to work of, 270–271
Boston Magazine, 262
Boston Teacher Residency, 143
bottom-up resource allocation, 212
Bower, Joseph, 212, 231
Bragga, Lynn, 50, 53, 65
bridal-type registry, in fundraising, 68
broad-based cost efficiency, 180–193
    audit of spending data and, 182–187
    cost-efficiency recommendations,
        187–190
    history of education spending and,
        181–182
    no central formula for, 191
    results and lessons learned, 191–193
Broad Foundation, 180
budget cuts, 1
    cost-equivalent, in per-teacher terms,
        82–83
    for extracurricular activities, 60–61
    learning undermined by, 264
    political protection against, 29–31
budget decisions, 213, 259–260, 301

budget development
  absence of sound information for, 269–271
  class size and, 244–245, 282
  community surveys in, 246
  creativity in, 14
  data collection and analysis in, 244, 259–260
  data on results of, 246–247
  executive coaching in, 243–246
  incremental, 273–275
  influence of stakeholders on, 274–275,
      279–280
  line-item reductions, 210
  power indicators, 108–110
  resource competition in, 87
  stabilizing process, 72, 91–94
  top-down decisions in, 213
  zero-based, 273–274
  See also school budgets
budget-stretching strategies, 16
building construction, 189, 190
building maintenance
  management layers for, 203, 204
  postponing, 9–10
  See also custodial services
built-in cost escalators, 92, 93
bundling, 185
bureaucratic inertia, 265, 273–275
Bureau of Labor Statistics, U.S., 150, 278
Burtless, Gary, 13
Busch, Carolyn, 13
business services. See auxiliary services

California, 30, 66, 155
California Department of Education,
    129–130, 137, 151
"cascading" method of delayering, 195
cash management, 109
categorical funding
  incremental budgeting and, 274
  inefficiency and, 185–186
  minimizing use of, 285
  reliance on, 265, 300
  Title I formulas, 226
Census Bureau, U.S., 267
Center on Reinventing Public Education
    (Univ. of Washington), 14, 72, 75, 83

Central Falls (R.I.) school district, 279
centralization, management of, 191–192
centrally coordinated teacher training, 140
central office support
  control of budgeting decisions, 213
  cost efficiency recommendations for, 189,
      190
  deep cuts to, 210–211
  delayering for efficiency (CPS example),
      193–201
  management of centralization, 191–192
  restructuring for organizational effective-
      ness, 194
  service-oriented, need for, 202
  shared services, 189, 190, 191
  shortened work week for, 59–60
  span of control for managers, 196–197
  See also administration
CGCS. See Council of Great City Schools
Chaconas, Dennis, 269
Chadwick, Jonathan, 3
Chalfant, James, 85
Chambers, Jay, 76
change
  fostering environment for, 289–290
  incremental v. transformative, 290–292
charter school management organizations,
    15, 286–287
charter schools
  academic results in, 299–300
  evidence on class sizes, 132–133
  expansion of, 41
  protecting enrollment from assault by,
      67
  resource competition with, 48
  traditional school closings and, 49–50
  virtual schools, 160–173, 282–283
cheerleading, 78, 82
Chicago Public Schools (CPS): delayering,
    193–201
  developing strategy for, 193–194
  organizational structure, 196–199
  outcomes achieved, 199–201
  systematic approach to, 195
Chicago Teaching Fellows program, 143
Children First reform agenda, 224–225

Cisco Systems, 3
Clark County (Nev.) School District, 48
    alternative education in, 64
    community meetings in, 69
    cost-cutting measures, 52, 57, 62
class formation, 133–136
classroom instruction model
    struggles with, 159–160
    whole-group instruction cycle, 160–161
classroom management skills, 141
class size
    budget development and, 244–245, 282
    evidence on, from charter schools,
        132–133
    online classes, 165–166
    state mandates on, 51–52, 77–78, 282
    unqualified teachers and, 129
class size increase, 2, 10, 51–52
    efficient use of teachers and, 126–133
    return on investment and, 122
    savings from, 126–127
    as smart strategy, 293–294
class size reduction
    expense of smaller classes, 130–131
    pressure to reduce, 127–133
    restrictive laws, 51, 152
    size caps on AP classes, 77–78
class size reduction (CSR) initiative, 129–130,
        137, 151
clerical work, 54
Clinton, William Jefferson, 128
cold calling technique, 142
collective bargaining agreements
    changing laws and regulations on, 285
    constraints of, 139, 146
    course consolidation and, 80
    district policy shaped by, 277–278
    media publicity on, 287
    multiyear contracts, 30–31
    personnel cutbacks and, 49
    "step and lane" raises, 294
    "terminating contracts," 58
collective scheduling, 245
Colorado State Finance Project, 47, 49, 50
Common Core of Data (National Center for
    Education Statistics), 183

communication
    with employees, proactive, 206
    trade-offs, 90
    using per-unit costs in, 72, 89–91
community
    awareness of spending and outcomes,
        266–267, 277, 281
    frustration with student achievement, 35,
        38–40, 41
    fundamental divide in, 240–242, 262
    per-unit costs in communicating with, 72,
        89–91
    political barriers to change and, 286–287
    role in public schools, 192
community-funded foundations, 68–69
community outreach
    in cost-cutting efforts, 69–70
    surveys, 69, 90, 246
    using per-unit costs in communicating,
        72, 89–91
compensation
    eliminating raises, 46
    for graduates of selective admission col-
        leges, 146–147
    higher for AP classes, 77
    historical increase in, 20
    international comparison of systems,
        145–146
    labor costs, 292–295
    lack of standardization in, 197–198
    as majority of spending, 10–12, 47, 125,
        158–159
    "master's bumps," 90, 144–145, 273
    pay-for-performance, 121
    performance management and, 199
    performance measurement and, 41, 145
    power indicators, 109
    realigning, 81
    rethinking, 263
    salary rollbacks, 49
    salary schedules, 8, 271–272
    savings due to online instruction, 174–177
    "step and lane" system, 121–122, 144, 294
    of support staff, 159
    teacher quality and, 294
    teacher salaries underestimated, 281–282

tenure-based salary increases, 199
  union proposals to defer, 223–224
compensation reform, 144–146
  differential pay, 146–147
  employee benefits, 148–149
  merit pay, 147–148
computer-assisted instruction, 7
computers, 62–63, 171
consultants
  learning support consultants, 215
  management consulting firms, 139
  use of, organization structure and, 199
content knowledge, 255–256
Cooperating School Districts consortium, 65,
    66–67
cooperative ventures among districts, 64–65
core courses, 80, 164–165
cost-benefit analysis, 16
cost containment specialists, 247
cost cutting, 1–17
  administration costs, 16, 239–240
  diverse views of, 7–8
  educational costs, 4–6
  encouraged by foundations, 286–287
  historical data on, 237–238
  lack of guidance for, 12–13
  large-scale (See large-scale cost cutting)
  opting for popular measures, 6
  political barriers to, 16
  potential models for, 14–17
  responses to challenges, 9–10
  rethinking model for, 10–12
  in special education, 16, 68
  structural barriers to, 16
cost-cutting example, 235–262
  addressing reading difficulties, 253–255
  changes in special education, 250–253
  effects on community, 240–242, 262
  external pressure for budget decisions,
    259–260
  financial management competency, 261
  Five Why analysis, 256–259
  lack of knowledge of budget, 236–237,
    238, 269
  resource allocation: shifting funds, 239–240
  school board term recommendation, 260

starting from scratch, 261
strong protests against change, 240–242
studying historical data, 237–238
"superintendent's cabinet," 242–246
task force for assistance, 248–250
teachers' content knowledge, 255–256
unintended consequences, 246–248
cost-cutting strategies, 45–70
  community outreach, 69–70
  cutting personnel costs, 47, 48–55
  effects on student and teacher perfor-
    mance, 46
  "everything else" strategy, 47, 59–65
  fundraising, 47, 66–69
  more effective use of teachers (See efficient
    use of teachers)
  trimming benefits, 47, 56–59
cost effectiveness, 298
cost efficiency. See broad-based cost efficiency
cost-equivalent budget cuts, 82–83
cost-of-living adjustments, 46
cost savings
  making commitment to, 199–200
  from online learning, 169–173
Council of Great City Schools (CGCS), 14, 290
  estimating costs and savings opportunities,
    113–114
  Performance Measurement and Bench-
    marking Project, 97–124, 270
  service costing, 75–76
counseling services, 156, 248–249
Covington, John, 9, 10
CPS. See Chicago Public Schools
cross-functional analysis of KPIs, 120
crossing guards, 240–242, 280
CSR (class size reduction) initiative, 129–130,
    137, 151
cultural norms, 239, 265, 273–275
culture-building skills, 141
curriculum, 64, 214, 224
Curriculum Computer Corporation, 168
Curts-Whann, Audra, 52, 64
custodial services
  analyses of best practices, 119
  comparing vendors, 79
  performance standards for, 118

custodial services, *continued*
  power indicators for, 106–107
  reduced, 5
  reporting chain for, 203, 204
  "team cleaning," 54
customer satisfaction with HR, 111, 112
"cyber" (virtual) charter schools, 160–173,
    282–283

data collection and analysis, 104–116
  absence of sound information, 269–271
  in benchmarking project, 102
  benchmarks developed from, 14–15
  in budget development, 244, 259–260
  decision making and, 14, 95, 100
  in delayering for reorganization, 202
  historical data on cost cutting, 237–238
  linking achievement data to spending data,
    298–299
  next-generation indicators, 117–120
  on results of budget development, 246–247
  in service costing, 75–76
  spending data (*See* audit of spending data)
  state-mandated compliance data, 72
  transparency of information, 284
  Web-based data dashboards, 119
decentralization, 28–29, 231–232
decision making
  about service issues, 280
  with better data, 14, 95, 100
  budget decisions, 213, 259–260, 301
  per-unit costs in, 94–96
  political considerations in, 210
  resource allocation decisions, 212
  See also strategic resource decisions
"decision rights," 198–199
"decision shopping," 198
Delaware public schools, 180–193, 270–271
delayering, 193–208
  for central office efficiency (CPS example),
    193–201
  district transformation example, 201–208
demand management, in purchasing, 185
Department of Education, U.S., 102, 183
Department of Educational Leadership (Univ.
    of Dayton), 68
differential pay plans, 146–147

"differentiated instruction," 133–136
differentiated practice, 163
distance learning, 15
district mandates, 253–255
District of Columbia Public Schools, 140,
    155–156
district policies
  for human resources operations, 200–201
  seniority-neutral layoff policy, 90–91, 294
  shaped by union contracts, 277–278
documentation of best practices, 100
*Does Money Matter? The Effect of School
    Resources on Student Achievement and
    Adult Success* (Burtless), 13
dropout prevention, 67
dropout rates, 158
Drucker, Peter, 209, 210, 224, 228, 232
"dumbed down" curriculum, 214
Duncan, Arne, 194, 279
duplication of key functions, 197, 206

early retirement, 56–57
Early Success Performance Plan, 222
economic conditions
  decline in support for education spend-
    ing, 266
  economic recovery, vigilance during,
    192–193
  education protected from, 26–27
  effect on education revenues, 2
  effects on urban school systems, 98
  employment levels linked to, 25–26
  general effects of, 155
  online learning and, 157–158
  as opportunity for reform, 2–3, 157–158,
    263
  resource use and, 123
  See also fiscal crises
Economic Impact Aid (Calif.), 215
economic recession
  effects of, 2, 155
  as opportunity for education reform, 2–3,
    157–158, 263
  as stimulus for operational efficiencies, 2–3
"economies of scale," 183–184
Edison-Learning, 15
Educating School Teachers, 12

education, privileged status of, 24–33
    constitutional privilege, 28
    decentralized operations and, 28–29
    employment linked to economic condi-
        tions, 25–26
    multiple revenue sources and, 31–33
    political protection of, 29–31
    protection from economic conditions,
        26–27
Education Commission of the States, 47, 49,
    57–58, 65
education employee unions
    ability to veto policy change, 278
    influence on elections, 276–279
    multiyear contracts, 30–31
    negotiations on merit pay, 278
    personnel cutbacks and, 49
    predisposition to voting, 30, 277
    proposal to defer compensation, 223–224
Education Next, 266, 277, 281
Education Next—PEPG survey on school
    quality, 266–267, 277, 281
education reform
    assistance of philanthropic community
        in, 153
    compensation reform, 144–146
    economic recession as opportunity for,
        2–3, 157–158, 263
    enabling, political barriers and, 283–287
    media publicity about, 263
    organizational challenges to, 15–16
    political pressures for, 40
    radical avenues toward, 7–8
    reform by addition, 295–296
    resistance to change and, 264–265
    tenure reform, 139–140
    Vision 2015 reform agenda, 180, 187, 191
education revenues
    decentralized operation and, 28–29
    direct funding to high-poverty schools, 296
    effectiveness of superintendents and, 268
    effect of economic recession, 2
    Fair Student Funding, 225–226, 229, 231,
        296
    flat or declining, 92–93
    limited ability to repurpose funds,
        282–283, 285–286

local funding of school districts, 31–32
multiple sources of, 31–33
per-pupil revenues, 19, 21, 24, 25, 32
protection of school funding, 30
questionable practices in public funding,
    7–8
shifting funds, in cost cutting, 239–240
education spending
    comparisons across schools, 88
    decline in support for, economy and, 266
    history of (See history of education spend-
        ing)
    impact of STAR initiative on, 218
    long-term commitments, avoiding, 94
    mediocre returns on, 158
    per-pupil (See per-pupil expenditures)
efficiency(ies)
    academic, per-pupil expenditures and,
        298–299
    broad-based cost efficiency, 180–193
    finding incentives for, 185–186
    inefficiencies, 50, 206, 287
    operational (See operational efficiencies)
efficient use of teachers, 125–153
    absenteeism reduction, 149, 150
    class formation and, 133–136
    class size and, 126–133
    compensation reform and (See compensa-
        tion reform)
    eliminating aides, 133, 294–295
    eliminating ineffective teachers, 138–140
    NAEP and, 123, 125, 129
    professional development and, 140–142
    program initiatives and, 150–151
    recruitment and training, 142–144
    teacher quality and, 137–144
    use of instructional technology, 136–137
    "3X" teachers, 148
Eisenhower, Dwight D., 147
elections and voting
    influence of self-interested coalitions, 264,
        276–279
    low-turnout school board elections, 264,
        275–276
    moving to on-cycle years, 275–276, 286
    union influence on elections, 276–279
    union predisposition to voting, 30, 277

elections and voting, *continued*
   views of elderly voters, 267
   vitriolic campaigns, 280
elective courses
   consolidating, 80
   eliminating language classes, 52
   outsourcing strategies, 78, 81
   scheduling changes, 81
   service costing, 75, 76–78
electronic assessment
   advantages of, 164, 165, 166
   grade placement by, 134
Elementary and Secondary Education Act
   (ESEA) of 1965, 33, 283
Elliott, Tom, 49, 68, 70
ELLs (English language learners), 222
Emanuel, Rahm, 2
employee benefits
   aligning with private sector plans, 148–149
   cost-efficiency recommendations, 188–189
   cost efficiency recommendations for,
      188–189, 190
   health care (*See* health-care benefits)
   pension-and-benefits system, 8, 10–12
   pensions (*See* pension plan benefits)
   reducing (*See* benefit cutting)
employment levels
   linked to economic conditions, 25–26
   upward trajectory in, 21, 23, 24
energy (utilities)
   careful monitoring of use, 62
   cost efficiency recommendations, 188, 190
   inter-district comparisons of spending, 183
   power indicators, 116
   savings on, 47, 59–60
English, intervention programs in, 244,
   255–256
English language learners (ELLs), 222
entrepreneurial ventures
   extra tuition and fees, 249–250
   in food service, 63–34
   for fundraising, 47
   investment pools, 65
   parking fees, 61, 68
   sale of advertising, 68
   school improvement and, 286–287
   solar power systems, 61–62

"equality of all subjects," 239
equity, 221
E-Rate program, 171
ESEA (Elementary and Secondary Education
   Act) of 1965, 33, 283
Essential Few indicators, 102, 104
"everything else" strategy, 47, 59–65
Excellence for All strategy, 214–215, 217
executive coaching
   in budget development, 243–246
   defending costs of, 247–248
experimentation
   lack of, 272–273
   Project STAR experiment, 128–131, 133
external pressures
   for budget decisions, 259–260, 301
   for class size reduction, 127–133
   for student achievement, 259, 301
extracurricular activities
   cheerleading, per-pupil spending on, 78, 82
   cutting budgets for, 60–61
   eliminating transportation to, 280
   elimination of field trips, 4
   fee-based afterschool program, 249
   participation in, for online learners, 173
   sports, 68, 74, 75, 78

face-to-face instruction, 170–171, 177–178
Fairfax County, Virginia
   "community dialogue meetings," 70
   increasing class sizes, 51
   planetariums closed, 61
   salary rollbacks, 49
   transportation savings, 54–55
fairness, in merit pay plans, 148
Fair Student Funding (FSF), 225–226, 229,
   231, 296
FCRR (first contact resolution rates), 114
federal funding of education
   grants (*See* federal grants)
   history of, 32–33
   shift toward, 43
   stimulus funds (*See* federal stimulus funds)
   Title I funding, 168, 215, 217, 272
federal government
   accountability policies, 265, 269, 285
   changes to restrictive policies of, 283–285

constraints on change, 281–283
E-Rate program, 171
role in education, 20, 153
support for change needed from, 298–299
federal grants
competitive, expanding use of, 284–285
grants management, 109
informal "owners" of, 240
power indicators in grants management, 109
federal stimulus funds, 3
ARRA, 33, 35, 37, 73, 156
end of, 45
role of government in education and, 20
shortfalls in spite of, 227
for solar power systems, 62
feedback, 163, 166
field trips, 4
finance, power indicators in, 103, 108–110
financial management
analyses of best practices, 119
efficient, as continual process, 291
power indicators, 109
superintendents' need for skills, 261, 270, 271
Financing Schools for High Performance: Strategies for Improving the Use of Educational Resources (Odden & Busch), 13
Finn, Chester, Jr., 11
first contact resolution rates (FCRR), 114
fiscal crises
changing spending in, 95
as common phenomenon, 91–92
reasons for perception of, 33–34
structural changes in schools and, 289
See also economic conditions
Fiscal Survey of States (2009), 45
Five Why analysis, 256–257
fixed costs, 92
food service
analyses of best practices, 119
change to bagged lunches, 63
comparing vendors, 79
entrepreneurial projects, 63–64
power indicators for, 107–108, 116
sale of advertising on trucks, 68
savings with online instruction, 171

foreign exchange programs, 249–250
foundations
assistance in reform, 153
encouragement of cost cutting, 286–287
in fundraising, 68–69
See also specific foundations
FSF (Fair Student Funding), 225–226, 229, 231, 296
FTEs (full-time equivalents), 87–88, 93
full-day kindergarten, 222, 231
Fullerton, Jon, 269
full-time equivalents (FTEs), 87–88, 93
fund balances, 110, 116, 118
Fund for Public Schools, 227
funding formulas
incentives in, 185–186
Title I formulas, 226
transportation funding, 187
weighted student formula, 215, 217, 225, 229, 231, 296
fundraising, 47, 66–69
community-funded foundations, 68–69
taxation, 66–67

Gallo, Fran, 279
GDP. See Gross Domestic Product
GED, 40
GFOA (Government Finance Officers' Association), 110, 118
Giuliani, Rudy, 224
golf classes, 78
Government Finance Officers' Association (GFOA), 110, 118
graduation rates, 40, 41, 201
Grand Rapids (Mich.) school district, 54, 64, 68
grants management, 109
Great Depression, 19, 21, 24–25
grievances filed, 112, 113
Griffith, Michael, 47, 65
Gross Domestic Product (GDP)
defense appropriations relative to, 26, 27
per-pupil revenues and, 19, 24, 25
Gross National Product, 157
Grubb, W. Norton, 13
guidance counselors, 156
Gustafson, Glenn, 59

Handbook of Research in Education Finance and Policy (Ladd), 13
Harrison School District No. 2 (Colo.), 145
Harvard Business Review, 209
Harvard University
    Program on Education Policy and Governance (PEPG), 266, 277, 281
    Public Education Leadership Project (PELP), 15, 211, 213, 229
Hassel, Brian, 148
Hassel, Emily, 148
Hawai'i, 156–157, 177
Hawai'i State Teachers Association, 156–157
"Hawthorne effect," 129
health-care benefits
    changing terms of, 57–59
    cost-efficiency recommendations, 188–189
    costs of, 42–43
    generosity of, 294
    planned cuts, 1
    study of, 267
health-care obligations, 5
heating and cooling budgets
    cuts in, 4, 9–10, 45, 59–60
    restructuring jobs and, 54
    solar power systems, 61–62
Heckman, James, 40, 41
Hewlett Foundation, 102
"Higher Education Strategies for Reducing Cost and Increasing Quality in Higher Education" (2005), 13
hiring freeze, 227–228
Hispanic students
    achievement-related challenges, 201, 214
    low proficiency rates, 220–221
history of education spending, 12–13, 14, 19–44
    broad-based cost efficiency and, 181–182
    cost cutting data, 237–238
    in Delaware, 181–182
    education's privileged status, 24–33
    long-run prospects, 38–44
    perception of fiscal calamity, 33–34
    per-pupil expenditures, 21, 22, 38, 39, 157–158, 266
    short-run prospects, 34–37

"hold harmless" concessions, 226, 232
human resources operations
    customer satisfaction with, 111, 112
    new policies for, 200–201
    power indicators, 103, 110–114
    study of, 101–102
hybrid schools, 173–175, 176, 295

IBM, 3
ideologues, 17
IEP (individual education plan), 251–252, 253, 256
"impact aid," 32–33
implementation, 208
incentive(s)
    in funding formulas, 185–186
    group-based, weakness of, 272
    job titles as rewards tool, 196
    merit pay, 13, 147–148, 200, 272, 278
    · monetary, against absenteeism, 86
    retirement incentive plans, 57
incentive systems, 245
incremental budgeting, 273–275
incremental change, 290–292, 295–296
independent learning, 136–137
"individual attention," failure of, 135
individual contributors, 197, 201
individual education plan (IEP), 251–252, 253, 256
ineffective programs, eliminating, 16
inefficiencies
    aggressive work to eliminate, 287
    categorical funding and, 185–186
    declining school enrollments and, 50
    removing, 206
    school district boundaries and, 192
    See also efficiency(ies)
information deficits, 269–271
information services, 101–102
information systems, 74
information technology, 103, 114, 116
innovation, opportunities for, 295–298
inquiry teams, 227
insolvent school districts, 21
Institute of Education Sciences, 153
Institute of Management, 108

instructional initiatives, 5
instructional reform facilitator (IRF), 215, 217, 219, 231
instructional techniques, 141–142
instructional technology (online), 158–160
    asynchronous instruction and, 165, 167–168
    core courses, 164–165
    engaging students with, 162–163
    independent learning with, 136–137
    potential savings with, 295
    productivity and, 174, 175–178
    software, 167–169
    student practice in, 163–164
instructional television, 64
inter-district spending comparisons, 183
interest group politics, 275–280
international comparisons
    of compensation systems, 145–146
    of student achievement, 131–132
    of teacher training, 142–143
Internet
    online community surveys, 69
    online courses, 64, 79, 81
    standardized tests online, 64
    Web-based data dashboards, 119
    See also instructional technology; online learning
interstate comparisons
    of cost-savings initiatives, 185
    of educational spending, 183
intervention programs, 244
Investing in Innovation Fund (i3), 284–285
IRF (instructional reform facilitator), 215, 217, 219, 231
i3 (Investing in Innovation Fund), 284–285

job titles
    lack of standardization in, 197–198
    reducing, 200–201
    as rewards tool, 196

K12 (online education company), 171
Kansas City school district, 9
Kennedy, Donald, 53, 63
key functions, duplication of, 197, 206

Key Performance Indicators (KPI), 98, 99–100, 116
    automation of, 119
    "leading" and "lagging" indicators, 117–118
    next-generation indicators, 117–120
    power indicators (See power indicators)
    trend lines in, 116
kindergarten, 222, 231
KIPP (Knowledge Is Power Program), 132–133, 140–141
Klein, Joel, 224, 225, 227–228, 229, 231, 232, 233, 278, 286
Knowledge Is Power Program (KIPP), 132–133, 140–141
KPI. See Key Performance Indicators

labor market, 11
labor model, 11, 12
Ladd, Helen, 13
"lagging" indicators, 117–118
Land Survey Ordinances of 1780s, 32
Langlois, James, 49, 53, 65, 70
language classes, 52
large-scale cost cutting, 179–208
    broad-based efficiency, 180–193
    central office efficiency: delayering, 193–201
    conditions for success, 179, 207–208
    school district transformation: delayering, 201–207
LEAD. See Leadership for Education Achievement in Delaware (LEAD) Committee
leadership
    expertise and focus in, 192
    opportunities for, 295–298
    strong, as condition for success, 207–208
leadership academy for teachers, 247
Leadership for Education Achievement in Delaware (LEAD) Committee
    cost-efficiency recommendations of, 187–190
    created to study spending efficiency, 181
    results and lessons learned, 191–193
    targeted analyses by, 182–187
"leading" indicators, 117–118

lean organizations, 5
learning
    online (*See* online learning)
    social dimensions of, 173
    undermined by budget cuts, 264
learning disabilities, 168
learning lab, 136
learning support consultants, 215
"least invasive interventions," 141
legal restrictions
    on class size, 51, 152
    on collective bargaining agreements, 285
    constraints of tenure laws, 139
    discouraging technology, 177–178
    prevailing wage laws, 185
Lemov, Doug, 142
Levenson, Nathan, 269, 296–297
Levin, David, 133
librarians, 52, 156
licensing costs, 172, 175
literacy, 163, 222
local funding of school districts, 31–32
Long Beach (Calif.) school district, 51, 60,
    67, 69
long-run fiscal prospects, 38–44
    adaptations to reality, 41–43
    early warnings, 38, 39
    resource competition and, 43–44
    student achievement and, 38–40, 41
long-term substitute teachers, 215, 219
Los Angeles (Calif.) Unified School District,
    85, 99, 115
low-income students, 137

management consulting firms, 139
management layers
    for maintenance function, 203, 204
    reducing (*See* delayering)
    in STAR schools initiative, 216
management organizations, 15, 286–287
managers
    budget autonomy, 213
    individual contributors in ranks of, 197,
        201
    oversupply of, changing, 196–197, 206
    professional judgment of, 186–187
    resource allocation decisions, 212

Managing the Resource Allocation Process
    (Bower), 212
Massachusetts Comprehensive Assessment
    System (MCAS), 134, 250
master's degrees in education, 90, 144–145, 273
mathematics
    intervention programs in, 244
    proficiency levels in, 220
    secondary-level special education, 255–256
    studies of, 125, 131, 142
mayoral control of school governance, 299
MCAS (Massachusetts Comprehensive As-
    sessment System), 134, 250
McKinsey & Company, 63
MCPS. *See* Montgomery County (Md.)
    Public Schools
measurement tools
    better use of, 291
    key performance indicators (*See* Key Per-
        formance Indicators)
    See also data collection and analysis
media publicity, 33–34, 263, 287
mental health partnerships, 248–249
merit pay, 13, 200
    compensation reform, 147–148
    negotiations with teacher union on, 278
    resentment against, 272
    See also incentive(s)
Michael, Kristen, 61
Microsoft Corporation, 3–4, 102
Miles, Mike, 145
Milwaukee (Wis.) school district, 50–51, 55,
    56–57, 62–63
Minner, Ruth Ann, 181
Modern Education Finance and Policy
    (Guthrie), 13
*The Money Myth: School Resources, Outcomes,
    and Equity* (Grubb), 13
Montgomery County (Md.) Public Schools
    (MCPS), 15
    coherence framework and, 228–233
    direct funding to high-poverty schools, 296
    red zone/green zone approach, 219–224,
        229, 231, 233
Moskowitz, Eva, 287
motivation, 162–163
music courses, 78

NAEP. *See* National Assessment of Educational Progress

"narrating the positive," 141

Nate, Michelle, 51, 56, 57, 62, 63

National Assessment of Educational Progress (NAEP)
  efficient use of teachers, 123, 125, 129
  lack of proficiency shown by, 158, 180
  public frustration with achievement, 40
  urban education, 97–98

National Association of Purchasing Card Professionals, 118

National Center for Education Statistics, 183

National Center for Policy Analysis, 12

National Defense Education Act (NDEA) of 1958, 33

national defense expenditures, 26, 27

National Education Association (NEA), 127

National Governors Association, 45

National Institute of Governmental Purchasing (NIGB), 118

National Products company, 212

National Reading Panel, 242, 253

NCLB (No Child Left Behind) Act of 2001, 2, 33, 50, 134, 269, 281

NDEA (National Defense Education Act) of 1958, 33

NEA (National Education Association), 127

Nelson Rockefeller Institute, 3

Newsweek magazine, 134

New Teachers Project, 142

New York City Department of Education (NYCDOE), 224–228, 229, 231–232

New York City Independent Budget Office, 227

New York City School District, 15
  ARIS (Achievement Reporting and Innovation System), 74, 227, 286
  autonomy/accountability exchange, 224–228, 229, 231–232
  Fair Student Funding (FSF), 225–226, 229, 231, 296
  influence of teacher unions in, 278
  principal-controlled budgets in, 213

New York City Teaching Fellows program, 143

New York State Council of School Superintendents, 46

NIGB (National Institute of Governmental Purchasing), 118

No Child Left Behind (NCLB) Act of 2001, 2, 33, 50, 134, 269, 281

"no excuses" schooling, 132–133, 141, 146

NYCDOE (New York City Department of Education), 224–228, 229, 231–232

Obama, Barack, 35, 156, 279, 294

Odden, Allan, 13

OECD (Organisation for Economic Cooperation and Development), 125

offsite meetings, 204–205

online learning, 155–178
  constrained by state regulations, 282–283
  cost savings from, 169–173
  "cyber" (virtual) charter schools, 160–173, 282–283
  economic downturn and, 157–158
  hybrid schools, 173–175, 176
  instructional software, 167–169
  opposition to, 300
  productivity and, 174, 175–178
  students and, 160–164
  teachers and, 164–167, 176
  technology for, 158–160
  virtual learning, 64, 295, 300, 301

"open source" books, 62–63

operational efficiencies
  economic recession as stimulus for, 2–3
  online instruction, 169–173
  straightforward efforts toward, 7–8
  as valued quality, 5

operational scenarios, for KPIs, 120

Organisation for Economic Cooperation and Development (OECD), 125

organizational challenges to reform, 15–16

organizational structure, changing, 196–199
  correcting chaotic, dysfunctional structure, 224–225
  "decision rights" unclear, 198–199
  delayering, 205–206
  duplication of key functions, 197, 206
  individual contributors, 197
  job titles and compensation, 197–198
  for organizational effectiveness, 194

organizational structure, changing, *continued*
　performance management and compensation, 199
　streamlining, 201
　too many managers, 196–197
　unclear structure, 199
organization charts, 199
Ouchi, William, 211–212, 213
outliers, 184, 291
out-of-district placements, 256–257
outsourcing
　counseling services, 248–249
　elective classes, 78, 81
　spending comparisons to, 185
　substitute teachers, 54

Palo Alto (Calif.) Unified School District, 56, 57
Paradise Valley (Ariz.) Unified School District, 49, 68, 70
paraprofessionals, 257–258
parent(s)
　reducing complaints by, 250
　resistance to change, 135–136
　role in trade-offs, 246
parent coordinator position, 224
parent liaison, 215
parking fees, 61, 68
pay-for-performance compensation system, 121
P-card transactions, 105–106, 118
PELP (Public Education Leadership Project), 15, 211, 213, 229
PELP Coherence framework, 229, 230
pension-and-benefits system, 8, 10–12
pension obligations, 5
pension plan benefits
　cost-efficiency recommendations, 188
　costs of, 42–43
　cutting, 1, 42–43, 56–57
　generosity of, 294
　study of, 267
PEPG (Program on Education Policy and Governance), 266, 277, 281
performance bonuses, 227
performance data, 14–15

performance evaluation
　compensation and, 41, 145
　return on investment measures, 283–284
　rigorous, teacher quality and, 139
　teacher salaries and, 41, 145
Performance Measurement and Benchmarking Project, 97–124, 270
　data collection and analysis, 104–116
　future of, 120–124
　next-generation indicators, 117–120
　project purposes and design, 98–104
Performance Measures, 102, 104
performance standards, 118
per-pupil expenditures
　academic efficiency and, 298–299
　calculating, 291
　declines in, 19, 21, 24–25
　for extracurricular activities, 78, 82
　historical, 21, 22, 38, 39, 157–158, 266
　limited analysis of, 71
　as percentage of GDP, 21, 22, 38, 39
　protection of school funding, 30
　in red zone/green zone approach, 223
　requiring disclosure of, 283–284
　short-run projections, 36–37
　weighted averages in, 80
per-pupil revenues
　inequalities in, 32
　upward trajectory in, 19, 21, 24, 25
personnel costs, 207
personnel cutbacks, 1, 34, 47, 48–55, 49
personnel operations, 110–111, 112
personnel protectionism, perception of fiscal crisis and, 33–34
per-unit allocations, 94
per-unit costs, 71–96
　as basis of school budgets, 72, 87–89
　in communicating with public, 72, 89–91
　in considering trade-offs, 72, 81–86
　to convey relative magnitude, 72, 73–74
　decision making and, 94–96
　in service costing, 72, 75–81
　stabilizing budgeting process, 72, 91–94
Peterson, David, 45, 47, 48, 54, 59–60, 61
Pew Center on the States, 267
Phi Delta Kappa/Gallup survey, 267

philanthropic community. *See* foundations
Phillips, Don, 46, 51, 54, 55, 60
PISA (Programme for International Student Assessment), 142
Pittsburgh (Penna.) school district
   changing pay and benefits, 58–59
   printing operations, 62
   renegotiated retiree benefits, 56
   school closings, 50
   use of tax liens, 67
planetariums, 61
"player coaches," 196
policy analysis, of KPIs, 120
political barriers to change, 263–287, 298–301
   bureaucratic and cultural inertia, 265, 273–275
   enabling reform and, 283–287
   federal policies, 283–285
   foundations, local officials, and community, 286–287
   information deficits, 269–271
   interest group politics within districts, 275–280
   lack of policy know-how, 271–273
   need for change, 265–268
   school productivity and, 275–283
   state and federal constraints, 281–283
   state policies, 285–286
   superficial barriers, 268–275
political barriers to cost cutting, 16
political capital
   implementing change and, 227
   losing, 242, 243, 247, 248
political challenges to education reform, 15–16
political pressures
   countering, 88–89
   decisions about service issues, 280
   for educational reform, 40
   interest group politics, 275–280
   lessening by longer school board terms, 260
political protection of education, 29–31
"poverty mentality," 236, 242
Poway Unified School District (Calif.), 49, 51, 55, 60

power indicators, 102, 103, 104–116
   business services, 104–108, 115–116
   finance and budget, 103, 108–110
   human resources and personnel operations, 103, 110–114
   information technology, 114
   next-generation indicators, 117–118
   return on investment, 114–116
pre-referral programs, 150–151
prerequisites for classes, 135
principals
   autonomy for, 225, 226
   school budgets controlled by, 211–212, 213, 229
private sector
   aligning benefits with, 148–149
   best practices comparisons with, 184–185
procurement. *See* purchasing
productivity
   enhanced by resource allocation, 264
   interest group politics, 275–280
   online instructional technology and, 174, 175–178
   politics and, 275–283
professional development, 140–142, 294
proficiency levels
   of minority students, 201, 214, 220–221
   in reading and math, 220
   shown by NAEP, 158, 180
   See also student achievement; student assessment
program cuts, 93–94
Programme for International Student Assessment (PISA), 142
Program on Education Policy and Governance (PEPG), 266, 277, 281
Project STAR (student-teacher achievement ratio) experiment
   costs of reducing class size, 131
   evaluations of, 128–129, 130
   use of teacher aides, 133
property taxes
   fundraising by, 66–67
   local, 32
   opposition to, 30, 263
   taxpayer overrides, 66

Proposition 13, 30, 66
protests
    against staff reductions, 240–242, 280
    against teacher layoffs, 85
    threats and innuendo, 259
prototypes, lacking for benchmarking, 99
public. *See* community
Public Agenda, 147, 276
Public Education Leadership Project (PELP;
        Harvard Univ.), 15, 211, 213, 229, 230
public funding, 7–8
Public Impact, 148
public policy
    budget items inconsistent with, 186
    constraints on school districts, 281–283
    lack of policy know-how, 271–273
    objectives of, audit of spending data and,
        186
    shaped by teacher unions, 278
purchasing
    analyses of best practices, 119
    automation of systems, 53–54
    best-practices comparisons in, 184–185
    cost-efficiency recommendations for, 188,
        190, 191
    invoice processing costs, 108
    leveraging better prices, 65
    power indicators, 105–106
    pronounced savings in, 207
    textbooks (*See* textbook purchases)
Putnam/Northern Westchester (N.Y.) Boards
        of Cooperative Educational Services, 49,
        53, 65, 70

quality review, annual, 226–227
questionable practices, in public funding, 7–8

Race to the Top, 284
Rainey, Tracie, 47, 64
Raisch, Dan, 68
raises, eliminating, 46
reading
    literacy, 163, 222
    proficiency levels in, 220
    remedial programs, 253–255
    trends in scores, 40

recruitment and training, 142–144
    centrally coordinated, 140
    constrained by state regulations, 282
    hiring freezes, 227–228
    international comparisons, 142–143
    teacher position vacancies, 111, 112
red zone/green zone approach (MCPS),
        219–224, 229, 231, 233
reform by addition, 295–296
relative magnitude, 72, 73–74
relief time, 54
Rennie Center for Education Research and
        Policy, 256
resistance to change
    costs of reform and, 264–265
    lack of experimentation due to, 272–273
    by parents, 135–136
    political and policy barriers, 298
    restructured programs, 253–255
    school district transformation, 206–207
    in special education programs, 256
    strong protests, 240–242
resource allocation, 95, 282
    alignment with strategic priorities, 123
    bottom-up, 212
    distributed approach to, 213
    to enhance productivity, 264
    equitable, 122
    formula for, 225–226
    shifting spending, 239–240
    staffing-based allocation model, 87–88, 93
    strategic decisions in (*See* strategic resource
        decisions)
    targeting highest priorities, 291
resource competition
    among schools and districts, 285
    budget battles, 87
    competitive grant funding, 284–285
    decentralized operations as buffer against,
        28–29
    long-run fiscal prospects and, 43–44
    in short run, 35
    traditional v. charter schools, 48
    See also resource allocation
resource plan, 231
retirement incentive plans, 57

return on investment (ROI)
    class size and, 122
    performance measures, 283–284
    power indicators, 114–116
rewards, job titles as tool for, 196
Rhee, Michelle, 140, 155–156
Richmond (Va.) public schools, 50, 53
"right is right" technique, 142
"right-sizing" infrastructure, 50–51
risk management, 109
risk-to-ROI ratio, 115
Rocketship Education, 137
Rocketship Mateo Sheedy Elementary School,
    137
Rodel Foundation, 180
ROI (return on investment), 114–116, 122,
    283–284

Sabis model of class formation, 134–135
safety issues, 55, 59, 108
salary cuts, 49
salary schedules, 8, 271–272
San Francisco Unified School District
    (SFUSD), 15
    coherence framework and, 228–229, 231,
        232
    STAR schools initiative, 214–219, 232
SAT test, 128
savings identification, 79–81
scale curves, 183–184
scheduling
    by administrator, in special education,
        258–259
    changes for elective courses, 81
    collective, 245
    eliminating block scheduling, 52
    uniform bell schedules, 55
school attendance, monitoring, 67
school boards
    lengthening term recommendation, 260,
        286
    low-turnout elections, 264, 275–276
school budgets
    breakdowns of, 72
    computer hardware and connectivity, 171
    for extracurricular activities, cutting, 60–61

items inconsistent with public policy, 186
    knowledge of budget, 236–237, 238, 269
    per-unit costs as basis of, 72, 87–89
    principal-controlled, 213
    stabilizing budgeting process, 72, 91–94
    See also budget development; heating and
        cooling budgets
school buildings
    construction of, cost efficiency in, 189, 190
    maintenance, 9–10, 203, 204
    smaller, for online learning, 170, 175
    See also custodial services
school closings
    "right-sizing" infrastructure, 50–51
    underused schools, 49–50, 263
school district brand, 221–222
school districts
    annual quality reviews, 226–227
    boundaries of, inefficiency and, 192
    consolidation of, 189
    cooperative ventures among, 64–65
    district-mandated programs, 253–255
    ending out-of-district placements, 256–257
    insolvent, 21
    interest group politics in, 275–280
    limited ability to repurpose funds,
        282–283, 285–286
    local funding of, 31–32
    operating environments of, 209–210
    oversight of, 29
    public policy constraints on, 281–283
    reviewing performance in, 102, 104
    spending by, 22, 88–89, 183
school district transformation: delayering,
    201–207
    changing organizational structure, 205–206
    recommendations for, 202–205
    resistance to change, 206–207
School District U-46 (Illinois), 280
school enrollment declines, 49–50
school governance, 13, 299
school librarians, 52, 156
Scottsdale (Ariz.) Unified School District, 45
    entrepreneurial projects, 61
    substitute teaching, 54
    utilities savings, 47, 59–60

Seattle (Wa.) Public Schools, 85
security services, 79, 108
selective admission colleges, 146–147
self-interest coalitions
    outsized influence on elections, 264,
        276–279
    as political protection of education, 29–31
self-management skills, 151
seniority, 144, 200, 294
seniority-neutral layoff policy, 90–91, 294
service costing, 72, 75–81
    benchmarking in, 79
    collecting and sharing data on, 75–76
    elective courses, 75, 76–78
    identifying savings, 79–81
service delivery
    Baumol's disease, 292–293
    changing models for, 78–79
    reorganization of, 94
    See also specific services
"service" mentality, lack of, 199
SFUSD. See San Francisco Unified School
    District
short-run fiscal prospects, 34–37
sick days, 85–86
Six Sigma processes, 101
Skelly, Kevin, 56, 57
skills levels, placement in grade by, 134–135
small-group tutorials, 166
social dimensions of learning, 173
social promotion, 224
solar power systems, 61–62
span of control, 196–197
special education
    aides in, 53, 256–257
    behavior management in, 258
    cost-cutting in, 16, 68
    Five Why analysis, 256–257
    increasing student achievement in,
        250–253
    online instruction for learning disabilities,
        168
    pre-referral programs, 150–151
    reading, 253–255
    secondary-level math and English, 255–256
    transportation, 55
special needs students, 168, 172

spending comparisons
    across schools, 88
    inter-district comparisons, 183
    interstate comparisons, 183
    outliers in, 184, 291
    to outsourcing, 185
    scale curves in, 183–184
    See also audit of spending data
"spending on services." See service costing
sports, 74, 75, 78
sports fees, 68
staffing-based allocation model, 87–88, 93
stakeholders
    effects on grant funding, 284
    explaining trade-offs to, 81–83, 85
    influence on budgeting, 274–275,
        279–280
    political power of, 210
    See also education employee unions;
        specific stakeholders
standardization
    lack of, in job titles, 197–198
    in purchasing, 185
    in school building construction, 189
standardized performance measures, 100
standardized tests
    merit pay based on, 272
    online, 64, 172
    See also student assessment; specific assess-
        ment instruments
STAR experiment. See Project STAR
STAR schools initiative (SFUSD), 214–219,
    232
state constitutions, 28
state funding of education, 32, 282
state governments, 298–299
state mandates
    accountability policies, 265, 269, 285
    changes to restrictive policies, 285–286
    on class size
     for AP classes, 77–78
     budget difficulties and, 282
     waivers from, 51–52
    compliance data, 72
    face-to-face instruction, 170
    freedom from, 300
    regulatory constraints, 281–283

seniority-neutral layoffs, 91
textbook adoption cycle, 60
Steiner, David, 142
Steinhauser, Chris, 60, 67, 69
step and lane compensation system, 121–122,
    144, 294
"step and scale" compensation tables, 199
Stevenson, Cindy, 70
strategic initiatives, 15
strategic resource decisions, 209–233
    autonomy/accountability exchange,
        224–228, 229, 231–232
    challenges in, 209–211
    framework for strategy in, 228–233
    management literature concerning,
        211–214
    red zone/green zone approach, 219–224,
        229
    STAR schools initiative, 214–219, 232
    See also decision making; resource
        allocation
"stretch it" technique, 142
structural barriers to cost-cutting, 16
student(s)
    African American, 150, 201, 214, 220–221
    effects of cost cutting on performance, 46
    Hispanic, 201, 214, 220–221
    learning needs, inquiry team and, 227
    online learning and, 160–164
    special needs, online schools and, 172
    supervision of, in online classes, 167
    unmotivated in classroom, 161
student achievement
    accountability for progress, 122, 283
    benchmarks for, 222
    challenges for minority students, 201, 214
    compensation tied to, 145
    control of budget by principal and,
        211–212, 229
    expectations for, 122, 283, 289
    extending power indicators to, 117
    external pressures for, 259, 301
    as goal of online instruction, 174
    goals for, upward adjustment in, 41
    increasing, in special education, 250–253
    international comparisons, 131–132
    linking data to spending data, 298–299

low-income students, 137
    by low-income students, 137
    online instructional technology and, 174,
        175–178
    organization design and, 205
    proficiency levels of minority students,
        201, 214, 220–221
    Project STAR experiment, 128–129, 130,
        131, 133
    public frustration with, 35, 38–40, 41
    stagnant, 38–40, 41, 42, 125
    STAR schools initiative, 214–219, 232
student assessment
    electronic, 134, 164, 165, 166
    MCAS, 134, 250
    NAEP (See National Assessment of Educa-
        tional Progress)
    PISA, 142
    SAT and ACT, 128
    subjectivity in, 166
    See also standardized tests
student behavior advisors, 215, 258
student practice, 163–164
Students and Teachers Achieving Results
    (STAR) schools initiative (SFUSD),
    214–219, 232
subjectivity in student assessment, 166
substitute teachers
    cutting personnel, 54
    long-term, 215, 219
    sick days and, 85–86
summer school, 60
superficial barriers to change, 268–275
superintendents
    effectiveness of, revenues and, 268
    need for financial management skills, 261,
        270, 271
    strong leadership by, 297
superintendent's cabinet, 242–246
Suppes, Patrick, 167–168
supplier relationship management, 185
support staff, compensation of, 159
surveys
    community surveys, 69, 90, 246
    Education Next—PEPG, 266–267, 277, 281
    Fiscal Survey of States (2009), 45
    in information gathering, 101

surveys, *continued*
  on merit pay, 147
  Pew Center on the States, 267
  Phi Delta Kappa/Gallup survey, 267
Sylvan Learning, 79

TABOR (Taxpayer Bill of Rights), 66
Taxpayer Bill of Rights (TABOR), 66
Taylor, Bernard, Jr., 54, 64, 68
teacher(s)
  content knowledge of, 255–256
  cost-effective use of, 15, 44
  efficient use of (*See* efficient use of teachers)
  "excess pool," 227–228
  explaining trade-offs to, 82–83
  historical growth in teaching force, 11, 21, 23
  ineffective, termination of, 138–140, 294
  lack of success by, 159
  leadership academy for, 247
  online learning and, 164–167, 176
  performance evaluation of, 121
  prone to subjectivity, 166
  recruitment and training of (*See* recruitment and training)
  substitutes, 54, 85–86, 215, 219
  "3X" teachers, 148
  unqualified, class size and, 129
teacher absenteeism, 294
  costs of, 149
  monetary incentives against, 86
  power indicators, 111
  reducing, 149–150
  sick days as significant expense, 85–86
teacher aides
  eliminating, 133, 294–295
  in special education, 53, 256–257
teacher certification, 282
Teacher Incentive Fund, 284
teacher layoffs
  considering trade-offs in, 83–85
  mass firings, 279
  proposals to avoid, 223–224
  protests against, 85
  seniority-neutral policy, 90–91, 294
teacher position vacancies, 111, 112

teacher quality, 137–144
  compensation and, 294
  online instruction and, 176–177
  terminating ineffective teachers, 138–140, 294
  value-added effects of, 137–138
teacher retention
  power indicators, 111–113
  titles as tool for, 196
  See also recruitment and training; teacher layoffs
teacher salaries. *See* compensation; compensation reform
Teacher U (Hunter College), 140–141, 142
teacher unions. *See* education employee unions; *specific unions*
teaching assistance, 257–258
team building, 243
"team cleaning," 54
technology
  adoption of, 42
  assistance provided by, 300
  cost control through, 64
  instructional (*See* instructional technology)
  for online learning (*See* online learning)
  virtual technologies, 15
tenure, 8
  legal constraints, 139
  need for reform, 139–140
  raising bar for, 247
  salary increases based on, 199
"terminating contracts," 58
termination of ineffective teachers, 138–140, 294
textbook purchases
  agreement on common textbooks, 65
  constrained by state regulations, 283
  deferred, 4, 5, 46, 60
  online instruction and, 171–172
  replacing books with laptop computers, 62–63
Third International Mathematics and Science Study, 131
Thomas B. Fordham Institute, 11, 16
"3X" teachers, 148

TIMSS (Trends in Mathematics and Science
    Study), 125, 142
Title I funding
    categorical formulas, 226
    for compensatory education, 272
    for online instruction, 168
    for STAR schools initiative, 215, 217
top-down budgeting decisions, 213
Torres, Jose, 280
trade-offs
    communication of, 90
    control of, 86
    fiscal reforms through, 297
    parents' role in, 246
    per-unit costs in, 72, 81–86
    in service delivery models, 78–79
TransACT Communications, 102
transaction costs, 29, 30
transparency in merit pay plans, 148
transportation
    bus replacement, 59, 187–188, 190
    cost efficiency recommendations, 187–188,
        190
    cost-saving strategies in, 54–55
    cutting bus routes, 10
    performance standards for, 118
    political pressures regarding, 280
    power indicators for, 104–108, 115–116
    restructuring bus service, 55
    sale of advertising on buses, 68
    savings with online instruction, 171
    to sports and activities, 60–61, 280
    subsidy for private school students, 186,
        188, 190
trend lines, in KPIs, 116
Trends in Mathematics and Science Study
    (TIMSS), 125, 142
truancy strike force, 67
tuition reimbursement plans, 58
turnaround strategies, 13
tutoring, 75, 166, 169–170

Uncommon Schools, 132, 140–141
uniform bell schedules, 55
United Federation of Teachers, 278
Urkevich, John, 67
utilities. See energy

vacation days, 57
value-added effects of teacher quality,
    137–138
vigilance, critical importance of, 192–193
virtual charter schools, 160–173, 282–283
virtual learning, 64, 295, 300, 301
virtual schooling, 2, 7
virtual technologies, 15
Vision 2015 reform agenda, 180, 187, 191
Vitale, David, 201
voluntary furloughs, 156–157

Wall Street Journal, 14
War on Terror, 26, 27
Weast, Jerry, 220, 221, 229–230, 231, 232, 233
weighted averages, 80
weighted student formula (WSF), 215, 217,
    225, 229, 231, 296
weighted student funding model, 87–88, 93
Weiler, Jeff, 48, 52, 57, 62, 64, 69
Weingarten, Randi, 278
wellness programs, 58–59
whole-group instruction
    instruction cycle, 160–161
    online instruction, 165–166
workmen's compensation claims, 59
work week, shortened, 59–60
World War II
    decrease in school spending, 19, 21, 24–25
    post-war baby boom, 43–44
WSF (weighted student formula), 215, 217,
    225, 229, 231, 296
WSF STAR bonus, 217

zero-based budgeting, 273–274